A clear blue sky over a blue-green ocean provides the pathway to a nation in conflict. From 30,000 feet, the approach gives little indication of the turmoil below. The beaches look calm and white. The concrete runways, visible along the coast, belie the devastation their inhabitants wreak in the countryside. The ground appears lush, green and peaceful. A tinge of purple covers the mountains, often surrounded by cumulous clouds. It was difficult to believe what occurred on the ground. There are many aspects of the war. Ours is only one—a detached one at best—seldom challenged until 1972. At night it changed; it was then possible to observe the firefights outlining the struggle below.

Where the
Buf Fellows Roamed

————— James Hooppaw —————

FIRST EDITION
Third Printing

 RED APPLE
PUBLISHING

Printed by Gorham Printing
Rochester, WA 98579

ISBN 1-880222-33-7

Library of Congress Catalog Card Number 99-74598

Disclaimer: Although the author and publisher have tried to ensure accuracy and completeness of the events, they assume no responsibility for errors, inaccuracies, omissions or any inconsistencies. Events are colored by the author's viewpoint and how they affected him. Names and places have been disguised when necessary.

Cover Design by James D. Hooppaw

AUTHOR'S NOTE

This collection of memories is about the men and women of the Strategic Air Command who spent a large portion of their careers and lives on Alert throughout the world to keep the peace. Peace was our profession. When the klaxon sounded, there was always the thought that it could be the real thing. Thank God, it never was.

I recognize and salute the sacrifices made by the families of these dedicated professionals. They gave us strength.

I also salute those who kept the faith. Following our departure from Southeast Asia, the military went through a hard time. The professionals who stayed gave strength to a force depleted in resources and too often in morale. This cadre, most who have never been recognized, are the ones responsible for the return of strength throughout a military which the nation has again supported.

It was not always easy. Most, like me, lived through it. Others did not. Some were lost in war, and some were preparing for war with the hope it would never come. The sacrifices are no less in either case. If any memories are evoked, I sincerely hope they are pleasant ones.

—JDH
JAMES D. HOOPPAW
COLONEL, USAF (RET)

COLONEL HOOPPAW is a retired command pilot with twenty-six years in SAC. He flew the Boeing B-47E and B-52,C,D,E,F,G, and H models. He served as a pilot, instructor, Squadron Commander, and Deputy Commander of Operations of a Bomb Wing. He served three ARC LIGHT tours in Southeast Asia and received the normal complement of decorations with gongs that everyone else received. Any success he has enjoyed is mainly the result of "working with and for a great group of people." He presently lives in Nine Mile Falls, Washington, with his wife Wendy and a variety of friendly critters.

"Oh, give me a home
where the BUF fellows roam . . .
and the skies are not cloudy all day."

—My version of *Home on the Range*

HIGH FLIGHT

Oh, I have slipped the surly bonds of earth
And danced the skies on laughter—silvered wings;
Sunward I've climbed, and joined the tumbling mirth
Of sun-split clouds—and done a hundred things
You have not dreamed of—wheeled and soared and swung
High in the sunlit silence. Hov'ring there,
I've chased the shouting wind along, and flung
My eager craft through footless halls of air.
Up, up the long, delirious, burning blue
I've topped the windswept heights with easy grace
Where never lark, or even eagle flew
And, while with silent, lifting mind I've trod
The high untrespassed sanctity of space,
Put out my hand, and touched the face of God.

—John Gillespie Magee, Jr.

"I have never found it expressed better."
—JDH

ORDER OF BATTLE

INTRODUCTION

There has always been a mystique about the B-52, affectionately known to its operators as the BUF. (I prefer this spelling although it has been spelled BUFF as well.) It has been described as the crate the B-47 was shipped in. It may be because of its size. It may be because most people think of it in terms of nuclear war and the shrouds of secrecy that surround that undesirable activity. It may be because of its capability to deliver large amounts of bombs. To those of us who spent many years just trying to get it airborne, it is more often than not spoken of with affection. She could be stubborn, and we all cursed her at times, but it was infrequent that she did not bring us safely home, even though wounded, sometimes grievously. Like a lover, we treated her with respect, did not abuse her, and she brought us home safely.

The first impression upon seeing the BUF is that it is big. It is. The original paint scheme was simple—silver aluminum, white paint coating the belly, underside of the wings and elevator, to reflect heat and light from a nuclear blast. Upon the advent of the war in Southeast Asia, the D models got a new paint job. It was ugly, but tended to grow on you. The top of the aircraft was camouflaged in shapes of gray and green; the underside of the aircraft and the sides were black.

When a crisis arises, along with the old call of *Send in the Marines!*, the same pundits often recommend sending the BUFs to bomb the antagonist into submission. A show of ignorance. They know little or nothing about the application of force, bombing targets, or the planning and support that must be done. It is easy to say *Send Them* when they know they will not be directly involved. To the marines and aircrews it is a completely different ballgame.

How do you describe flying to anyone who has never slipped the surly bonds of earth alone, nor enjoyed the highs or endured the lows of flying? The thrill of the takeoff is always questionable, in that men do not have wings and the environment is still alien and often hostile to them, no matter what their experience. In itself, flying is still dangerous.

Formation flying can be the most intense experience for a pilot aside from combat—maintaining a position in the sky in relation to at least one other aircraft and pilot in which you have given complete trust not to fly you into the ground while you engage in in-trail acrobatic maneuvers. At times you pull so many G's that the tailpipe of the aircraft in front of you is reduced to just a black hole, resulting in tunnel vision. It can also be most satisfying—especially a night heavyweight air refueling with weather, turbulence, and an engine shutdown or into the sun with nothing to decrease the intensity of light to the point of barely being able to make out a faint outline of the tanker to which you are connected, and knowing you dare not fail.

Instrument flying has its own intensity. The ground is not visible and the pilot's trust is transferred to a set of man-made instruments which he must interpret to safely navigate the skies.

High speed means little at high altitude, for it is not in relation to anything static. But move to within a few feet of the ground or ocean and it becomes a rush hard to describe. Low level flight just above the terrain and sometimes below the surrounding ridges and mountains viewing nature's wonders can only be experienced, not related to another. I have seen a lot of this country up close and personal at an average of about four hundred miles an hour and am in awe of its beauty and majesty.

This narrative began as an attempt to put down on paper an explanation to family and friends why I missed important events such as birthdays, anniversaries, Christmases and Thanksgivings—where I was and what I was doing. Like Topsy, it just grew.

Everyone tells a story a little differently. Each person recalls events as he sees them or how they affected him. I have done the same and relate them as I recall them. They are true, only colored by my own viewpoint. Therefore, it is not an artistic attempt to describe events, but a personal chronology of experiences of a pilot that strapped a BUF to his butt and went where the BUF fellows roamed.

—JDH

EXPLANATION OF TERMS

ABC—Airborne commander—exercised control of the wave. This was often the pilot in the lead aircraft but also could be a staff pilot flying along with the crew.

AC—Aircraft commander—a pilot in charge of a crew

ADO—Assistant Deputy Commander for Operations

Alert—Duty which involved the crew living in the alert facility and responding to the klaxon when it sounded. Each crew was assigned an aircraft which was loaded for nuclear retaliation against an aggressor nation. The crew's activities were restricted while on alert.

Arc Light—Code name for the B-52 operations in Southeast Asia

ARCP—Air refueling control point—a point on the air refueling track at which the tanker and receiver theoretically arrive at a given time ready to refuel. The tanker orbits the ARCP awaiting the arrival of the receiver.

ARIP—Initial point of the air refueling track upstream from the ARCP

ATO, JATO—Assisted takeoff, sometimes referred to as jet assisted takeoff. Used on the B-47 for EWO launch. A rack, fitted on the lower rear fuselage, held a maximum of thirty bottles of propellant which could be fired and produce a thousand pounds of thrust each for approximately fifteen seconds. The rack was jettisoned after burnout.

BUF—Big Ugly Fucker. In gentler company Big Ugly Fellow. This became an appellation of respect and endearment.

BUFF—Big Ugly Fat Fucker. Often used rather than the above. I prefer the first and use it exclusively.

Cell—Three aircraft in formation, stacked up 500 or 1000 feet and in trail, one mile between aircraft.

Charlie—Code name for the Deputy Commander for Operations. Also a representative of the DCO, well experienced and qualified in the B-52 aircraft and mission. He ran the coordination and launch of the BUFs during Arc Light operations.

CC—Commander

CINC—Commander in Chief. Normally refers to the Commander of SAC, TAC, MAC, etc.

Chapkit—Survival kit worn by crewmembers especially designed for use in a theater of operations

CCRR—Combat crew rest and recuperation. As referenced in the text, it refers to the one half day off SAC crews received for each day of alert duty.

CCTS—Combat crew training squadron

Chrome Dome—Airborne alert by the B-52 force. Nuclear armed B-52's flew twenty-four hour missions ready to respond if required by national authority. This mission normally rotated among the wings for a period of several months. Several wings were involved and responsible for assigned areas. Each aircraft was responsible for a given period of time until relieved by another.

CP—Co-pilot

Cocked Aircraft—Aircraft, usually on alert, loaded and ready to start and take off with the minimum amount of activity.

DCO, DO—Deputy Commander for Operations. Director of Operations. Also referred to as Charlie. Usually a full colonel.

Dash 1—Manual for operation of a specific aircraft

EGT—Exhaust gas temperature of a jet engine

EPR—Engine pressure ratio. The ratio of engine inlet to exhaust pressure, used to measure engine thrust.

EVS—Electo-optical viewing system. A system in the G and H model which provides the crew a remote visual display of the terrain ahead of the aircraft in a closed curtain environment when the crew has no outside visibility. It provides a low light television and an infrared capability. Basic flight data is also displayed on the screen.

EW, EWO—Electronic warfare officer. Defensive member of the crew, evaluates and counters enemy radars and offenses.

EWO—Emergency War Order—the plans under which the execution of nuclear war would be conducted

FNG—Fucking new guy. Anyone new to a unit. This reference is made when a name cannot be recalled or the individual does something questionable.

GCI—Ground control intercept. Radar units on the ground which direct, advise and control aircraft.

Gig line—An imaginary line from the throat to the crotch which takes in the shirt, tie, belt and buckle, and pants fly. All should be in one straight line. Cadets are given demerits if this alignment is not correct.

Groundpounders—Air Force personnel not rated or on flying status

High cone—Point directly over a radio aid, usually at twenty thousand feet, used as a reference point for holding and a point to begin penetration for an approach and landing

Hold line—Line at the intersection of the runway and taxiway leading to the runway which the aircraft holds in anticipation of clearance for takeoff

Horse holders, counts and no accounts—Aides, assistants and others who are not directly involved but are in attendance because of their relationship to the commander or senior staff member

IFF/SIF—Identification Friend or Foe/Selective Identification. Electronically emitted signal which identifies aircraft to ground radar

ILS—Instrument landing system

IP—Instructor pilot. Also the initial point for a bomb run

LC, Lt Col—Lieutenant Colonel

MA, DCM—Deputy Commander for Maintenance

Nav—Navigator. Responsible for aircraft navigation.

O-6, Bird Colonel—Colonel—bird refers to the insignia which is an eagle. O-6 refers to the pay grade. Interchangeable with full bull as well

OER—Officer Effectiveness Report

Preflight—Inspection of the aircraft prior to engine start

Pre-IP—A point prior to the initial point of a bomb run

RN—Radar navigator. Bombardier. Responsible for target identification and release of the weapons

RPM—Revolutions per minute

RTU—Replacement training unit. Refers to B-52 crews qualified in the G and H models who were checked out in the D model and sent to Arc Light

RM—Deputy Commander for Resources

Rolling takeoff—takeoff in which the aircraft lines up and continues its takeoff without stopping on the runway

Secrets Box—Metal container,always locked and sealed, which contained EWO classified mission materials such as maps, targets and other supplemental items. A special locked and sealed container was attached which held the strike documents. The pilot and radar each had a lock on the box; neither knew both combinations. The box was never left with one crewmember.

T-bird—T-33 aircraft

TDY—Temporary duty. The individual or unit could be sent to another duty station without making a permanent change of station.

TGT—Target

TA—Terrain avoidance. The B-52 is equipped with a system which allows the aircraft to be flown at low altitude in conditions in which the ground may not be visible.

Two man policy—The policy states that two qualified individuals must be present with nuclear weapons or components. One lone individual is prohibited.

UT—U-Tapao, Thailand

Wave—One or more cells of aircraft. Usually two cells with a short timing space between them

PREFLIGHT

The sky was still dark when I arose and went into the bathroom to clean up for the coming day. I was looking forward to the day with mixed emotions. I was scheduled to fly what would probably be the last flight I would have in the BUF. We had shared many experiences together, the old girl and I. I had never wanted to fly her, but fate put us together and the association had become one of respect and affection on my part.

I donned my flying suit which I had prepared the night before with all the items I would carry with me. It was an old habit born out of years of early rising in a dark house and many tours of alert duty in which the sound of the klaxon demanded immediate response, with no time to look for things to take along. The coffee was ready and I watched the early news as I drank my ritual cup prior to leaving the house.

I would meet the rest of the crew at base operations where we would review last minute items and file our flight plan for the day. As the Deputy Commander for Operations and a full colonel, I could have waited and arrived at the aircraft at engine start time, but I wanted to savor the whole experience for at least one more time.

The mission was a standard SAC profile. We would meet a tanker for a token onload of fuel, fly a navigation leg to a low level entry point, fly a terrain avoidance route terminating with a simulated bomb release, climb out and return to Fairchild AFB for some approaches and landings.

The weather was dreary. The ceiling was about three hundred feet with occasional light mist. It was not the weather I would have scheduled for a final flight. However, I had little influence with the weather maker.

We arrived at the aircraft, and the crew chief got on the bus with the forms and handed them to me. He mentioned the bird looked good and had no problems which would delay us. This reminded me of the times when I had arrived at the aircraft and it was not ready or had a maintenance problem. In those cases, the person presenting the forms always seemed to inform me that he was not the "regular crew chief." This was common, and we all wished for the day when we would meet the "regular crew chief."

I reviewed the 781, noting items which other crew members should be aware of, and then briefed the crew chief. We left the bus with our equipment and began the exterior preflight. I recalled the first aircraft which I had preflighted many years before.

I LEARNED ABOUT FLYING FROM THAT!

I always wanted to play second base for the St. Louis Cardinals. I had other dreams as well, which seemed just as farfetched. It seems I had more talent for dreams then turning the double play or hitting a baseball. But then, that is what dreams are all about, isn't it?

The dream I was able to fulfill was that of being a pilot, although there were times when it appeared that dream was not attainable. I got my first opportunity while in college. I had always had an interest in drawing and design. I enrolled in the School of Visual Design at Southern Illinois University at Carbondale, Illinois. This was very handy since I also lived just outside of Carbondale. All male students were required, with a few exceptions, to take ROTC (Reserve Officer Training Corps). SIU had an Air Force unit that was one of the largest in the nation. At the end of my sophomore year I took the Air Force Officer Qualification Test and was fortunate enough to pass it and be accepted into the advanced program which, if completed, would result in a commission as a second lieutenant in the Air Force Reserve. There was the possibility of becoming a pilot.

The unit at SIU was a good one with inspirational instructors, admittedly pro Air Force, but with the ability to make one want to succeed in any endeavor. They all had experience in World War II or Korea or both. Most were pilots and their enthusiasm for flying rubbed off on the students. They took us for flights out of Scott AFB and the enthusiasm grew. Our primary instructor my senior year was not rated (read pilot or navigator) but was one of the most inspirational officers I have known. He recognized we were not all pilots to be and some would wash out of flying school. He concentrated on making us responsible and knowledgeable officers.

He appeared in class one day with an examination on etiquette, which he proceeded to administer. He had arranged with an instructor from the Home Economics Department to assist him with the review and subsequent instruction. We spent a week on situations, social and otherwise, which we could possibly face in the future. The one item I always remember (probably because I alone got it correct) was that a wrist watch was not worn with formal attire. In the following thirty years I found many officers wore their watches, probably out of habit, for a watch is a necessity for a flyer. I kept mine in my mess dress pocket.

The detachment commander had many connections and arranged for many speakers to come to the campus. They would speak to the community in the evening, and when possible, spend the day with the ROTC upperclassmen during their periods of instruction. I remember two in particular: Alexander P. de Seversky and Kurt von Schuschnigg.

Alexander de Seversky, an early proponent of airpower, was an interesting speaker who sprinkled his ideas with past experiences as a civilian aeronautical expert.

Schuschnigg was the more interesting to me. Here was a man who was present when history, that has affected all of us, was made. The Chancellor of Austria when Hitler was on the rise, his experiences and impressions of one of history's most infamous dictators was riveting. He spoke of the situation in Europe at the time, the atmosphere and conditions which led him to agree to Hitler's demands and resign two days later. It was a heady, learning experience.

The Air Force began a program for potential pilots during my senior year. Seniors who expressed a desire and met the qualifications were entered into a flying program of forty hours of flying instruction culminating in the student's receiving a private pilot license if successfully completing the checks. The intent was to acclimate the future trainee to flying, and weed out those whose future was not in the cockpit. Only about fifty percent finished that first class with their license, partly due to the academic pressures of completing their education with little time to plan for flying instruction. Following classes had more time to plan. I had one classmate who did not like the instructor yelling at him. I took his place a lot and got yelled at all the time. In fact, the instructor, Glenn Sheets, threatened to make me fly barefooted until I could correctly feel the pressures required on the rudder. He taught me a lot, although my first instructor at pilot training did not seem to believe it.

We were required to pass a flight check to get our private pilot license. Most of us were not going to let anything stand in our way of receiving the reward of forty hours of verbal abuse. The flight school required each potential pilot to complete a flight check with the head instructor prior to the ride with FAA. We planned a cross country flight similar to what would be required for the FAA flight check. I received my flight date and planned my flight. It was a cross country from Murdale to Cincinnati and return. We had been briefed to plan a good mission, but be prepared to break off and complete the required maneuvers at the direction of the check pilot.

The day I arrived for my pre-check ride I got a surprise. A friend and neighbor of mine, Roger, who had a private license prior to entering the AFROTC program at the University of Illinois, had received his instructor check and was present. He was waiting for his orders to active duty and in the interim was going to work as an instructor at Murdale Airport. The check pilot asked if I would mind if Roger accompanied us and observed. Naturally, I would rather not have had anyone else with us in case I blew the check ride, but how could I refuse? I found I could not and the pressure of the ride seemed to double from that point.

The takeoff and departure were normal and I answered each question correctly. Twenty minutes after I had demonstrated the ability to maintain a heading in the general direction I had planned, I was told to demonstrate my skill in flight maneuvers. Following each instruction and demonstration, the check pilot would explain to Roger why he required each activity and what he was looking for.

He asked me to set up a thirty degree banked descending turn to the left. I rolled into a thirty degree bank and began a descent to the left. It quickly became obvious that I had a problem to solve. The airspeed began to climb. I held the turn until it reached a point where I could not continue without exceeding some limits, so I rolled the wings level, slowed down, and rolled into the turn again awaiting further instruction, which came immediately. He told me to return to the airport. He then turned to Roger and told him the point of the exercise was to see if I had enough sense to recognize the potential problem and correct it, or continue to turn until I corkscrewed into the ground. Apparently, I had done it right, for the rest of the flight was easy and I received my real check ride the next week. I passed that one also.

I learned about flying from that!!!

I was attending summer school and taking a photography class. My interest in flying was still great, but I could not afford it. One of the other classes had constructed a geodesic dome next to the building where we held class. It was the result of a visit and seminar held by Buckminster Fuller. One day a discussion of aerial photography came up and someone mentioned that aerial shots of the dome would be nice to have and work with. I immediately volunteered to fly the aircraft if the department would pay for the rental; to my surprise, they agreed. Most of the class volunteered to go along but we had only three seats available in the Cessna 172, in addition to the one I was not about to give up.

The selection of passengers was made and I thought nothing about it at the time. I, of course, was the pilot and weighed about 140 pounds. The others varied—one about 150, one about 170, and the instructor who grossed out at close to 300 pounds. We loaded in with the two smallest in the front and the others in the rear. It was a close fit.

I opened the throttle and we began to roll. The bird wanted to fly so I pulled back on the controls and we became airborne. About fifteen feet in the air the stall warning began to sing to me. The others had no idea what the noise was and were not concerned. I knew and was very concerned. I leveled off and prayed for airspeed. Fortunately, the prayer was answered and we continued at a slow rate of climb. That was my first lesson in weight and balance. The rest of the flight went well as I kept the airspeed as high as safely possible, especially on turns and final approach. We got our photos and I got the flying time, and more importantly, a valuable lesson.

I learned about flying from that!!!

I received my commission and was eagerly awaiting my orders. I had enrolled in graduate school in order to keep my job as a surveyor with the university. I also was working as a janitor and in a service station on weekends. I began to wonder how I was to support a wife as the wedding date rapidly approached. I received my orders on the day of the wedding. I was to report to Lackland AFB, Texas, on 29 April 1958. The wedding went off as planned and Wendy and I made plans to travel.

The time at Lackland was referred to as Preflight. Actually, it was a gradual introduction to the Air Force. We spent what seemed like days filling out forms. There were finance forms, travel forms, personnel forms, medical forms, forms for dependents . . . and on and on. The program had been reduced to four weeks from six weeks and had not been shaken down well when we went through it. We were tested and retested. We had physicals to ensure we were still qualified to fly. It became obvious the program was new. My flight was scheduled for the obstacle course three times instead of the one required.

The training we received was directed toward the eventual arrival at, and entry into, flying training. The most exhilarating was the visit to the parachute training area. The day consisted of practicing the proper fit and operation of the parachute, and what seemed like hours of practicing parachute landing falls and recoveries. The best was left until last. This area consisted of several high towers with lines of cable running out several hundred feet where they terminated about seven feet above the ground against another cable which terminated the descending ride.

The idea and operation was to don the parachute harness and climb the tower, which appeared twice as high as it was. Once safely on the platform near the top, the risers of the parachute harness were attached to one of the cables. Each of us inched forward in line until we were standing with our toes on the edge of the platform. We were then directed to continue to look at the horizon, and, while holding the risers above us, step off of the platform. This was not an easy thing to do, and while no one I know of was pushed, everyone completed the jump. I'm sure the practice is a little like the actual thing and I have never had to test my skills. I kept my eyes on the horizon and reluctantly stepped into space. The drop was only a few feet before the harness jerked me upward and then settled into a long smooth ride to the end of the cable where I was abruptly brought to a stop and barely had time to make a passable landing.

We had all put in our preferences for the bases we would like to attend for primary pilot training. The reality of the assignments we received about a week before the end of preflight had little or nothing to do with the requested preferences. In fact, most seemed to be as far in the opposite direction as possible. (This has seemed to be a constant in my experience with assignments.) I had not asked for it but received Bartow Air Base at Winter Haven, Florida. I'm probably the only one who did not ask for it. It was considered a choice assignment because of the location and it was an officer-only base with no aviation cadets.

Bartow Airbase

Class 59-H was unusual. The class had eighty-eight pilots to be, and twelve of us were brand new second lieutenants. The balance consisted of first lieutenants who were rated navigators with a wide variety of experience in the Air Force. The largest group had been in airlift, generally in C-119's and C-130's.

The base had no facilities for married students. Therefore, we lived off base in Winter Haven for the most part. I was in a carpool with four first lieutenants and was reminded almost daily of the three most useless things in the Air Force: the runway behind you, the altitude above you, and second lieutenants.

Our training was done in the T-34 for the first thirty hours; if qualified, we advanced to the T-28. Both aircraft were prop driven. The class which followed us was the first at Bartow to fly the T-37, a new jet trainer which is still in service.

The class was divided into two sections. One would fly in the morning and attend academic classes in the afternoon. The other section had classes in the morning and flew in the afternoon. This was alternated every week throughout the training period and we got experience in morning and afternoon weather, which in Florida in the summertime could be challenging.

There were two flying periods each morning and afternoon of about one and one half hours each. The training in the T-34 was conducted out of Drane Field, an auxiliary to Bartow. Those scheduled for the first period would takeoff from Bartow and complete their activity by landing at Drane. The students not flying the first period were taken by bus to the auxiliary where they acted as ground crew for the recovering aircraft. Once everyone had soloed, it took a load off of the instructors, and the flying schedule was not as intense for the students. The mornings held few problems, but the afternoons were a different story.

The summer weather in Florida is nothing if not consistent. Each day about fifteen hundred (three p.m.), thunderstorms would build in intensity to the point flying would be terminated until they had dissipated. It was not uncommon to lose the second period to weather. The aircraft would sit on the ramp until the storms had passed; they would then be cranked up and returned to Bartow, often with no time but to go direct and in line. The stream would have both student and instructor-student teams and stretch from Drane to Bartow.

Bartow had two runways. The inner was for the slower T-34 which flew a rectangular pattern; the outer was for the faster T-28 which flew a pitch pattern. The outer was shared with the T-37 until the first class began training and then it was solely for the T-37. The three different aircraft made for interesting activity.

A pitch pattern, flown by the T-28 and T-37, consisted of flying the approach directly to the end of the runway at a constant altitude and airspeed. Upon arriving over the end of the runway, the pilot would pitch, sixty or more degrees of bank turn, and upon rolling level one hundred and eighty degrees from the original heading, lower the landing gear and start a descending turn to final approach while slowing and starting flap extension to roll out on final at approach speed.

The canopy on the T-34 could be opened (it slid backward) when on downwind. It was not necessary to open it, but in Florida in the summer any type of air-conditioning was welcome, so it became a quasi-requirement, especially if there was an instructor on board and it was not raining. It was difficult getting the checklists in order and memorized in the first few flights. Therefore, it was kept in readiness and referred to until all items came naturally. The instructors knew this and some had a twisted sense of humor. As you rolled out on downwind, they would ask where the airfield was, and without thinking the student would point to the airfield. If you happened to point with the hand that held the checklist, the odds were the checklist would be caught in the slipstream and more often than not, disappear. If one did not think quickly and followed the checklist by turning the head and looking for it, there was the slim chance the headset would be caught in the wind and join the checklist. This would open one up for continual abuse from the back seat. I had heard of this and took great care to avoid it.

Transition into the T-28 was a big step, actually and figuratively. The aircraft itself sits high above the ground, about twice as high as the T-34. There is no truth to the rumor that the height could cause vertigo. It certainly seemed a lot larger. The larger engine turned out eight hundred horsepower, four hundred less than the Navy version which would occasionally land at Bartow. They did show off on takeoff by doing a chandelle on their turn out of traffic. We envied that engine.

The aircraft was spacious inside. It had tandem seating for two pilots. The seats were wider and deeper, forcing some smaller pilots to use two back cushions. The canopy was wide and high, creating a feeling of openness. It could be opened in the air; the instructors often did it in the pattern to cool off. The students were forbidden to open it because of the increased rate of descent required to maintain airspeed, and someone in the past had landed short rather than use the throttle.

My instructor had a theory which I agree with for the most part. He felt once we had attained some level of competence in the aircraft we would learn more solo trying to kill ourselves than when we were with him. If he was in mobile control, he would not allow us to terminate until everyone else had landed. At the table he would critique our activity without sparing anyone. He made sure we all learned from each other's mistakes.

It was not unusual to get a view of the future while we were flying. I recall attempting a loop one day, and as I approached the top with the airspeed low, I looked to my left and there on approach to Pinecastle AFB was a B-47. If I had known then, I might have looked closer rather than complete the loop.

The most spectacular views were to the east. Cape Canaveral was in that direction. We often saw the remnants of an aborted missile launch. The contrails were terrific. The good launches were straight up, with only the wind patterns changing the contrails to a graceful corkscrew. Others went in circles, loops and wild turns before they were destroyed and the contrails would linger until the winds blew them to nothingness.

The instructors were known for their lack of sensitivity and had little regard that they might be teaching a future Chief of Staff. Most were veterans. They seemed to enjoy reminding us of our inadequacies over and over. The attention they gave us in this respect probably has saved numerous lives. I came to this conclusion about halfway through the program when I was being berated unceasingly about my inability to feel what the aircraft was telling me. I glanced in the rear view mirror and while he was chewing me out he was laughing. Here's a belated thanks, Mac.

Then there was Whispering Smith. He briefed in almost a whisper and seemed very subdued. Once the interphone was plugged in he became a screaming terror. He could have communicated without an interphone, maybe even the radio. I flew the return of my out and back cross country with him. He was constantly yelling and screaming until we leveled off, and then he said very little until we were almost back at Bartow. He then asked me where we were, and I pointed to and identified the Bartow rotating light beacon. He took the aircraft, told me to put away my maps, and as I bent to do so rolled the aircraft upside down and split S into the downwind pattern from eight thousand feet. He racked it around the pattern and pitched out as I sat fat, dumb and happy. He flew final approach to about one hundred feet above the runway and told me to take it and land. I reacted automatically, took the stick, reduced the power and flared. The touchdown was very smooth. I'd like to say it was skill, but every pilot who might read this will know it was luck. Did I mention it was nighttime?

I learned about flying from that!!!

The T-28 was a good trainer—fast enough to build confidence, and slow enough to be reasonably safe. In the six months at primary we had only one accident in all the classes, and it was in a T-34. No one was hurt. More about that later.

The T-28s worked between five and ten thousand feet for transition and acrobatics. The entry into the traffic pattern was unique in most cases. The entry consisted of intercepting downwind at a forty-five degree angle, turning base leg, and an initial approach to a pitch pattern for landing. This pattern would get extended toward the end of a flying period as the aircraft returned. The approach to downwind would sometimes reach almost to Lake Okeechobee. We would fly along the forty-five to the downwind in the opposite direction about eight thousand feet until the end of the stream was located.

Recognizing the end of the stream, the pilot would raise the nose, kick a rudder, and hold it until the aircraft began to spin. The spin was held until about twenty-five hundred feet, where spin recovery was initiated to roll out right behind the last aircraft in the stream. The unlucky pilot who had to break out of the pattern had the difficulty of re-entering without making it a cross country trip. If a touch and go was made, a game of chicken often occurred on downwind.

One of the flying hazards was the buzzards. They were large. They flew between one and two thousand feet above the ground. The hot Florida atmosphere was full of thermal currents and the buzzards would find one;

with their wings spread wide, they would glide and soar in what looked like effortless flight. They had been there forever and we were new on the scene. Of course, we were much larger and moved much faster.

They had to be aware of us and it appeared they played a game with us. They would glide at the same altitude as the aircraft, and when it appeared as if a collision was imminent, their wings would fold and they would drop quickly to a lower and safer altitude. At times, when the buzzards' reactions were slow, a collision did occur. The buzzard is a large and tough bird, but a collision with a metal airplane, especially the prop, makes the bird the loser. The airplane did not get off without damage. The prop could be thrown out of balance or bent. The hairiest was a punctured fuel tank, which, along with the rapid loss of fuel, presented the potential for fire. That was the price for entering their airspace. They did have to adjust with the advent of the faster T-37.

I learned about flying from that!!!

Instrument flying is probably the hardest for which the pilot has to adjust. In preparation for flight, hours were spent in the Link Trainer, a mock cockpit, fully enclosed, on a pedestal. It moves about the pedestal as the pilot makes his pitiful inputs. It is difficult to believe you are flying when in the trainer; deep down you know better. That is not to say one could not get totally confused and have no idea what was going on or even what should be occurring. It is not difficult to break a sweat in the box. The debriefing which followed the session confirmed what you knew all along—that you had absolutely no comprehension as to what you were supposed to be doing.

The aircraft was better in some respects. Instrument flight was conducted with the instructor in the front seat to provide clearance from other aircraft. The student would fly in the rear seat. Just prior to taking the active runway, he would pull a canvas hood, attached to the back of the headrest, forward over himself and attach it to the instrument cowl. The student's world became reduced to the area immediately around him—the seat to the rear, the instrument panel in front, and the cockpit rails and fuselage to the sides. The hood was white, and supposed to reflect heat. The heat of the sun did not appear to reflect outward but burn right through and create a living hell. The temperature was in direct relation to the difficulty the student was experiencing.

The procedure was to takeoff, depart, and complete a series of aerial maneuvers under the hood with no reference except the instruments in front of you. The only thing not accomplished under the hood was the landing, which was made by the instructor in the front seat most of the time. After the first few periods under the hood, the old axiom "one peek is worth a thousand crosschecks" began to make sense.

Instrument flying is a slower process than the other phases; you are learning to trust your mind to interpret and accept what your eyes are seeing on the instrument panel and take the appropriate actions with no outside references. Later, when you had mastered the concepts and were able to apply them—to do exactly what you wished (most of the time)—there was no greater feeling of accomplishment than to break through a 200 foot ceiling on centerline and glidepath to land the aircraft gracefully on the awaiting runway.

OK. Most of the time you landed smoothly . . . at least part of the time. The road to that confidence was often rough and rocky, and failure was not impossible to contemplate.

Instrument flying with foreign students was always interesting. We had them from many nations. You could identify them by their accents on the radio. Selecting the interphone versus the radio seemed to be difficult for them. All transmissions were halted when one was reading the checklist on the radio instead of interphone.

Takeoff under the hood was always a trial. The instructor would line up on the runway centerline. When cleared by the instructor, the student would advance the power and with reference only to the heading indicator, turn and slip indicator, and airspeed, attempt to keep the aircraft on the runway centerline until the proper airspeed for liftoff was attained. Rudder trim was set to assist in overcoming engine torque, but rudder action was still needed as the aircraft began its roll. It was easy to imagine careening from one side of the runway to the other and ending in a fiery crash at the end of it. The instructor was constantly and sarcastically confirming these fears. Of course, he had a distinct advantage, he could see outside!

The most vivid memory I have is of the early morning first period flights. Fall had come. It was cool enough to warrant wearing the summer flight jacket. Our aircraft were not heated and the jacket was welcome for the first ten minutes. It could be worn with little discomfort on other flights, but an hour under the hood and it was miserable. As the sun heated the rear cockpit, sweat poured into the eyes and life became barely tolerable.

I was flying with a substitute instructor as my regular instructor was recovering from conjunctivitis, possibly brought on from the thought of flying with me and needing to constantly keep his eyes peeled.

I would preflight and then we would board the aircraft, start engines and taxi out. I would put up the hood. The aircraft would still be cool. With no time to remove and stow my jacket, we would be off defying gravity again. Shortly afterward, the temperature would begin to rise. At this point there was no way to remove the jacket without giving the instructor control of the aircraft and praying that when he returned it, it would not be in an unusual position, requiring recovery and a lengthy discourse on the lack of forethought and planning on my part. While I may not have had good control, at least I had some with a general idea of the attitude and position of the aircraft. The sweat poured down.

This particular instructor had a habit I will never forget. We had learned that as altitude increases, gasses also increase in volume. Therefore, to preclude acute discomfort, we were taught what food and beverages to ingest prior to flight. Our wives, if we were married, were also given the same information. We were also taught the two ways to reduce the discomfort and encouraged to use them regardless of what was accepted in polite society. My instructor had learned the lessons well.

The flight progressed. We gained altitude. As I began to gain a little confidence, he would become flatulent—not just flatulent, but big-league flatulent. It was all I could do to concentrate on the instruments with my eyes tearing and shallow breathing as the green fog crept silently under my instrument panel and rose on the warm air currents of the enclosed cockpit. Obviously, I survived, but have often wondered what would have happened had I declared that I had fumes in the cockpit, declared an emergency, and attempted to return to the base. Unfortunately, we did not have oxygen available either.

I learned about flying from that!!!

Primary flight training came to an end in November 1958. The last requirement prior to graduation and assignments for basic flight training was to pass a checkride. No one wanted to have a military checkride, for the military pilots were considered to be much tougher than the civilians. Whether this was true or not, it was the accepted conventional wisdom. Since my instructor had been ill, we were some of the last students to get our checkrides; mine was the day prior to graduation. Did I feel pressure? Does a bear crap in the woods? One other student was also scheduled for a military checkride at the same time.

I appeared at the appointed time at the military evaluator's office. He sat down and explained to me what we would be doing and what he expected of me. We took our gear and proceeded to the aircraft. The fear of any pilot, especially one undergoing a checkride, is to hear the evaluator say the dreaded words: "I have the aircraft." This generally indicates that the pilot committed some unforgivable act which guarantees that he has failed the ride. I preflighted the exterior and we got into our seats. The engine was started; we taxied to the runway for departure. So far, so good. The takeoff was perfect. I made the first turn out of traffic, and as I rolled out of the second turn I heard it: "I have the aircraft."

My world fell apart. I could think of nothing that had not been by the book. We continued to climb, and the evaluator made clearing turns keeping the airfield in sight. My mind was racing, trying to determine what had gone wrong and what, if anything, I could do to correct it. The interphone came alive and the voice asked, "Can you keep a secret?" It was at that time I realized I had passed my checkride.

I immediately assured him I could. He replied that he was going to jump the other evaluator as soon as he broke out of traffic. This comment reaffirmed my knowledge of successfully completing my ride unless I spun in on final. As the other aircraft turned out of traffic, we were on his tail. For the next twenty minutes we rat-raced around the sky, chasing each other and flying closer at times than I had ever imagined. My emotions went from close to terror to complete elation. This was what it was all about.

It ended too soon. He finally broke it off indicating that he had better see if I could actually fly the aircraft. The maneuvers I executed were quite tame compared to the ones we had just experienced. The forced landing was completed, and as we climbed up he noted the other aircraft just beginning its approach to a nearby field. He again took the bird, and for the next ten minutes or so we were again on the roller coaster. Eventually we broke off and returned to Bartow.

I learned about flying from that!!!

I graduated with my class the next day and was assigned to Greenville AFB, Mississippi, for basic flight training. I had my ticket to the T-Bird.

GREENVILLE

Greenville, Mississippi, in 1959 was not the garden spot of the United States. It was cold. It was damp. It was the South in 1959. It was also a place with friendly people. The Air Force was economically good for the town, and they generally reflected their appreciation. Adequate housing was in short supply. We were fortunate we had some friends we could stay with for a few days while trying to find a place to live. Arriving prior to the departure of the class we were replacing did not help the situation.

We found three houses for rent. One I refused to live in. The second was rented by the time we found it, ironically by one of my carpoolers. The third was a brand new two-bedroom house built in the middle of a junk yard. I kid you not, it was surrounded by stacks of junked cars, aircraft canopies, and other various and sundry items which could only be described as junk. The owner assured us he was going to clean it up. Desperate for a place to live, we rented it, rationalizing that if we kept the drapes closed we wouldn't notice the junk. He kept his word; the junk was removed well before our six-month tour was complete.

The house was furnished with everything but a refrigerator, which we were told would arrive the next day. We expected an apartment size and were pleasantly surprised when a very large one was delivered. He had a carport built as well, right in front of the front door. He was an excellent landlord and nice gentleman as well. However, we did keep the drapes closed.

The next month was spent anxiously awaiting the arrival of our first daughter. Jami arrived in January 1959. I spent most evenings studying for the silver wings. Wendy helped me with the procedures. I think she still knows the emergency procedures for the T-33. All in all, it was one of the best periods of our lives, junkyard and all.

We acclimated to basic flight training much easier than primary. The biggest difference, other than the aircraft, was the all-military instructor force and the presence of flight cadets. Aviation cadets were student pilots who had not received a commission but were receiving flight training. If they completed the course successfully, they would be commissioned as second lieutenants the same day they received their wings. Second lieutenants were not the lowest on the pecking order at last. However we all suffered the same; to some extent, even the first lieutenants who outranked the instructors received a ration of grief. In retrospect, it was worth it.

The T-33A single engine jet trainer, commonly called the T-Bird, was a two-seat version of the Lockheed F-80 Shooting Star modified for flight instruction. It was one of the most enjoyable planes to fly; there may still be a few in the inventory. Our instruction would be similar to what we had in primary, with the addition of formation flight. Normally, we did not start formation until we had soloed (on the average eight hours of time in the bird) and collected about twenty hours and the confidence of our instructors.

The first flight was an opportunity for the instructor to demonstrate the aircraft capabilities and for the student to begin to get the feel of the differences. This was commonly called the *dollar ride* because some students lost about a dollar's worth of lunch during the ride. Most of us did not.

My first flight was on a beautiful, clear, crisp Monday in December. It had rained over the weekend but the sky had cleared and the weather was great for flying. The sky was blue forever, the temperature below freezing, and yes, it was in Mississippi.

Everything went well. I started the engine and did not get much of a whump when I pulled the throttle back and released the emergency fuel system checkout switch . . . that in itself was progress.

I taxied and took my position for takeoff. My instructor was talking me through each step as I was released by runway control and advanced power for takeoff. The instruments checked and the aircraft accelerated very smoothly. I began to add back pressure on the stick as we reached 85 knots. The airspeed reached 100, 110, and as it reached our takeoff of 120 knots, I noticed the altimeter unwinding, indicating we were below sea level. My "outstanding pilot knowledge" told me the altimeter was wrong since it was obvious we were climbing into what was to become the wild blue yonder. I calmly brought this to the attention of the instructor and added that my airspeed indicator was also decreasing although we were accelerating. He grasped the situation (and the stick!) immediately and advised control we were without two of the required instruments for safe flight. He had no sooner completed the transmission than others began to call in similar problems.

This situation is considered an emergency and the corrective action is to remain under visual flight conditions, if possible, and wait until another aircraft, hopefully of the same type, can rendezvous and lead you to a safe landing. The only requirement of the emergency aircraft is to fly formation right down to the runway. We were advised to proceed to a holding point and wait until we could be escorted back to the airfield. It became apparent quite rapidly that there were a lot of birds with a problem and only few without it. The radio chatter was great. We had solo aircraft and dual aircraft, some with formation experience and some without. Getting together with the right combination of competence was just short of a miracle. Eventually, the formations were put together and given landing times. Some instructors were adamant about not leading a formation with a solo student who had never flown formation before. Initially, some aircraft were put together, which had the same problem, but in the end it all worked out.

I spent my dollar ride receiving my first formation ride. We had plenty of time to practice simple maneuvers. It proved to be much more instructive than a dollar ride could ever have been. We flew the wing of an aircraft with reliable instruments, and although ours gradually came back, they were intermittent and unreliable. At our appointed time we descended to pattern altitude, flying the wing of the lead aircraft down to just above touchdown where it executed a missed approach, and we landed; that is, the instructor landed, I just rode it out. We recovered everyone with no incidents. I was probably not smart enough to recognize the full problem at the time, especially with the number of aircraft involved, but in retrospect it was pucker time.

I learned about flying from that!!!

The program was fast-paced, or at least it seemed like it to us at the time. We initially flew contact, mastering the flight maneuvers required to become familiar with the aircraft and its limitations as well as building confidence. This involved takeoff, climbs, turns, descents, pattern work, landings and aerobatics. I don't know a pilot that does not enjoy a tight pitch pattern to a touch-and-go landing followed by a closed pattern to another landing. This is one of the events where you become a part of the bird. The other is aerobatics, either solo or in formation, and air refueling is another, but that came later in a different bird.

When the instructor thought you were safe enough to fly in the pattern alone (or was scared to fly with you!), he would clear you for a solo flight where you stayed in the pattern and practiced landings, normally three. This generally occurred when the student had about eight hours in the aircraft. Once you had soloed and convinced the instructor you could handle the bird reasonably well, he would start in the formation phase.

Formation flying involved a formation takeoff and departure with the instructor close on the controls to ensure you did not overcontrol and become entangled with the lead aircraft. When the student demonstrated some competence, he would be allowed to fly solo in formation. Some got very little solo formation. The maneuvers consisted of all of the contact activities. The wingman attempted to maintain a position a few feet off of the lead's wing, or in trail a few feet below and behind his tailpipe. This was done at speed up to just short of the Mach. As the flight number increased to three or four ships, it became more interesting and intense. It seemed my instructor was always in a three or four ship formation; I got a lot of experience in all positions, mostly solo. Instrument flying was introduced after a few more hours of experience.

Several times a week we had an event that was magnetic and scary. Of course, it was not scary while we were in flight training. We would hear the call:

"Attention all Greenville aircraft. Use extreme caution! A B-47 and KC-97 are conducting refueling operations in the south transition area. All aircraft stay away from the south transition area between the altitudes of twelve and twenty thousand feet."

This would be repeated several times until all aircraft had the opportunity to hear it. Almost immediately, all solo aircraft would head for the south transition area to see the show! This did not bother me until about a year later when I was in the B-47 and knew what was going on all around me.

The first night solo flight in the T-Bird was enlightening, no pun intended. I had flown at night before in primary, but this was a new environment. The procedure went somewhat like this. The instructor flew with the student for several approaches and landings until he felt comfortable with the student's ability; then he got out and the student went off on his own. The second flight was solo, and the student was assigned an altitude in the transition or formation area and a penetration time. A normal instrument departure was flown to the altitude, and radio checks were made at given intervals to ensure all was well. At the penetration time the student was expected to be over the high cone of the VOR and report starting his penetration from twenty thousand feet to the traffic pattern for a full-stop landing.

The first night penetration alone at Greenville kept the adrenaline level up. The initial heading was to the northwest toward the White River bottoms in Southeast Arkansas. There were absolutely no lights on the ground for reference. It was pitch black, and the rate of descent was 4,000 feet per minute. The only lights were on the instrument panel until the penetration turn was completed and the aircraft was inbound to the pattern. A real confidence builder!

We did many things that did not seem dangerous at the time, but when we thought about them later, wondered how we could be so stupid. One of the scariest parts of flying was the formation reforming. This activity was practiced after someone had fallen out of formation; the whole gaggle just went to shit or to practice so it could be accomplished. It was a simple procedure; the intent was to get the formation back together. The lead would set up an orbit with a thirty degree banked turn. He would hold this until each aircraft rejoined the formation in its original position and in order. The process could get lengthy when everyone was new or someone was having difficulty. The wingman would approach the lead, or in case of three and four, the respective aircraft that had been between him and the lead.

The proper airspeed differential and closure rate were critical. The lead had to hold his position and altitude while the rejoining aircraft aimed at him and tried to smoothly return to position. It was not uncommon for the rate of closure to be too high. When this happens the closing aircraft may raise his wing to slow the closure. If this happens, he loses sight of lead, and lead can only see a rapidly closing piece of metal. If the closing aircraft elects to drop the wing and go under lead, he can still see the lead but the lead can only hope he does not try to correct back, for the lead's belly is vulnerable. It even gets more scary when number four is having difficulty finding the slot. It is somewhat like a mass Mongolian goat rope. Some pilots can do it easily; others make the lead's hair turn gray. I spent a lot of time in orbit as lead; I have a lot of gray hair!

As the program advanced, the student would fly different missions each week with fewer and fewer contact flights. It was not unusual, due to instrument flying in the rear seat—weather, illness, or combination of factors to go for seven days without a landing in the front seat. When this occurred, the student could not fly solo until he had a flight with an instructor and made some front-seat landings.

This was obviously called a front-seat ride. Everyone had one at some time. I do not recall the reason but found myself in need of a front-seat ride and was scheduled with the flight commander. Normally, several students would be scheduled and the instructor would give each three landings and thus update their front-seat date. I had flown with the flight commander before and remembered he had difficulty, or so it seemed to me, completing a good coordinated chandelle.

I was the second student to fly that day. He taxied in and I replaced the other student. I strapped in and made my hookups to oxygen and radios while he taxied to the runway. We ran through our pre-takeoff checks and he gave me control. He told me to stay in the pattern and do a series of touch-and-go landings—simple instructions for a simple student who did as he was told. I flew initial, pitched and kept it tight (it was allowed in those days), reduced my airspeed to 140 knots plus 5 knots for each 100 gallon increment over 200 gallons (yes, the T-Bird fuel was measured in gallons not pounds), turned final and set my speed at 120 knots plus the required amount for fuel. I completed the touch-and-go and requested a closed pattern to another touch- and-go.

The instructor critiqued my approach and said I flew my final too fast. I quickly checked my figures and was sure I was correct, but rogered him and set up to improve this time. As I rolled out on final and set my airspeed, I was told I was too fast. Everything still checked with my calculations. On the go he took the aircraft and informed me he would show me how it was done.

I did not argue; I was a student, a second lieutenant, and he was a captain. I was there to learn. We had learned that we did not question the instructor unless we were absolutely positive we were right. I have since changed my approach to that idiocy!

He turned to final, and I noticed the airspeed was 15 to 20 knots higher than what I had held, but assumed he knew what he was doing. The airspeed did not drop off as we came down the chute. I noticed the throttle was in idle. I ran a quick cockpit check, and before I could say anything, the flares were in the air from runway control and we were advised: "On final, go around! No flaps!" The interphone in the T-Bird is always hot and it was all I could do to keep from laughing. It was very quiet and I was told to take it and make a full-stop landing. I did. Nothing was said until the ride in from the flight line when the instructor looked at me and said, "Well, we had fun today, didn't we?" I agreed.

I learned about flying from that!!!

I enjoyed basic much more than primary and my progress showed it. The time passed rapidly, but the specter of the graduation and silver wings always seemed to be far off in the future. The pace was faster, and before I knew it, it was time for my mid-phase formation check. I was scheduled to fly with another instructor; in the second aircraft was an instructor returning from Squadron Officer School receiving a requalification checkride. I knew I was in for a ride when, after we leveled off and ran our checks, the lead began a slow climb and I saw the landing gear doors crack open and the gear come down. Without thinking, I lowered my gear and noticed lead's flaps had begun to extend. I followed with mine, although I had never gone through this drill before. The lead's flaps had no sooner fully extended than the retraction process began. After this little exercise, all the normal maneuvers, including aerobatics, seemed like old hat, and the flight went well. When my turn to lead came, I did not reciprocate. I passed with flying colors.

The final checkride was the one we all faced with some dread, and rightfully so. The worst thing we could imagine was to get to the last flight and blow the whole course. In reality, few who got that far were washed out unless they could not put it all together. If you blew the ride, and were not dangerously unsafe, you got another chance. I flew a second ride.

Instrument flying in training is not the same as the real thing, but is close in that you have no outside references. The feeling of space is not available under the hood. The pilot learned to set up a crosscheck of the instruments without becoming fixated on just one. This included the engine instruments, radio instruments, and flight instruments. Disorientation is not uncommon. The final checkride was basically an instrument ride.

Instrument flying is different. It is not unusual for a pilot to master most phases of flight and have problems with others. For example, the presence of another voice giving instructions sometimes is calming and a pilot will have little difficulty flying a GCA (Ground Controlled Approach) precision approach, but an ILS (Instrument Landing System) without the voice means reliance upon one's own skills completely. It may be more difficult. I had no more problem than most. The one which I found the easiest was the aural null procedure. Basically, this involved tuning and identifying a radio station, rotating the loop to locate the null, determine the direction and degrees to turn to put the null on the wingtip, set the radio compass azimuth needle to the nearest wingtip and turn to that heading. Upon rollout, determine the direction of the station by the direction the needle moves. Time, distance and heading to the station can be determined. The pilot receiving the check runs a commentary to the flight examiner as to what he is doing and what he plans to do. He then accomplishes it to the best of his ability.

The standardization flight wore black hats and tried to live up to their reputation as tough but fair evaluators. The tension could be cut with a knife, but the atmosphere was built intentionally. If you dealt with it well and succeeded, it was not only the final step to the silver wings but created a sense of accomplishment and confidence in your abilities. Stan-eval helped build the apprehension. If and when the student successfully completed this checkride, he would put his name on the full length, *check your gig line* mirror in the front corner of the room with any comments he felt appropriate.

My examiner briefed me on the flight and the order in which we would complete each required phase. We picked up our helmets and chutes and proceeded to the aircraft. The departure and cruise to Little Rock went well. I flew my ILS approach well enough to pass, continued my missed approach and climb to return to Greenville. Enroute, the instructor took control of the radio and tuned in the local station at Greenville. I was then told to complete an aural null procedure. I confidently went through the procedures and advised him of our distance and time to the station and that it would require a turn to the left. He acknowledged and told me to home in, so I turned . . . right. We flew for about two minutes when he told me to pop the hood. I knew I had done something wrong, but did not know what. He told me to look around and think about what we had just done. It dawned on me. That terminated the mission as far as a checkride was concerned. The one thing I had not worried about was the thing that got me. I felt lower than whale poop.

The amazing thing to me was that no one—the examiner, my instructor, the flight and assistant flight commander—seemed too concerned. I think that approach kept my confidence high enough that the second flight was completed with minor discrepancies. I had earned the silver wings.

The Air Force had taught me to fly, paid me for it, and were going to continue to do both. I put my name on the mirror . . . "wrong way" Hooppaw.

I learned about flying from that!!!

I had never had to worry about flying pay because I had been flying continuously since I had entered flight training. My graduation date was 10 June 1959, and I had not received enough flying time in June to qualify for flight pay. The wing had made a few T-Birds available for those who were interested and had the time to fly. Many of us could not get on the schedule.

I could find no way until my friend Joe approached me and asked if I would be interested in flying in a C-47. Joe was a rated navigator as well as a brand new pilot. We had been at Bartow together. He found that a C-47 was flying checks on the radio aids in the area and had a spot for an extra pilot to log time. He said he was willing to log navigator time and I could log pilot time; we would both get paid.

I agreed. I always thought it interesting that my first rated time (that accumulated after winning my wings) was completed in a Gooney Bird which had been flying almost as long as I'd lived. I even got some stick time and have a soft spot in my heart for the old girl.

ENGINE START

The preflight went well, and we found no discrepancies with the air craft. I hoped this was the way the crews always found the aircraft, not just because an 0-6 was on the schedule. In reality, I knew the maintenance people wanted things to go well, but when you are working with machinery and electronics, strange things can happen. Equipment may work fine, and then for no apparent reason just refuse to operate.

The weather held steady. The ceiling was low; no change in the forecast was predicted until well after our departure. We had a short break before engine start time. I got out of the aircraft and into the vehicle with the Supervisor of Flying. We discussed the weather and other unimportant items until it was time to reboard the aircraft.

I climbed into the aircraft and up the stairs to the pilot's seat. I slipped into the parachute and connected the shoulder straps and seat belt. I then put on my helmet and connected the oxygen hose to the chute. The copilot was also ready and called the tower:

"Fairchild tower, Maggie 11 starting engines, spot twelve."
"Maggie 11, roger; altimeter 29.89; temperature 59 degrees; wind 250 at 5. Call ready to taxi."
"Maggie 11, wilco."
I started the checklist.
"Parking brakes, set."
"Battery." CP— "On."
"Interphone, on."
"External power." CP— "On."
"Ground, start external air."
Ground— "Roger," CP— "30 psi."
"Ground, stand by to start engines."
Ground— "Fire guard posted and clear."
"Starting number four."

The copilot put the number four starter switch to start, and at 15% RPM I advanced the throttle to what should be 90% RPM while monitoring the EGT and fuel-flow gauges. We did the same for number 5 engine; when it reached 85%, we began to start the remaining engines. When they reached idle, I reduced the power on 4 and 5 to idle and continued the checklist:

"Starters and light." CP— "Off and out."
"Nav, close entry hatch." Nav— "Locked."   "Light out."
"Manifold valve." CP— "Closed."
"Generators." CP— "On. Battery lights out."
"Air conditioning." CP— "7.45."
"Anti-ice set climatic."
"Liaison radio." CP— "On."
"Ground, clear aircraft for taxi." Ground— "Roger."
"IFF/SIF is set standby."
"Body standby pumps off."
"Rudder-Elevator. On, lights out."
"Hydraulic pressure checked."
"Stab trim checked, takeoff trim set." CP— "Set."
"EVS, on." CP— "On."
"Crew equipment on and adjusted, pilot." CP— "On and adjusted."
"Oxygen set, pilot." CP— "Set."
"Bomb doors clear?" Ground— "Clear."   "Closed." Ground— "Closed."
"Ground, remove wheel chocks, disconnect interphone and stand by to taxi."
Ground— "Roger, wheel chocks removed leaving interphone. Have a good flight, sir."
"Anti-collision and nav lights." CP— "On and steady."
"Fairchild tower, Maggie 11, spot 12 ready to taxi."
"Maggie 11, roger. Altimeter 29.89, wind 260 at 6. Turn right, taxi to runway 23."
"Maggie 11 copies."

The crew chief had moved across the taxiway directly in front of me. I flashed the landing lights and he began to motion me forward. I called for the taxi checklist as I applied power, released the parking brake and applied the brakes. "Brakes checked."

CP— "Flap lever down."

I approached the centerline of the taxiway, and as I crossed it applied full right rudder and turned to the right. "Turn and slip indicators checked, pilot."

"Checked, copilot."

I turned onto the parallel taxiway. "Crosswind crab."

I pulled up the control handle and checked the crab right and left and used the centering button to bring it back to center and pushed the handle down. "Checked and down, pilot."

"Checked and down, copilot."

We continued to the end of the runway and stopped in the number one position. The supervisor of flying asked for clearance to check the exterior and I cleared him in. I asked for the Before Lineup checklist.

"Brakes." "Set."
"Pitot heat." "Set."
"Control surface trim set, copilot."
"Set, pilot."
"Stab trim checked for takeoff setting, copilot."
"Checked for takeoff setting, pilot."
"Airbrakes."
"Off."
"Flaps, 100%, lever down, copilot."
"100%, lever down, pilot."
"Fuel panel switches set."
"Checked, pilot."
"Windows and hatches closed and locked, copilot."
"Closed and locked, pilot."
"Flight instruments set, copilot."
"Set, pilot."

"Set, nav."

"Radar altimeter set 500 feet, copilot."

"Set 500 feet, pilot."

"Radio navigation instruments checked and set, copilot."

"Checked and set, pilot."

"Air-conditioning head outlets set, copilot."

"Set, pilot."

"Generators checked."

"Starter selector flight start."

"Takeoff data."

We reviewed the S1 speed and timing as well as the takeoff speed and emergency best flare speed.

"Reviewed, pilot."

"Reviewed, copilot."

"Reviewed, nav. 15 seconds."

"Yaw and pitch SAS switches."

"Engaged. Lights off."

"Autopilot power switch on."

"Seat, rudder pedals and controls column adjusted and checked, copilot."

"Adjusted and checked, pilot."

"Arming lever safety pins removed, copilot."

"Removed, pilot."

"Removed, EW."

"Removed, gunner."

"Trigger ring."

"Unstowed, radar."

"Unstowed, nav."

"Zero delay lanyard hooked, copilot."

"Hooked, pilot." "Hooked, EW."

"Hooked, gunner."

"Crew, standby for takeoff."

"Fairchild tower, Maggie 11 ready for takeoff."

"Maggie 11, squawk 321, maintain runway heading, climb to flight level 210, contact departure control on 284.6. Cleared for takeoff."

"Maggie 11 copies cleared as requested, contact departure control on 284.6, cleared for takeoff. 11's rolling."

"Maggie 11."

"IFF/SIF." "Set."

I realized this would probably be the last time I made a takeoff in the BUF. I wondered how many times I had been in this position at the end of a runway.

B-47

The one event we all looked forward to with great anticipation once we were assured of completing flying school and receiving our wings was the day the follow-on assignments arrived. Anticipation in some ways, dread in others. A lot depended upon where you were in class standing as to whether you would receive an assignment to the aircraft of choice: your choice, not the Air Force's. We all took our flight training in single-engine aircraft with basic training in T-Birds and were one of the last classes to fly the T-34 and T-28. The Air Force was on its way to an all-jet force to include initial flight training. A portion of 59-H had been in the Air Force and were rated as navigators with experience in other aircraft. The majority of us had never flown any aircraft other than the trainers. Selecting our follow-on assignments had more to do with visions of our own abilities and wishes than the more practical matter of which we were more suited to fly.

The proposed assignments took up a good bit of discussion. This was our future and had to be planned accordingly. We talked among ourselves as to what we thought we would like to fly and the good and bad points of each potential aircraft and command—even going so far as to ask those who daily ridiculed and railed at us about our lack of ability to walk and chew gum at the same time, much less consider flying and thinking. It still came down to the luck of the draw.

The procedure we were briefed on follows: The Air Force would provide each training base with a list of aircraft available for class assignments. This list would be put on the board for all to consider. Each new pilot would list three aircraft in the order of preference. Each instructor would list each of his pilots and the aircraft and order in which he thought the pilot would be most suited. The flight commander would do the same. The class standings, in flight and academics, were combined for an overall standing. This information would be forwarded with the selections for consideration and, after what seemed like an eternity, the assignments would be posted.

The general trend was that the pilot who was number one in class standing was expected to request and receive a fighter assignment. Pressure was often applied to someone who considered anything with more than one engine or other than centerline thrust. Our student flight commander had been a navigator in C-124s. When asked what he wanted to fly, he replied: "Multi-engine. When the pilot tells me to shut down number four, I want to be able to ask, 'Which wing?'"

The precedent at the time was that if you did not receive your first choice, or if it was not available by the time your position in class standing arrived, you were assigned to B-47s. Most classes had a better than 50% assignment to the Stratojet. It was not an assignment many asked for or desired. Although many tried to work the system to get their choice, no-body seemed to win unless they were high in the standings or selected something that was not too desirable, such as the B-47 and the KC-97.

It seemed everyone wanted the F-86, F-100 or C-135 (Air Force version of the Boeing 707)—not to be confused with the KC-135 which belonged to SAC. It should be noted that Strategic Air Command aircraft were not considered desirable. It was not the birds, but the duty. We could not even apply for the B-52 even if we wanted. My class standing was 12th.

I had it made. Right?

I had a friend in 59-G who thought he had a system to get his first choice. He really wanted SA-16s which had an air/sea rescue mission. Since many had not received their first choice, especially fighters, he altered his choices: F-100, helicopters, and SA-16. Naturally, his assignment was to F-100s. The last I heard he was still with PanAm.

Our assignments came in on a Sunday and I received a C-135 assignment. A correction came in on Monday and I was reassigned to B-47s. It took several days before anyone told me that I had originally been assigned to C-135s and changed to B-47s. In retrospect, it was probably the best thing for me. Everyone else had received an end-base assignment. Since mine had been changed, it took some time for me to learn I was going to Little Rock AFB, Arkansas. Additionally, because of the change, I would go to McConnell AFB, Kansas, for academics only and receive my flight training at my assigned unit, the 384th Bomb Wing. Enroute to McConnell, I was to attend USAF Survival School at Stead AFB located a few miles north of Reno, Nevada.

Wendy and Jami stayed with our parents, since they lived in the same town, while I went to Stead. Wendy was with a group of other young married women one day when they asked what I did for a living. She replied I was a pilot in the Air Force. They all thought this was really something. She told them most of our friends also flew jet aircraft and it did not seem like a big deal to her.

Four of us from my flying class met in Kansas City and drove to Stead in one car.

The course was about seventeen days in duration. At times it seemed longer. We arrived in the afternoon and were assigned quarters. The airman who checked us in told us we might be picked up later to help fight some forest fires up on Peavine Mountain. We discussed this among ourselves, cleaned up, and went into Reno for the night. Fire fighting was not our specialty.

School started with academics and preparation for the seven-day trek we would spend in the field. The preparation consisted of exercise and running. Fortunately, we were in pretty good shape and the altitude did not bother us too much. As we went through our course, many of the civilian firefighters were housed in the same containment area we were. Most were Indians from Arizona, and we rarely saw them except in the shower area. They would strip, throw away their clothes, wash up, dress in clean clothes, and go back to work.

Escape and evasion were an integral part of the training. Each class was required to pass through an area which contained border-type obstacles and other potential dangers to a downed airman in enemy territory. This area also contained roving guards, and to make it interesting, there were many booby traps that set off flares when initiated. This was done at night. The area was just off the end of the runway, which made it even more interesting. Stead was a helicopter training base and they flew around the clock. Many evaders were in mid-stride when a helicopter approaching the runway turned on the landing lights. Actually, it added a touch of reality.

We began the exercise as soon as the sky was dark and had until midnight to complete it. The object was to pass through without detection. If detected or captured, the evader would then be put into a prisoner of war camp. The Tactical Air Command guys went in it regardless. They could become POWs. I guess we were written off. If the evader followed the guidelines and approached the evasion properly, it was not too difficult to get through it. I know, for I did it without capture.

I was lying on the edge of a ditch which was about six feet deep and more that ten feet wide. As I lay there trying to determine the best method to cross, I heard someone running. They stopped; the sound of a body hitting the far side of the ditch was evident. Even the guards who tended to allow some margin of error for the evaders could not miss it. How else were we to learn? This was followed by some real-life moaning and groaning until the guards took him away, while I made like a bush and was not detected. I found another way to cross.

The trek started with an *oh dark thirty* get up. Our instructor met us with our survival rations. The same we would have if we bailed out of an aircraft equipped with a survival kit. We had each been given an old parachute the day before and made backpacks. We threw nothing away, for we would use the canopy for shelter later. We were to operate in a group of five plus the instructor. We had been issued a pound of beef each, some potatoes and a live rabbit.

Our instructor did us a favor, he thought. He got two rabbits.

We were to make the beef into jerky and split the rabbit among us after butchering it. No additional food could be taken into the field.

The first day we spent in a static camp. We each built a shelter from our parachute. A fire was built and we learned the proper way to prepare the beef and smoke it for jerky. While the jerky was smoking, we drew straws to see who would be the executioner of the rabbits. The instructor, who we learned later was on his second trek, suggested we might want to slaughter only one rabbit and have the second one the next day. We decided to follow this suggestion. He also attempted to convince us that the fluid in a deer eye tasted like Coke and that a rabbit eye was tasty. One survivor was convinced and ate an eyeball of the rabbit. He admitted it tasted more like snot.

Bright and early the next day (daybreak) we started out. Our route was about five miles to the next point. We listened to our instructor and went around the mountain instead of using a more direct route—each of us taking a turn carrying the rabbit which was in a slowly deteriorating cardboard box. We were also practicing evasion as well as survival. The temperature went up. It was the latter part of July. The route was difficult, tempers grew short, and a distinct hate for the rabbit was developing. This may have been an intentional act by the instructor, but I doubt it. We got lost, all of us, instructor included.

We had walked for about two hours without water when we came upon a spring. The water was ice cold and clear. The instructor made sure we used our purification tablets when we filled our canteens. We shook the canteens and waited for the tablets to dissolve. He walked away and we immediately began to drink directly from the spring. Needless to say, we had lost some confidence in him. He left to find another group or identifiable point while we rested and argued over who was to do the dirty deed to the rabbit. We each had a definite hate for the little beast, but no one really wanted to kill and clean it. Someone pulled rank and assigned it to the newest lieutenant.

The next several days went well and we were back on track. One night we set up camp near a stream with beaver ponds along it. It was an area which was popular with civilian campers. The rules stated that we could not approach them except in an emergency and must do our best to keep from being seen. I do not know if they were aware we were around, but I have always wondered what they thought when they saw these scruffy-looking people sneaking through the brush, fishing under cover, and trying to bathe in a beaver pond.

We lost all confidence in the instructor the next day. We followed his advice and got lost again. We finally arrived at the moveout point for the last night. This part of the trek was to be made at night to an area where we would be picked up and transported back to Stead. The instructor left us in the afternoon and joined up with the other instructors to become a defensive force against us as we attempted to evade them while traveling to the last checkpoint. The experiences we had helped us make up our minds to follow the road on our map and travel about one third of the way between it and the ridgeline. The objective was to not be caught and to have your card punched. We left as the sun set.

The instructors set up checkpoints at road intersections and maintained roving patrols on foot and in vehicles. We had to evade them and arrive at the end point sometime before dawn. Most groups left at dusk. Some traveled in groups and others split up into two's. We split up but kept within communication distance. We ran into another group after dark and were talking to them when a jeep with instructors came around a bend in the road and stopped. They turned their spotlight toward the group and we all hit the ground. The instructors called out that we had been seen and were to come down and have our cards punched. Several evaders went down to them.

I guessed correctly. It turned out they were not sure how many of us were in the brush, so I just stayed on my stomach and did not move. They moved on looking for other evaders. I learned a little about evading that night.

We arrived at the checkpoint with no other interruptions. The area was spread out along a gentle hillside. We met others and set out to prepare a shelter for the night. I had noticed that there had been cattle in the area in the recent past and was trying to be careful where I stepped. I had started down the hillside when I stepped on a large cowpie with a crust on top. It was very wet inside and I slid about six feet. I spent the rest of the night dreading what the morning would bring. I just knew I was covered with cowflop from my shoes to my knees. I did not look forward to spending the next eighteen hours smelling like a barnyard. I spent a somewhat restless night and was pleasantly surprised when the sun came up and I could find no trace of the dreaded substance. The world was good again and the coffee, orange juice and sweet roll we had before boarding the trucks for return to Stead was like a banquet.

McConnell AFB

We decided that I would attend B-47 academics alone and Wendy and Jami would stay with our parents. This would give us an opportunity to save some money and the grandparents the opportunity to continue to spoil the new grandchild. The grandparents were more successful.

Prior to starting the academic phase, we were all sent through several weeks in the Special Weapons School, in a concrete building surrounded by a chain link fence with razor wire at the top. Each student was listed on a control roster with his security clearance. The school was taken seriously, as it should have been. We received indoctrination into nuclear weapons and their effects as they pertained to our mission and their application. We had to know the wiring and firing sequences. It could get very sleepy in the classes when the lights were turned off and the slides began, even with air conditioning which kept it like a meat locker. In order to keep the attention, slides of nude ladies were interspersed with the class material. SAC got smarter in later years and did not require the memorization of the wiring of all the weapons.

Although it may not be common knowledge, a nuclear weapon was dropped over the Carolinas in the 50s. There was no nuclear detonation and very little damage. The instructor began to explain to us what had happened when a voice spoke up and said: "That's not the way it happened." When asked to explain what he meant, the student informed us he had been the navigator on the aircraft involved and went on to explain in greater detail. A modification of the release system was made to preclude further incidents.

We became familiar with new terms and procedures which were alien to us at first, but rapidly became part of our vocabulary. Compared to the aircraft we had been flying, the B-47 was very complicated, especially when the mission requirements were added. We began to hear the term "big picture" and hoped someday to see it. We persevered and began to put it all together.

The school went well, with many acquaintances from preflight, basic and primary present. One of the problems we faced was the lack of flying time. Unless we flew four hours a month, we did not get paid our flight pay. It was possible to miss two months and fly twelve hours the third month and then receive the three month's pay all at once. In order to keep some kind of a budget, it was best to fly each month. At McConnell we flew the C-45 for this purpose until we either went to the flightline or left for our assigned base, as in my case.

The flights we took were planned long enough for the instructor to ensure we extra pilots received enough time to qualify for our flight pay. Two to four pilots would be on board, depending upon the length of the mission. The flights all consisted of a cross country to another base, a short stop, and recovering back at McConnell, usually late at night. We knew little and were told less about the aircraft. The pilot always briefed me to stay off of the controls on takeoff unless he told me what to do; this would occur only in case of an engine loss. At that time I would be required to provide additional force on the appropriate rudder pedal to help him control the aircraft.

My first flight in the Bugsmasher (C-45) was to Laredo AFB, Texas. It was described as a whiskey run, since Laredo was on the Mexican border.

I do not know if this was true, but we did return with some cargo. I was in the copilot seat for takeoff from McConnell. Once we leveled off, the pilot told me to monitor the autopilot, maintain the course, and make all position reports. He also informed me not to touch anything else and to wake him when the fuel tanks need to be changed. When I asked how I was to determine this, he told me to monitor the gauge. The pilot then proceeded to succumb to the arms of Morpheus, and I monitored the bird while passing our position to those who were interested.

The engines began to sputter and backfire. I did not need to wake the pilot. He calmly made the appropriate changes to the fuel switches, said, "Good job." and promptly went back to sleep. At the termination of my four hours, I notified the other pilot and woke up the real pilot to monitor the autopilot while we changed seats.

I went to the rear of the aircraft to use the relief tube before taking my seat. The relief tube was located on the bulkhead at the rear of the passenger cabin on the right side facing aft. The entrance door was to the right. In order to complete my activity I had to scrunch down and lean against the door, which proved to be no problem. I finished and took my seat.

The aircraft was on final approach when we were advised to make a 360 degree turn to the left for other traffic. Laredo was a flight training base with the typical pattern full of T-Birds. The pilot began his turn and when the aircraft stabilized in the turn, the entrance door fell open. Yes, the one I had been leaning against was now swinging in the slipstream. I felt a little weak for a minute or two.

I learned about flying from that!!!

I had my assignment to Little Rock AFB, but I had never been there. I happened to read on the bulletin board that a flight was going from McConnell to Little Rock on the following Friday, returning on Sunday. Anyone who was interested could sign up. The takeoff time was scheduled for 1630 and I got out of my last class at 1500 so I signed up. When I came out of class a sign of the board had changed the time to 1530. I ran back to the BOQ and quickly finished packing and left for base operations.

I ran into the counter and asked about the flight to Little Rock. I was told it had just taxied out for takeoff. I was resigned to missing it when the

Aerodrome Officer said he would run me out in his vehicle if the tower could get the bird to hold at the end of the runway. I grabbed my bag and we set out. When we arrived at the end of the runway, the C-47 was waiting for us. The side entrance was open. I ran to it thanking the AO as I left.

I arrived at the door and was assisted on board by an officer in a flying suit. He was wearing eagles on his shoulder and told me to sit down and strap in. He then went forward to the cockpit. We immediately began to roll. I spent the next two hours wondering why they had changed the time or if I had read it correctly. I knew I had.

We arrived at Little Rock just before dark. The colonel briefed us on the takeoff time on Sunday and that it was firm. He also advised us not to be late for they would not delay takeoff again. I did not argue the point about the time change. I made sure I was on time for the return trip, very much so.

I spent the weekend getting acquainted with the base and was especially interested in the housing, which was new. Base Operations had a picture board of the senior people at the base. The colonel who assisted me on board the aircraft was the new base commander.

I learned about flying from that!!!

I had been assigned to the B-47 since the first of June, and the closest I had been to the cockpit was the simulator. I left McConnell in October for Little Rock, with a short stop at gunnery school and a few days of leave to pick up the family. The time between McConnell and my sign-in at the 384th Bomb Wing was ill boding for future pilots in the Stratojet.

There were three accidents involving B-47 aircraft during that short period. They were all in the news. They were even more disconcerting since each one had a flying school classmate on board. Two of them fatalities. It was difficult to convince my family and parents that it was unusual. I do not believe I succeeded. I have to admit I had some reservations of my own.

LITTLE ROCK AFB

The best assignment I ever had in Arkansas.

I arrived at Little Rock with the family and immediately went to the housing office. A crusty old captain sat behind the desk and asked if he could help. I told him I would like to have a place to live. I also explained that I would be a first lieutenant as soon as I had confirmation with a set of orders.

He looked at me for what seemed forever and then asked how many dependents I had. I replied that I had two and would like a three-bedroom house if one was available. He continued to look at me for a while. He then turned to a board behind his desk, scooped off a handful of keys and told me to go pick one out.

We looked at all of them and finally selected one. They were brand new with air-conditioning and all the appliances except washer and dryer. To us it seemed like a mansion after six months in the junkyard. As the years passed, it did get smaller.

I signed into the bomb wing and was assigned to the 545th Bomb Squadron. I immediately began my checkout in the aircraft. I thought I had learned a lot at McConnell. I was in for a shock. I received ground training in nuclear weapons, electronic countermeasures, gunnery systems, communications, simulators in all of the above, Emergency War Order (EWO) training, target study, navigation to include celestial navigation, and last but not least, flying the aircraft which I had thought was the reason for the copilot. In addition, I was constantly tested.

The ground standardization tests had to be passed prior to receiving a flight check. This consisted of a three-hour mission in the simulator emphasizing normal and emergency procedures, a gunnery simulator which involved identifying, tracking and destroying radar targets, demonstrating the gunnery postflight, and identifying radar signals as to whether they were GCI, AAA, missile, or airborne in search and track modes by listening to an audio tape. In addition, each copilot had to take written tests. These included open and closed book exams on aircraft general, normal and emergency procedures, ECM, gunnery, nuclear weapons, and tactical doctrine. All in all, there were more than four hundred questions to answer; then, you had to fly.

My first flight was interesting to say the least. I was in the fourth man seat and had no way of seeing where we were going or where we had been. We were on a bomb run, and the copilot told me to flip up the AN/APS 54 switch on my interphone panel and I could hear the bomb plot tracking us. I did, but was not aware of the significance at the time. I later learned that the copilot was responsible for monitoring and countering the radar lockon within a given time frame. He was scored on this activity just as the navigator was scored on his bombing.

My second flight was in the same position. I was on board to read the checklist for the pilots, one of whom was requalifying in the aircraft. The flight was a mass gaggle. In other words, a large number of B-47s took off and were to rendezvous with a similar number of KC-97s for air refueling, somewhere in the vicinity of Missouri. The idea was that the tankers would be spread out, a mile apart, in echelon. The bombers were to assume the same formation. At the ARIP, the bombers would descend below the tankers and slowly climb until each was positioned below its tanker and in the pre-contact position.

In theory it worked.

The weather was atrocious. The tankers were semi-identified on radar by the bomber lead navigator, and we began our descent through the weather to hopefully arrive below and behind them. I could not see out and could only relate to what I heard on the interphone and UHF radio. I learned why it was called a mass gaggle. Some aircraft got the gas, some even got the assigned tanker, others got neither. If I had been smart enough to know what was going on, I would have been scared; as it was, I wasn't. It is a wonder we did not have mid-air collisions. We got part of the gas. We also spent the night at Bunker Hill AFB.

TAKEOFF AND DEPARTURE

I advanced the throttles and the aircraft began to move forward. The co-pilot turned on the landing lights, turned the air-conditioning switch to RAM and checked the crosswind crab at zero. As the nose of the aircraft lined up with the runway centerline, I moved the steering ratio selector to Takeoff and Land and set the throttles. The copilot gave me a thumbs-up indicating the throttles were adjusted. I hit the water switch and checked the lights. Fuel flow and EPR instruments increased. The aircraft accelerated and I checked my airspeed.

"Seventy knots——now!" I called.

The nav replied: "Nav hack."

Everything was smooth as the airspeed increased and we approached decision speed. Little lateral control was needed to keep the wings level and the nav began the countdown of timing. He called: "Ready, S-1 now."

I replied: "Committed."

The copilot took control of the throttles and set the throttle brake. I made a slight correction to maintain the centerline and added some right control pressure along with back pressure on the control column as the copilot began his call: "Unstick speed, now!"

We lifted off and began our climb. I applied the brakes to stop the wheel spin and called for the gear to be retracted. "Up," the copilot called, and after a short pause added: "Six up, lights out."

We entered the overcast and it was as if we were flying in a milk bottle. I was on instruments as we were enveloped by clouds. What a way to start a day, much less a flight. I checked the panel and gave the same response.

The copilot told departure control we were airborne, and they rogered his call and cleared us to maintain heading and climb to 28,000 feet. We continued to accelerate; as we reached one thousand feet with 180 knots, I called for flaps up. I stayed on the flap retraction speed schedule and the copilot called: "Up and lever off." I confirmed it. The water injection began to burn out. The copilot adjusted the throttles for our climbout of 280 knots and picked up the checklist.

"Starter switches—off."

"Water injection switches."

"Off and open."

"Air-conditioning master switch, 7,45."

"Slipway doors coming open for thirty seconds . . . closed."

"Radar altimeter—off."

"Off."

At twelve thousand feet we had our oxygen check. The cabin pressure was steady. I disconnected my mask and let it dangle beside my cheek. We were still in the weather; although it was gray and thick, there was no turbulence. As we continued to climb, the clouds began to lighten; then suddenly we broke through into a brilliance which almost hurt the eyes . . . what I call real Air Force Blue. My mood began to change rapidly with the sunlight—a feeling that cannot be given justice with words. Leaving the gloom of the weather and being surrounded so quickly by sunlight and blue sky presents a freedom earthbound people can never know. I know I will miss it greatly.

The altimeter was set as we passed through 24,000 feet and we leveled off at 28,000. I looked across the sunlit clouds and recalled many other flights.

CREW DUTY

I had been at Little Rock for less than two months and had not even checked out in the aircraft when there was another accident. This time it was in the 384th Bomb Wing. The wing was involved in an exercise and an F-102 collided with a B-47. There were three fatalities, two in the B-47. The other accidents had been elsewhere and could be observed from a more distant perspective even though they involved acquaintances. This was at home and had to be dealt with differently.

The possibility is always there, but it is not something a pilot can dwell on. I have always felt if the aircraft was not airworthy I would not fly it. I never approached a flight with the feeling I was going to have an accident or have to bail out. Instead I tried to prepare myself so that I could deal with any problem, do what was needed to ensure a safe flight and return. There were four accidents at Little Rock while I was there, one a year. There were other accidents at other bases . . . an average of about one a month overall. I never got comfortable with the losses. There were too many friends involved. However, if you let it eat at you, you cannot do your job properly, and chances were, you could be the next statistic.

Bomber aircraft require the crews to work together to operate them properly and effectively. A B-47, for example, had a pilot (aircraft commander), copilot, and radar-navigator. The B-52, a more complex aircraft, added a navigator, an electronics warfare officer, and a gunner. A good crew is a safe crew. Each member must be attuned to the mission—not only what it is but how to accomplish it correctly and safely.

Trust is the most important factor. The crew must trust the pilots to fly the aircraft safely and assist them when required. They must know when to assist and when to question. No question is too dumb when the mission or crew survival is at risk. The pilot must trust the nav team to get them from point A to point B correctly and on time, as well as properly identify and attack the targets. They must trust the EW and gunner to identify and counter threats. The more knowledgeable each member is of the mission and duties of the other crewmembers, the better the chances of success.

The pilot is the leader and must be able to ensure the crew works together. Knowledge and diplomacy are his best tools. Some succeed; some do not.

The typical mission in a B-47 was seven to nine hours long—some shorter and some longer. The takeoff time always seemed to be at *oh dark thirty* in the morning. The aircraft would fly a normal instrument departure. They would fly to a rendezvous point with a KC-97 or KC-135 and refuel. Following A/R, a two-hour navigation leg, usually celestial navigation, was flown. The crew might have a high altitude bomb run, followed by an entry into a low level navigation route, culminating in a bomb run on a Radar Bomb Scoring site (RBS). The bomb run would be a Short Look, which was a slight climb for a simulated weapon release, or in the early days a Long Look, which was a climb to around 18,000 feet for a simulated release of a different type of weapon. ECM runs were made in conjunction with the bomb runs. The crew might then fly racetrack patterns from the target to the IP and then back to the target. The departure from low level was followed by a radar nav leg back to home station. Arrival at high key was followed by an instrument penetration to the traffic pattern where approaches were flown until the scheduled landing time.

These missions were flown in all types of weather, day and night. Severe icing, turbulence, and thunderstorms were about the only thing which cancelled or delayed the flight, or portions of it. Imagine taking off and flying the whole mission in weather and on instruments. It has been done with the exception of air refueling and landing which require some visibility. It is a confidence builder and a mission necessity. If the call had ever come, the launch or mission would not have been delayed for better weather conditions as long as it was possible to get the birds in the air. It was not uncommon to enter the low-level route in instrument conditions, fly the route and exit, and never see the ground. This was done between 280 and 325 knots indicated on most flights depending upon the aircraft, although some called for higher speeds. This was done with equipment which seems primitive compared to today's technology.

The annual high speed flight was always a fun ride. The drop tanks were removed and the aircraft became even more streamlined. The flight called for a low-level bomb route and run at EWO speeds. The navigation portion of the low level route was flown at 390 knots indicated and the bomb run at 425 KIAS. Just touching the throttles at that speed could increase the airspeed 10-15 knots. This had to be watched closely, for as the B-47 increased its speed past 425 knots, the ailerons became less effective until about 444 knots when aileron reversal occurred. In short, when turned left, the bird went right. This required close attention to the miracle of flight if one wished to survive.

The aircraft was underpowered on the ground. It could eat up a lot of runway. Water injection was used for additional thrust on takeoff. If one of the outboard engines failed to take water, the pilot had three seconds after liftoff to get in full rudder or the aircraft became uncontrollable and cart wheeled. Once it was in the air and cleaned up, it was very aerodynamic. In fact, if the throttles were not set and level flight maintained, it could accelerate enough to tear the wings off. It was not a very forgiving aircraft. There was a saying: "The man who says *no sweat* has never flown the Stratojet."

The aircraft was not easy to land from the back seat until one became accustomed to limited visibility. As the aircraft approached the runway, the pilot in the back seat was continually looking out of each side of the canopy to align the bird with the center of the runway. Because of the pilot's ejection seat and the IFF/SIF mounted on the copilot's instrument cowl, both directly in the copilot's line of vision, it was necessary to try to look around them to see through the windscreen. At the flare point, the copilot rotated the aircraft until the canopy rail was parallel with the side of the runway, reduced power and held on. If all went well, he greased it. If not, he bounced, sometimes very high and very often.

I approached the day when I would fly my stan-eval ride. The schedule had me going on alert the day after, for I had already been assigned to a crew pending my successful completion of the checkride. I passed and went on alert, which was a new experience altogether.

Alert. It became a way of life. Unless you have done it, it is sometimes difficult to comprehend. Each wing had an EWO mission. This was basically the delivery of nuclear weapons on predetermined targets when ordered to do so by the appropriate civilian authority. Obviously, much more complicated, but that is the essence. As missiles came into the Soviet inventory, the warning time for a response before possible annihilation was severely reduced. The answer was to preload a certain number of aircraft in each wing and have the crews immediately available to respond within the warning time. This would ensure at least the survival of a portion of the force. "Alert" was continuous. The crews changed over at different intervals depending upon the desires of the wing. Most of the units I was in stayed with the seven-day cycle, although during the spring of 1960 we tried all combinations at Little Rock.

Once qualified in the aircraft and certified in the EWO, a crewmember begins the new and never ending duty.

Alert was held in three ways—home alert, reflex, and airborne—for the B-52 force.

Reflex was held at bases outside the contiguous forty-eight states. The B-47 crews went to Spain, the United Kingdom, Morocco, Alaska and Guam. Regardless of location, the tour was spent waiting for nothing to happen. Deterrence was our reason for existence. Recent history seems to bear out the success of the program.

The cycles we tried were "one day on, two days, three days and four days." We returned to the seven-day cycle. The crews would report for alert duty at eight hundred on Thursday morning. The new crews would receive an assumption of alert briefing which consisted of a time hack, weather for local, enroute and target areas, intelligence, maintenance requirements and other pertinent data. We would then proceed to the aircraft with professional gear and any changes to the EWO bag in the secrets box. The new crew would sign for the EWO bag, nuclear weapons, and aircraft. Once this was complete, the old crew would be released and the new crew would assume the responsibility of nuclear alert.

Several hours of target study would follow. Some ground training might occur during the next seven days, but generally the crews had only to attend the morning briefing and respond to the klaxon when it rang.

This was the way it was in 1960. It changed in later years.

The best thing about alert duty was C square (CCRR), combat crew rest and relaxation. The rules read that for each day the crew spent on alert duty, they would receive one half day off. In short, when we came off of alert on Thursday at 0830, we were not required for duty until twenty hundred (eight P.M.) Sunday night. At that time we could enter crew rest in order to fly on Monday. There were exceptions: a real alert, an Operational Readiness Inspection or similar exercise, or if we waived it for any reason, such as an upgrading ride. It was possible to fly off of alert on Thursday and the C square would then start one hour after landing.

The alert facility had not been completed, and we lived in a BOQ which had restricted entry and was continually guarded. Our meals were taken in a regular mess hall with a reserved area for the alert crews. If we wished, we could eat at the Officer's Club next door to our quarters. We had freedom of the base, which meant we could only go where there was an operational klaxon. The base had alert lights throughout the routes we followed, and they would illuminate and flash if an alert occurred. These were tested daily and if not operational were off limits to us until the klaxon was repaired.

The seven days were spent in a flying suit, a comfortable piece of clothing which, if not changed often, could acquire a life of its own. The flight suit and identifying alert tag was acceptable dress for any base function including formal affairs. It also permitted the wearer to go to the head of any line for immediate service.

Crewmembers met families at the exchange, clubs, movies, parking lot of the alert facility, or any other area which was in sound of a klaxon. Privacy was limited to those who owned a truck with a camper.

The "mole hole" as the alert facility became known, was a two-story structure. We moved in early summer. The upper level, which was above ground, contained the administration offices, dining hall, briefing room, target study rooms, a game room, officer and enlisted lounges, and a library. The lower level, underground, contained the crew quarters.

Crewmembers engaged in many activities to pass the time. The TV was always on, football the favorite viewing. Movies in the briefing room usually drew a crowd. Someone always seemed to be playing some form of pool. A poker game went on forever, only changing participants when changeover day came. The library offered books, current magazines, record player and records, and conversation. Many evenings were spent drinking coffee and hangar flying. Some, like my AC, played bridge. He replayed each hand verbally to me the next day. I never wanted to learn after that. Board games were popular. Many of us engaged in the base softball and basketball leagues. Some bases had a swimming pool in the area. Even with the many activities and some freedom of the base, it got boring very quickly; then the klaxon would sound and we'd all respond.

Regardless of what was occurring, when the klaxon blew, activity stopped. We left in the middle of meals or movies; games were left abruptly while crews gathered flying suits and ran. Sleep was often disturbed in the "mole hole." Crews left in their vehicles with the lights flashing, drove to the loaded birds of prey with the thought in the back of our minds that it could be more than just an exercise. I did this for thirteen years, broken only by an occasional training to qualify in a different aircraft and three almost all-expense-paid trips to Southeast Asia.

Alert was hardest on the families. It not only disrupted normality but came before it. Some marriages did not survive. Family illness, unless serious, did not excuse one from alert. Assistance from the families of the squadron and friends was common.

A DNIF (duty not including flying) crew member often found himself on alert. This always created interesting discussions; we were on alert to fly if we had to. Colds, sprains, and minor illness were no deterrent. I had a friend who came down with chicken pox; as soon as he was non-contagious he was put on alert, pox all over his body. He spent most of the tour in bed.

It was about this time in B-47s my navigator decided his hemorrhoids were too painful to endure a seven-day-alert tour. The flight surgeon sent him to the local VA hospital where they commenced to shove the "steel

eel" up his rear end to check him out. He said his immediate thought was how good alert was compared to the proctoscope. He never complained about them again.

Christmas, Thanksgiving, birthdays, anniversaries, graduations, births and many other normal activities took a back seat to the alert schedule. If someone was available to replace the individual, the birth of a child was a reason to get out of an alert tour. The squadrons did try to help out. We were never overmanned to the point replacement was a foregone conclusion. It was the luck of the draw and the cooperation of the child. The crew force was made up primarily of family men, and when one stops to think of the number of family events missed over the years, it is difficult to comprehend the dedication of the men, much less the families. In many ways, it made them stronger. It was a way of life, and I do not miss it, although there have been times when I could have used the seven-day break.

Each crew had its own vehicle and used it to respond to the aircraft when the klaxon blew. Crew members could ride with others to attend other activities. There was an exercise each day when I first started alert duty. We had three different types of exercises: alpha, bravo and coco. We never knew which we would have until we were on the aircraft with power and radios on the command post frequency.

The alpha exercise consisted of only answering a roll call when polled.

A bravo exercise was an engine start, but no movement except to rotate the tires.

A coco consisted of engine start and taxi to the runway.

Each aircraft, when polled, would respond with their time of engines started, ready to taxi and crossing the hold line, as appropriate to the exercise. Time frames for these activities had been established and exercise times were compared for evaluation reliability. It was not unknown for a crew to adjust times to meet the criteria, although it was not a common practice.

A coco exercise was a thing to behold. In the B-52, it was referred to as the elephant walk, because of the ponderous way the aircraft moved. The aircraft would be starting engines and taxi as quickly as possible. Number-one position was desired for they were the first parked when the aircraft returned to the parking area. Last place could take up to half a day if things did not go right. About six months after I started alert duty, the alpha exercise was dropped, and the sound of the klaxon itself was clearance for the alert aircraft to start their engines.

A B-47 was not an easy aircraft to alert start. The cocking checklist called for the generators to be reset manually. This involved descending the entrance hatch ladder part way and entering the crawlway to the bomb bay—long, narrow, about two feet high, two feet wide, and twenty feet long. The generator control panels were located along this space and attached to the aircraft structure. Halfway down, there was a place which allowed one to almost stand upright. This contained several generator control panels. There were six in all, and after power was removed from the aircraft, each one had to be reset by a small lever on the panel. Normally, this was done with switches in the cockpit. However, if one failed to come on line electrically (I never had it occur), it was possible to reset it manually in the crawlway, not what one would want to do during an alert start, for everyone had to remain in view of each other to maintain the two-man policy. One person could not be alone in the crawlway or cockpit. In most cases, after the copilot demonstrated the ability and had some practice, most AC's allowed them to reset them in the back seat.

Sometimes, the alert start was a nightmare. The pilot and copilot went up the ladder into the aircraft while the nav stayed on the ground to assist the crew chief with the start and removal of power equipment in anticipation of taxi. When the engines were started, the nav came up the ladder while the crew chief buttoned up the entrance hatch. The nav immediately went forward to his seat and got his secrets out to check the validity of the alert message. In most cases, the pilot was too busy to do this. No action past engine start could be accomplished until the message had been validated by two crew members.

The aircraft was cocked, or prepositioned, so that only the minimum actions were required to start engines and proceed to a launch. Checklist items pertaining to donning crew equipment, such as parachutes, could be done after takeoff. Survival of the force was paramount. The pilot's first action was to turn on the battery switch and the copilot would reset the generators from the rear seat. The pilot would engage the number four engine starter, when cleared by the crew chief. He'd select it with the selector switch and hit the starter switch also for two seconds. At six percent RPM the copilot notifies the pilot, and the throttle is moved to start and monitors the EGT. As the engine accelerates to 25% RPM, the copilot called, "starter dropout"—the pilot selected number five engine and repeated the procedure in the sequence six, one, two and three. The pilot, monitoring the EGT of each engine then advanced the throttles to 40% (idle). It could be a slow process, as the engines tended to overtemp when advanced rapidly. It was possible to have six throttles between start and idle, while the pilot juggled each one to maintain the EGT within limits.

This took three minutes under ideal conditions.

Conditions were seldom ideal.

Checklist items were cleaned up, and if required, the aircraft would begin to taxi. This could be a spectacular display at night when there were twenty or more aircraft and a few had engines torch. This occurred when fuel would pool in the tailpipe and ignite when the engine was started. The result was a long stream of flame (torch) out the rear of the engine.

The crew equipment was left in the aircraft for the crew to slip into quickly. The helmet was necessary for communications through the interphone/radio hookup. B-47 crews were not authorized headsets because of the location of the crew positions which were such that direct observation of each other was not possible. The crew was supposed to be on oxygen in the air except when permission of the pilot was given and the mask could be unhooked to dangle by the side of the face. Since direct view of each other was impossible, most flew with the mask unhooked except during critical phases of flight or when stan-eval was on board.

The aircraft were parked on the ramp in the sun, rain and snow. The canopy provided a hothouse effect on all equipment. The need to have visual reference for start, taxi and takeoff did not allow for the thermal curtains to be used as shade. This also tended to wear them out rapidly. The pilots tried to keep their helmets out of direct sunlight, but they still retained a great amount of heat. It was always an unpleasant surprise to respond to an alert horn in the afternoon in Morocco, when the outside temperature was above one hundred degrees, and slip on a helmet. It felt as if the earphones and lining had melted and were on fire. The helmet was bad and compounded by sitting on the metal buckles and fasteners of the chute which could not be moved and had been in direct sun all day.

My first alert tour was the first time that I was to work with my crew. We had all week to plan the mission we were to fly when we came off of alert. We were scheduled to fly a typical mission and would have an evaluator from Second Air Force on board. Takeoff was scheduled for early evening with an air refueling shortly thereafter. We would then go to St. Louis Bomb Plot and make a simulated synchronous bomb run, followed by a non-synchronous run. A celestial navigation leg would then be flown and the mission would terminate at Little Rock. We table flew the mission all week. The nav was especially concerned as the evaluator was a navigator and I was a brand new copilot. We built my map with annotations as to when I would make the radio calls to bomb plot, what I would say, when I would make the sextant shots, and on which stars. We also precomped the celestial information. We did not have a scheduled release time and were just betting on the possibility of getting our releases with no delay. A delay would throw the celestial information off by the amount of the delay and have to be recomputed.

The flight went exactly as planned. No delays. The celestial navigation was almost perfect, a three miler which would have been zero except the nav terminated on his watch. We had been using mine for all the shots and references. Most navs would take that any day. The only change was the landing at Forbes AFB, Kansas, due to weather at Little Rock. We received our debriefing the following day. The comment I recall from the evaluator, an experienced LC, was, "That was the best flight I have ever observed for a copilot." All credit must go to the nav and pilot for they had spent the time to get me ready. Also, the fact that everything went on schedule was a minor miracle. We returned to Little Rock and were feeling pretty good. The squadron operations officer asked how the flight went, and the pilot and nav told him everything and topped it off with the evaluator's comment about me. He put it all in perspective. His comment: "That's a typical 545th Bomb Squadron job." He was right. I can recall few other flights going as well.

The base had an open house that spring and we were "selected" to assist—standing by a B-47 and answering any questions the public asked. We were required to be in flight suits. Two farmers from the area came up and asked some questions about our low-level activities and then asked for a better look at my boots. I pulled up the leg of my flight suit and showed them. The boots were quick-donning, all-weather, flying boots. Many crew members did not like them, but I have always found them more comfortable than regular combat boots. They were a simple, insulated boot with a zipper laced in the lace holes. They could be slipped on quickly and zipped up—thus the name quick-donning. The boots impressed the gentlemen more than all the airplanes and equipment they had seen all day!

We were scheduled for our annual live drop of a weapon. The weapon used was an MB-4 practice bomb. It was about four feet long and weighed between one and two hundred pounds. It contained a ten-pound black powder charge which aided in the visual scoring by the bomb range crew when it detonated on impact with the ground. We flew down to Matagorda Island Bomb Range for the drop. The flight was to terminate with an hour in the local pattern for low approaches for the pilots, and the squadron commander was on board as the instructor pilot. He stayed in the fourth man position until we were back in the pattern.

The bomb run was uneventful and the MB-4 was released. The bomb plot did not give us a score for they did not observe smoke for the charge. We descended to a lower altitude, and I prepared to go down the crawlway to check the bomb bay and ensure it was clear. If it was not clear, we could do no other activity. The squadron commander told me to stay in my seat; he would conduct the inspection. I readily agreed. The trip down the ladder and then the crawlway was bad enough on the ground; in the air it was worse. He gave us the thumbs up when he returned. We climbed back to cruise altitude and returned to Little Rock for our pilot activity.

We made our approach as planned and landed at the termination of our flight time. I was in the fourth man position and the squadron commander was in the front seat. We pulled off of the runway, stopped, and ran our after-landing checklist which included opening the bomb doors. The pilot got taxi instructions and began to taxi to our parking area. We felt a big bump. The pilot turned the aircraft on the taxiway and looked back to see what we had hit.

You guessed it. The squadron commander called the command post and advised them we had dropped the MB-4 on the taxiway and taxied over it. All hell broke loose. We were advised by the tower to prepare to abandon the aircraft and the fire trucks were on the way. Everyone was excited but us, for as the commander told the tower: "If it did not explode on impact and when we taxied over it, I'm not concerned that it will blow now." I was just glad I wasn't the one who had checked the bomb bay.

The weapons class in our squadron building had an old MB-4 with no charge, used as a visual aid. It kept finding its way to the top of the squadron commander's desk. Fortunately, he had a sense of humor and took the heat.

I learned about flying from that!!!

The B-47 cockpit was arranged in a straight line with the navigator in the nose with no outside visibility. The pilot and copilot sat in tandem above and behind the nav under a canopy, with the copilot in the rear. The fourth man position was in the aisle, or walkway, which ran from the copilot position past the pilot's left to the nav position. The pilot and copilot each had a relief tube for disposal of liquid body waste; the tube was located under the seat pulled up when needed. Each tube drained into a container behind the nav's position. A relief tube was also located in this position for the nav and fourth man. The nav had to get out of his seat to use it. Each relief tube had a horn at the end of it to hold the liquid; many had a control valve which released the fluid into the tube. It was normal to hold the control valve open to preclude spills.

The system often developed malfunctions. I can recall having a full horn which would not drain, in one hand, my personal equipment in the other with the flow pinched off, and the pilot demanding I change the channel on the radio. I could not even use the interphone to tell him my problem. I ended up dumping it into the hell hole under my seat, praying the maintenance people would forgive me. I know why it's called the hell hole.

Entry into low level could be hectic with the radio calls, checklists and other items that had to be completed. If the need arose and time permitted, it was best to use the tube before the last minute. It could also be painful if haste caused one to catch his equipment in the zipper of his flight suit. Believe me, that gets your attention, for you know the pain will be worse when it is unzipped.

I learned about flying from that!!!

The container for body waste other than fluids is in the front of the aisle and is stored to the side, behind the nav. The pace of the missions left little time for its use. There was also an unwritten law that if you used it, you cleaned it.

There were no females on the flightline in those days and it was normal to complete the engine shutdown checklist, climb down the ladder, walk to the wingtip and relieve oneself. This practice has been discontinued.

The copilot in the B-47 was the critical crew member, the glue that held it all together. He was also the busiest. His duties consisted of the following:

1. Reading all checklists for the pilot and navigator and ensuring all responses were correct; he had to have some knowledge of all the equipment and procedures.

2. Operating the HF and UHF radios and making most of the radio transmissions. The main radio control boxes were in the rear cockpit.

3. Monitoring the pilot as he made the fuel sequence changes, keeping the weight and balance within limits, controlling fuel distribution during air refueling and keeping a fuel log.

4. Pre-computing and checking the computations of the nav for celestial navigation. Maintain a working knowledge of the stars of the heavens and use the sextant to shoot them for a position fix. Keep a time sequence for fixes, plot them and compare them with the nav's plot.

5. Maintaining the capability to identify any radar signals (ground, gunlaying, missiles and airborne) which could endanger the aircraft and take the appropriate action to deter them with jamming and chaff, done during any phase of flight in or near hostile territory.

6. Operating the twenty millimeter guns in the tail. This required turning the seat around to use the radar and gun controls for the system.

7. Being able to operate the aircraft within set standards. In other words, fly the aircraft.

The copilot had an interesting set of instruments. The pilot had a complete set of engine instruments; the copilot had only RPM gauges. The later models have a six-inch blank area in the center from the top of the instrument panel to the bottom. The attitude indicator, vertical velocity indicator, clock, and flap position indicator were to the right of this space. The directional indicator (which had to be reset after each large turn), airspeed indicator, turn and slip, and altimeter were on the left. The ID-249 and 250 for VOR and ILS were on the lower left at knee level. This made for an interesting crosscheck. It was always a pleasure to get into the front seat where the instrument layout was much more practical. When the pilot received his instrument check, he had to get into the rear seat under the hood. It usually took a while before he got his crosscheck down pat.

The copilot also ran the hydraulic panel located on a long side panel to his right. It was simple—just follow the checklist and turn it on and off when required.

We were scheduled for an early-morning takeoff with a full complement of activity. CEVG (Combat Evaluation Group) had arrived on base for their annual unannounced visit, and we were met at base ops by a navigator evaluator. When we arrived at the aircraft it was spread out across three parking spaces and maintenance was in the process of putting it back together. We had always been instructed to help them and preflight around them where possible in order to save an on-time takeoff and the mission for the overall good of the unit. The assumption was that this was reciprocated when the final results were evaluated.

We did preflight around them. The last problem to solve was a hydraulic one. The maintenance team asked us to assist with the repair while we preflighted, to save time. We agreed. I was the copilot.

The ground crew asked me to turn on the emergency hydraulic pump switch; I did as they asked. I was then asked to turn it off. This occurred several times. We were told the diaphragm was broken and would have to be replaced. An hour or so later, with the hydraulic system repaired, we started engines and flew the mission, late, but completed the scheduled activity.

A squadron commander from another squadron met us when we returned and asked why the copilot caused the late takeoff. His information came from the daily standup meeting with the wing commander. Maintenance briefed him that the copilot had turned on the emergency hydraulic switch and burst the diaphragm, causing replacement of the pump and the late takeoff. We tried to explain the condition of the aircraft when we arrived and that the only time I positioned any hydraulic switches was upon the request of the maintenance team. He seemed reluctant to accept this until the CEVG evaluator spoke up and confirmed our explanation. It was one of the few times when I was glad to have an evaluator on board. We also made sure our squadron commander, the DCO and CC got the word.

I learned about maintenance and flying from that!!!

It was about this time that the movie *Dr. Strangelove* came out. It took it a while to get to Arkansas, like everything else. A theater in North Little Rock finally got it and Wendy and I went to see it. I had read a little about it and therefore was prepared for the black comedy aspect of it. The theater was about three quarters full, and I swear the others took the movie seriously. The lead-in music, *Try a Little Tenderness*, playing while picturing an air refueling is exquisite. I sat and laughed and giggled at things, which to some extent were what I did for a living. The only laughter I heard from the crowd was when the crew was going through the survival kit, which in itself was funny; in reality they were all sealed and never opened in the air. The discovery of condoms set everyone teeheeing. As I said, this was in the early sixties and Arkansas. It is still one of my favorite movies.

The B-47 force had a responsibility to disperse when the tensions of the world demanded the increase of the Defcon level. We had a commitment to go to Memphis International. This was exercised at least once a year with two aircraft flying into the airport and the local Air Guard or Reserve unit providing support. The game was played as if the aircraft were on alert with guards—the whole nine yards.

In order to get the maximum training, we would fly a mission and recover at the dispersal base, in this case Memphis. The mission we had was a pilot proficiency which consisted of numerous approaches and other activity pertaining to the proficiency of the pilots. We elected to make these approaches at Memphis. The traffic controllers were great. Apparently, they did not get this kind of activity very often. We put out the approach chute, a twelve-foot parachute which, when deployed behind the tail, provided enough drag to keep the throttles at a higher setting, precluding engine stalls when the throttles were advanced. It also helped to burn off fuel faster.

We landed and prepared to turn the aircraft over to the Guard unit. Prior to shutting down the engines, the traffic control people asked if they could go through the aircraft. We told them unfortunately we could not permit it and asked if we could get a tour of their facilities. They readily agreed and set up a time for us to appear. We were interested in how they operated and they were interested in the B-47. The subject of landing came up and were told how gracefully the aircraft had looked upon landing. We laughed, for we had bounced solidly and did not consider it a very good landing. They asked when we were leaving and we gave them a time, wondering why; they would get our flight plan when we filed it the next day.

They told us they were inundated with calls as to why there were bombers flying over Memphis; half the calls asked if they knew someone had bailed out and was caught on the tail. They had asked if we had any difficulty during the approaches, and we had assured them all was fine.

Little did we know. We explained the function of the drag chute. We also made the Sunday front page of the Memphis paper, approach chute and all.

We performed the mission on the ground, spent the night, and prepared to leave. We taxied out and looked over at the traffic control center. The roof was lined with people. They had gone to a skeleton crew for our takeoff. I hope they enjoyed it, for it was just a normal, medium weight takeoff for us.

I was on alert when I got a call from Wendy that our second child was on his way. The call came in the middle of the night, and I had to wait until the next morning to notify the squadron. A replacement was sent out about the time Wendy called, and the doctor said it would be about two more weeks. I sent the replacement back to the squadron and stayed on alert. At 0400 the next morning she called again and informed me she was on the way to the hospital in Little Rock and Bret was also on the way. He arrived shortly after she did. I had to call the squadron again, a lucky pilot came to replace me, and I went to welcome my son.

REFLEX

The B-47 force was large and in the early years the entire unit of some 45 aircraft would deploy to a forward base for a six-month period. These bases were in Morocco, Spain, and the United Kingdom in the European Theater. This spread out the force and made it more difficult for any potential enemy to make a successful strike against the U.S. without sustaining tremendous damage to themselves. This duty rotated among the wings and was referred to as Reflex.

This changed by the time I began to enjoy the pleasures of life in the Stratojet. The 384th had not had Reflex duty for several years and our time came in 1961. The new process sent a reduced number of aircraft and crews to each base, and the TDY period was reduced to four weeks. The new crews would arrive and relieve the old crews, spend a week on alert, get five days off, go back on alert for a week, get two days off, a final week on alert, and then deploy home. There was little training and our days were made up of many enjoyable activities. The five-day break was spent in a variety of European cities, depending upon where the crews voted to go.

There were two methods of deployment. The crew either flew a B-47 in a cell of two or three, which replaced a like number that had been deployed for a given time, or they flew on a KC-135 as passengers.

My first tour of Reflex was in the fall of 1961. We went to Sidi Slimane, Morocco. It was a new experience. I swear you could smell it from twenty thousand feet at high cone. We were scheduled to spend a week on alert, get our five-day break, return to Sidi, and proceed to Nouasseur Air Base, a few miles from Casablanca, and finish the tour.

We went to Madrid for our R and R. The first thing we did when we landed at Torrejon Air Base, Spain, was to go to the counter and put our names on the list for the return flight. It always worked out that the list would only contain about half of the names when we appeared for the return flight. It would be filled with dependents and civil service personnel. The people at the counter would insist we had not put our names down and that we would not be able to take the flight. We always told them to call the 16th Air Division at Torrejon and explain that the alert crews in Morocco would have to remain on alert and possibly delay a redeployment because we were being refused passage. To my knowledge, no one ever called them. We were always put on and others were bumped. Needless to say, this caused some animosity toward the Reflex crews. It always seemed ridiculous to me for we had priority anyway, and the flight was made with Reflex crews every week.

We were told if we got into trouble in Spain, the first thing we should look for was a member of the Guardia Civil, identify ourselves and follow their instructions. Fortunately, I never had to test this. They are very serious looking policemen, especially the motorcycle types who carried an automatic weapon and had the authority to stop and talk to anyone at anytime. The Spanish took them seriously, very seriously. I have been in a loud establishment when two Guardia Civil walked in. The silence was deafening until their intent was known or they left.

We returned to Sidi Slimane to find almost everyone from our wing had moved to Nouasseur. We were told to gather our gear and take a civilian bus. We balked. I had seen Moroccan buses and there was no way we were going to ride several hours through the countryside with a bag full of secret material and three .38 revolvers, in addition to our other baggage. After several heated phone calls, we were told we would be transported in a vehicle with a Moroccan driver. An attorney from the legal office had to go to Nouasseur and would accompany us.

We loaded the station wagon and left Sidi Slimane. We passed through the main gate and were immediately waved over by a local gendarme, who informed us through the attorney, who spoke French, that he wished to search the vehicle. I asked the attorney if that was necessary since we had classified material and weapons. He said he would handle it. He spent about ten minutes with the man with the gun, some money changed hands, and we were on our way. The attorney explained that the gendarme was not interested in what we had in the car. He wanted to make the point that he had the authority to stop and search it if he wished.

We made a point to bring this up with our squadron commander who was at Nouasseur, for we would have been in a difficult position if the gendarme had insisted.

The route took us to Rabat where we were driven into an underground garage. The driver got out and disappeared. After the incident at the gate, we began to wonder if we would ever arrive at our destination. The driver returned after ten minutes or so and we continued our journey. I noticed that every two or three minutes the driver was reaching into his coat pocket with his left hand and moving it to his mouth. The manner in which he was doing this was somewhat covert. I began to wonder what exotic drug or substance he was using. When we arrived at our destination several hours later I watched him empty his pocket. He had been eating grapes. I felt a little foolish.

Alert duty on Reflex became boring after a while. We had a morning briefing at eight o'clock, followed by a daily preflight of the aircraft. Other than an occasional briefing, target study the first day, and an alert exercise every other day or so, we had little to do. The rest of the time was ours, to do as we wished, as long as we stayed within areas which had a klaxon. We saw a lot of movies, spent a lot of time at the pool, shopped at the Base Exchange. Everyone had something of his own to take up the time.

One pilot's hobby was electronics. He had built a radio-controlled vehicle which he constantly played with. The vehicle was about eighteen inches long. It had pneumatic tires connected by rods which held a series of batteries. At the rear, a long antenna stuck up about four feet. At the front, the vehicle had a light which could be moved up and down and back and forth. At the alert shack at home he would go outside and hold the control unit behind his back while casually leaning against the building. He would run the vehicle down the ramp onto the taxiway and toward an aircraft until he got the attention of the guard. As the guard approached it, usually with his rifle ready, it would back up a few feet. If the guard stopped, it would stop. If the guard retreated, it would advance. If the guard advanced, it would retreat. This would continue until the guard got the attention of his roving guard vehicle. In those days the guards did not have radios. The pilot would then move the vehicle away from the aircraft. The guard could not leave his post. He wasn't sure where it went or what he should do. This went on until most of the Security Police were aware of it.

They would occasionally ask the pilot to use it when they got some new guards.

The alert facility at Nouasseur was a series of connected one-story barracks surrounded by a chainlink fence and concertina wire. There were two gates, controlled by one guard post. This was located between the housing area and the Officer's Club. Many local women worked in the housing area as maids, babysitters and so on. Every evening about 1630, these ladies would leave the housing area and walk by the alert facility to the main gate. Most of them were dressed in the long robes and a few wore veils. Carl would get his vehicle and run it up the road toward them. When they saw it they would stop, and it would stop with the antenna waving. It would advance and they would retreat off the paved road. The vehicle would then retreat and stay with them, keeping them off of the road, until they were past the O Club . . . somewhat like herding sheep. Eventually they lost their fear and he began to use it after dark, running it up and down the road with the light moving back and forth until a car left the club and promptly drove off in a ditch. He retired it with the resulting complaint.

We came off of alert for our two-day break and went to the club for a breakfast of steak and champagne. Those were the days to pull Reflex. I was talked into renting a vehicle since I had an American Express card and was sober, I think.

Four of us piled in the VW and took off for Casablanca. We had traveled about ten miles when the engine quit. We determined we were out of gas. The car had no gas gauge so how was I to know? The fourth man owned a VW and showed us how to activate the reserve tank. I filled it at the nearest station. As we approached Casablanca, I began to question whether I should have rented a car or should be driving at all. The streets were full of cars, trucks, buses, donkey carts, and people, none of which appeared to be going in the same direction. We spent the day touring, saw a Soviet officer in uniform in a street cafe, and drove down to Miami Beach to watch the ladies in bikinis. We returned safely.

Redeployment was the big day. We were returning home, hopefully in one leg of flight. The tankers were usually out of Lajes, in the Azores. No one wanted to abort, for that meant we would leave the next day and probably not get a tanker, forcing us to fly through another base on the return trip. This base was usually Pease, New Hampshire. This meant we would have to pass through civilian customs at a strange base. I never had any difficulty with customs. If you put down what you had brought back, they could either charge a fee, if appropriate, or waive it. The chance of getting caught breaking the rules was not worth it. Not everyone felt that way. The item most people tried to get by with was booze. Each aircraft deployed with a rack in the bomb bay rather than bombs. This rack held baggage and cargo. The trick was to set cases of booze on the bomb bay doors, under the rack, so that if they were detoured through Pease they would open the bomb doors and get rid of the booze. Of course, this could also result in the loss of additional items from the rack if they were not secured properly.

I know people who brought back sports cars in the bomb bay until the command put a stop to it. The cases I know of were declared and legal. A Triumph TR-3, for example, could easily fit if the windscreen was removed prior to loading.

Each aircraft was scheduled through an RBS site for a high altitude synchronous bomb run to have a current check of the systems, as the aircraft had been on alert for an extended time. The bomb run was made with extreme caution; opening the bomb doors was something that was not desired. All down the bomb run the copilot read the checklist and kept reminding the nav not to open the bomb doors. The pilot usually chimed in as well, especially if he had items of value in the bomb bay. At least one crew forgot and never got their items back when the doors opened at high altitude. It could be considered a live release, but the ballistics were so bad it could not be scored.

The second tour we were still going to Nouasseur. Our regular AC was at Squadron Officer School, and we were scheduled to go with a new pilot in the squadron. He had flown F-100s out of flying school, just long enough to become qualified, and was then transferred to SAC and B-47s at Dyess AFB, Texas. He was then moved to Little Rock when Dyess closed the B-47 unit. He had just upgraded to the front seat and the trip to Reflex was his first. Three first lieutenants.

We launched as number two in a cell about 2100 hours. The preparation for a month TDY away from the family did not always mean that we got all the crew rest required prior to flight. We made contact with the lead tanker, a KC-97, as we coasted out over South Carolina. He took the info for the A/R and said he would meet us at the ARCP. Our A/R was to occur in the vicinity of Bermuda.

We approached the ARCP and lead aircraft again made contact with the tanker lead. It was beginning to get sleepy out. The tanker told us that our tanker had not launched and we would not receive any fuel. We could not make Morocco without the fuel. We would have to abort into an enroute base. In this case, the only option was Pease. The nav got busy plotting a course and I began to trying to get clearance. Everything was so confusing to Lajes Airways; I just asked for clearance direct to the Lajes VOR direct Pease. We got it immediately. Although we asked several times, the lead tanker never gave us a reason why he did not tell us when we contacted him hours earlier that the number two tanker was not with him. It would have saved us quite a bit of flying time.

We arrived at Pease at *oh dark thirty* and had a three-hour turn-around for fuel and launched for Morocco. We began celestial navigation for the trip across the pond. The sun began to come up and the effort to keep the eyelids open became increasingly more difficult. If you have not been up all night, at altitude, with the sun rising in your face and the heat under the canopy increasing, you don't know sleepy. Everyone drinks coffee continuously, smokes even when they normally don't, and does everything imaginable to stay awake. There were scattered clouds below us, with dark shaded areas below them. The AC, trying to stay awake and make conversation, asked the nav what the island at two o'clock was. We immediately heard the radar banging back and forth in the nose as the nav tried to locate the island. He finally replied there was no island, and if there was, we would have been several hundred miles off course. That woke us up for the rest of the flight.

We redeployed a month later with the squadron commander as the fourth man. Immediately after the flaps were retracted, the air-conditioning system went to full hot and the fourth man's interphone failed. All efforts to lower the temperature were to no avail, as were those to repair the interphone. He could not hear or speak. It got hot, especially with the sun beating down on the canopy. The AC and squadron commander agreed to proceed rather than return to Nouasseur. Everything was hot to touch. We approached our tankers near Bermuda. We were all soaked with sweat as we began our descent for A/R. When we leveled off and the AC advanced the throttles, a rush of cool air flowed through the bird. The air-conditioning system had repaired itself. The rest of the flight was in comfort as far as temperature was concerned.

We coasted in over South Carolina and immediately were in heavy cirrus. The AC coordinated with lead and moved in from our normal separation of one mile to close formation. He flew all the way to the Mississippi River in close formation. No big deal . . . except we did not have to and it was frowned upon to a great extent by the command. We descended in loose formation, flew initial and then pitched, just like fighters. The squadron commander had said nothing until he saw the attitude indicator at 45 degrees of bank. The maximum bank in the traffic pattern was normally 30 degrees. He began to point at my attitude indicator and yell. I just shrugged and tried to indicate everything was under control. It was, but the people on the ground did not think so, even though they admitted it did look good. The DO took the AC aside and had a one-sided conversation with him.

Our families met the aircraft with other wing staff members. They said when we opened the hatch, the odor that came out almost knocked them over it was so foul.

The crews looked forward to the five-day break with great anticipation. Several days prior to the break the crews who would be going from the three Moroccan bases would vote as to where they wanted to go for R and R. We could go to almost any city or country in Western Europe. The Air Force provided the transportation to and from the location, and the base pilots could stay current by flying the aircraft. Some of the favorite places were Madrid, Rome, Munich and Palma, on the island of Majorca. Palma was the favorite . . . inexpensive and a lot of fun.

I had a good friend on one of the other crews who spent a lot of tours with us. The dress in those days was reasonably formal compared to today. In Madrid, for example, a coat and tie were worn even in the daytime. Gary and I each had a black, all-weather coat. We bought black berets and small black umbrellas. We fit right into the local population, even though neither of us could speak Spanish. One day we went to the Prado, Madrid's world-famous art museum. We spent the better part of the day viewing the Goya exhibit as well as the works of other great Spanish artists. Seeing them was much better than studying them. We walked back to the hotel in the late afternoon, stopping at most of the tosca houses we passed. There were several in each block, or so it seemed. It was a long walk. Tosca houses served a glass of beer or wine for five pesetas, the equivalent of a nickel.

One of our favorite pastimes was to spend the afternoon and early evening in the Castellana Hilton. The drinks were ridiculously cheap unless you drank scotch or bourbon. The quinine water cost more than the gin. We would move out to the rotunda and watch the world go by. All types of celebrities passed by, movie stars the most prevalent. Since most restaurants did not open until late, it was sometimes hard waiting until ten in the evening to eat, especially after an afternoon in the bar.

One night in Palma, Gary and I had been with a group who decided to call it a night about one in the morning. He convinced me we should look for the Saddle Bar, which he swore was one of the best he had ever been in. We wandered into and out of every bar in the old part of Palma. While neither of us could speak the language, we had fun. He introduced me as an American Indian, blue eyes and all. He actually could have passed for Spanish if he had spoken the language. We decided we had better find a cab and go back to the hotel about three in the morning. We heard footsteps behind us; they stopped each time we stopped. We were not in the best part of town.

The next morning he came to my table while I was having coffee and explained the reason we could not find the Saddle Bar; it was in Lisbon.

I have always had a problem with the way my last name is spelled by others. I have had them argue with me that they had spelled it correctly when it was obvious they had not. I have numerous sets of orders where it is spelled with only one "p" or one "o." One "p" seems to be the most common. I have always made sure the important ones, such as pay records and promotions were corrected. I have three different sets for promotion to first lieutenant with three different spellings.

In 1962 the training wing at Little Rock closed and many of the people were transferred to the 384th. We had two LC's and a major running the alert facility at one time. This is overkill. They ran the administrative area, which was responsible for completing the Form 380s. This form had to be complete with no erasures. It was used for access into the alert aircraft; without your name on the list the guard would not allow you inside the red area without an escort listed on the 380. The guard was required to check your badge against the 380 and, if there was a discrepancy, access was denied. The Security Police strike team was called to straighten it out. The names, rank and serial numbers had to be correct. This form was given to the pilot prior to the changeover briefing. He would check it for accuracy and sign it. All errors required a new one to be accomplished. After the pilot signed it, it would then be sent to the Security Police who would deliver it to the guard.

It would seem to be a simple task to copy a name from one form to another; apparently, it was not. The LC who gave the briefing would be given the 380 with my name spelled incorrectly, and he had to have it reaccomplished. This tended to slow the changeover process. This occurred on a regular basis for several months. We went to and returned from Reflex. On our first alert tour back home, the LC brought the 380 to the pilot and proudly informed him that my name was spelled correctly. "Two o's and two p's."

Mac looked at it and replied: "You're right, but he's a captain now. It has to be redone." The LC was not a happy camper.

OCTOBER-DECEMBER 1962

The wing changed Reflex bases in 1962.

We were assigned to Zaragosa AFB, Spain. Our crew deployed on the twenty-sixth of September. The tour was eventful. The intelligence reports dealt mostly with the war in Laos. Vietnam was not yet of great interest. We were mission planning to come home when we were told to forget the mission planning and report to the briefing room at 1500 for a special briefing.

The meeting was brief and serious. The briefer explained the situation with Cuba. He told us the Navy had a line of ships in the Atlantic and would attempt to stop the Soviet ships enroute to Cuba. If the Soviet ships did not stop, the Navy would sink them. He then told us that we could imagine where that put us. We were part of the nuclear deterrent force and there was no question what our duty might be. It was very sobering news and a subdued group of crews that heard it. We were told the Defcon level was raised and we should be prepared to be launched at any time.

The base changed. The increased security was obvious; traffic was minimal. There was a little more respect for the alert crews and our movements were more restricted, self-imposed to some extent. We did not go far from the flight line except to quarters and to eat. No one wanted to be the last to launch and face the possibility of being on the receiving end of a nuclear strike. Chess became the game of the day, and night, for we played around the clock, one game after another. We had enough crews to give every crew a day off every seven days. CCRR was forgotten.

A stan-eval crew flew in on a tanker and was assigned a target. They had to draw up their own route and mission plan, a task which was normally done by the staff. They were assigned a B-47 which had been used as a courier aircraft for 16th AF. The aircraft did not have a bombing radar, only mapping. It also did not have any ECM equipment or tailguns. But, hey, they were stan-eval and could handle it.

Time passed slowly and we had no contact with Little Rock other than official business. We had no idea how our families were coping, and they had no idea how or what we were doing; we were gone and on alert. This lasted several weeks before tensions eased enough that we were scheduled to redeploy on a KC-135 along with crews from other bases.

The morning of the redeployment, we arose about 0400 and loaded our gear on a truck which delivered it to a C-47; we unloaded the truck and loaded the airplane. The plane took us to Moron AFB near Seville. A truck met the airplane, we loaded our gear onto it, and followed it to a KC-135. Again, we unloaded the truck and loaded the aircraft under the supervision of the boom operator. This may not seem like much, but we had our flight gear, military and civilian clothing, plus items purchased during our tour. Most of us had few items, but several people had purchased pieces of marble. They were heavy, several hundred pounds in some cases, and awkward to handle. I began to hate marble with a passion not felt since the rabbit at Survival School.

We had only begun refueling with the KC-135 on a regular basis. We still had many KC-97s around. For most of us, this was our first time on board the Stratotanker. The aircraft was not loaded and did not use water injection for the takeoff.

The B-47 lifted off with the nose only slightly above the horizon. This was assisted by the aircraft's slightly nose-high attitude when parked and taking off. It was then accelerated to 310 knots for climbout. This acceleration was done in a slightly nose-high attitude depending upon the aircraft weight. The KC-135 lifted off in what appeared to us to be a very nose high attitude; when the gear and flaps were retracted, power reduced for climb, the nose was raised into what we thought was an exaggerated climb. We knew we were light, but this caused many anxious glances among the bomber troops on board. We flew to Brize-Norton AFB in the United Kingdom.

We were met by a previous operations officer of the 545th, now assigned to Brize-Norton. He got us squared away with transportation to the club for food and brought us up to date on the situation. Crews from other U.S. bases on Reflex duty in England were also scheduled to return on the same aircraft we were on. They were loading their gear while we were chowing down.

We arrived back at the aircraft as the refueling was completed. It was loaded with baggage from the front cargo door to the boom pod, shoulder high. There was just enough room on the sides for the troop seats. I overheard the boomer tell the pilot he had no idea what our weight was and just made an educated guess on the weight and balance Form F. The takeoff roll for a heavyweight B-47 was generally between fifty and sixty seconds. I checked my watch as we started the takeoff roll. When it passed 110 seconds and we were still on the ground, I turned my wrist over and prayed we would make it. We did.

The flight was straight to Barksdale AFB, Louisiana. We went through the unloading process, customs, loaded the truck, and then transferred it all to a C-47 from Little Rock for the last leg home. The Gooney Bird pilot questioned whether we could fit everything on board along with the oysters he had to take back to the O Club. The senior man explained the first thing to go would be the oysters, followed by a call to the Wing Commander to ask why we were having problems. We had had no contact with our families for weeks and were not in any mood to play games. The flight was made with no further difficulty.

The situation with Cuba had not improved greatly and the wing still had every airplane on alert or deployed to civilian airports. We were given two days to become reacquainted with our families and then began alert duty again, thankfully at home station.

Wendy told me when the crisis broke, things changed. The men had left the housing area at 0730 as normal. Two hours later the cars began returning, flying gear was loaded, and they left again, everyone in a flying suit. The families were told nothing and learned of the situation that evening when President Kennedy addressed the nation.

Time passed. December, and we were still on alert. Many of us had not flown for two months and had not received flight pay for that period. If we did not fly by the end of the month, we would begin to lose it completely. In addition, most of us were approaching the time when our currency for critical items would be passed. This could all be waived, of course, but there were more important things going on in Washington.

The question of maintaining readiness with no training began to surface. Finally, several aircraft were made available and those of us who had the longest time on the ground were able to begin flying again. It just happened the flights were scheduled for four hours each, which was the monthly requirement for flight pay. In those days, if you did not fly as proscribed you did not get paid. The rules have changed since to preclude such problems.

The crisis was resolved and by the end of December we began to return to some degree of normalcy.

Turning Points

We returned to Reflex in 1963. This tour was split between Spain and Morocco. Mid-tour we downloaded the JATO, reduced the fuel load, and ferried them to Benguerir Air Base near Marrakech, Morocco. Our route was set up to pass through the Strait of Gibraltar in order to not overfly land anymore than possible. The flight was a night takeoff from Zaragosa. We were no sooner off the ground than the base socked in with weather. All the Moroccan bases did the same. We continued on our flight plan; fortunately, the sun rose and burned off the fog as we arrived over our destination.

Benguerir was different. It was hot and dusty and seemed more isolated than the other Moroccan bases. We replaced another B-47 wing. Our crew replaced one which, at the time, we thought had been there too long. The navigator was really different. Little did I know that five years later we would be on the same crew and become good friends.

We had been on alert for several days when we had a moving exercise. Everyone taxied but us. The number five engine overtemped on start and would not accelerate properly. It backfired, and according to our engine instruments was in bad shape. Naturally, we were considered ineffective, which did not sit well with everyone. The line chief and the AC got into a hot argument as to the reliability of the engine. The line chief insisted there was nothing wrong with it; the AC insisted there was. The fact we were to redeploy with that aircraft in a few days had something to do with the AC's position. He had put it in the Form 781 and it had to be cleared. The line chief wanted to sign it off and the AC informed him he would not accept the aircraft back on alert until the engine was repaired.

The argument was resolved when an LC from maintenance climbed up on the engine stand, looked into the tailpipe, got down and told the line chief to, "Change the goddamn engine, chief!" They did.

The runway was over thirteen thousand five hundred feet long. We redeployed as scheduled. Our takeoff roll used thirteen thousand five hundred feet of runway. The AC told us, after we were safely airborne, that number five had lost power after decision speed. Takeoff rolls which exceed the expected length by several thousand feet can get your attention.

The wing was then assigned to go to Greenham Common Air Force Base in the UK. The base is a small one located at Newbury, west of London. The route of flight we took was north, past Chicago, into Canada, and coasting out north of Goose Bay, Labrador. We then went just south of Greenland and Iceland, to coast in over Northern Ireland and into Great Britain. The navigators always went north of course intentionally so they could get a good radar fix on the tip of Greenland; that fix would carry them into the coast of Ireland with the help of celestial navigation.

We were in the number two position. I was making position reports on the HF radio all the way. It was a job no one liked because very seldom could anyone be contacted except Santa Maria. I passed our positions and ETAs as lead gave them to us. When we got within UHF range of Ireland, the lead took over the position reports. He called traffic control and gave our position. A very calm English-accented voice answered with: "Oh no, old boy, we have you 200 miles south of course. Please turn left at this time."

The English have the smoothest controllers I have ever worked with. An hour passed and we were approaching our descent point into Greenham Common. Lead reported our position and again was told: "I'm sorry, old man, I have you over a restricted area. Please turn right immediately and start your descent." No violation, just cooperation.

Greenham was a good Reflex base. It was also interesting. There was a house just off of the base with all sorts of antennas on the roof. We were told it belonged to the Communist Party and they monitored all radio transmissions made in that area and to consider what we said before transmitting from the aircraft.

We noticed each day a B-47 arrived or departed, a man dressed in black on a motorcycle outside the fence beside the runway was evident. He had binoculars and appeared to be taking notes. He was there rain or shine, with each arriving and departing B-47 . . . until the day they changed the schedule. He missed the arrivals. However, he did not miss the subsequent departure the next day and thereafter.

I had a friend from ROTC stationed in France. I hoped to see him during our crew rest break. However, several days prior to the break, a B-66 strayed into East Germany and was shot down. The pilot was a good friend of my AC and had given me my mid-phase formation and instrument checks in flying school. This complicated everything since the B-66 flew out of the same base as my friend was stationed. I opted, instead of trying to get to France, to go with the rest of the crews to Munich.

We were told the C-54 we rode in would fly as far as Weisbaden, but no further, even though we were supposed to go to Munich. Wiser heads did not want to chance losing a planeload of SAC crew members to the East Germans/Soviets. However, they would fly to Munich and pick us up for the return trip since the heading would be westerly. We were on our own to get to Munich. We spent several days at Weisbaden and then began to consider how we would get to Munich. Someone came up with the brilliant idea that I could rent a car and we could drive down the autobahn and engage in a little tourism. This sounded vaguely familiar to me but I agreed.

The autobahn was not very busy that Sunday morning we set out for Munich in a small Ford sedan. We stayed in the right lane as the other vehicles were traveling much faster than we were. The autobahn turned south at Frankfort. It began to snow, lightly at first, and then at a steady rate. I was driving at the time; the intent was to share the duty. The other three began to tell stories of never driving in snow, always ending in a ditch, and so on. I ended up driving all the way with only one stop to get some coffee, about halfway.

The snow came down even harder, and the road became rutted as the snow reached four to six inches in depth. The car we were in was under-powered with only a four-cylinder engine. As long as we were on level ground, I could stay with traffic. As we got into the hills, we were slowed to what we felt was a crawl. I was finally able to tuck in behind a Bentley for most of the trip. He provided a path through the snow and easily pulled ahead on grades, but he maintained a steady speed which allowed me to catch up on the level or downgrades. We followed him all the way into Munich. When we pulled up to the hotel, I felt as if I had been in the same position forever. Actually, it took us about eight hours. Since I had driven the complete trip, I insisted the passengers provide the refreshments. We spent two nights in Munich, met the C-54, and returned to Greenham Common and alert.

While we were in Germany, Mac, my AC, decided he should go to France and see the family of his friend and offer any help he could, while they awaited word from the East Germans. He checked into the BOQ and tried to call the family, but could not make contact with them. Instead, he received visitors he claimed were CIA, OSI, and other initials he did not recognize. They wanted to know what his intentions were. It took him a long time to convince them he was harmless and his intentions were honorable. He was told to leave immediately or face consequences he could only imagine. He complied. He went to base operations to see if a flight was available and ran into my college friend who flew him back to Greenham where he spent the rest of his CCRR. Our friend was eventually released by the East Germans.

Shortly after the crews assumed Reflex alert, they were given target study and required to brief the commander on their sortie. We were always represented by a member of our home wing, who was assigned for several months. He always sat in on the briefings. An operation officer from a squadron other than mine was filling this position.

The commander took the briefing and signed off if he felt the crew was knowledgeable and could perform the assigned mission. Each crew member had specific areas of responsibility and covered them. The commander obviously had the authority to ask questions at any time. They generally waited until the crew was finished unless a glaring error was introduced. He would then turn to the wing representative and ask if he had any questions. Normally, the representative would reply in the negative or ask a reasonably easy question. This guy was different.

He turned to me and gave me a time and position. Then he asked what my IFF/SIF setting would be. I pulled the charts out to establish the information necessary to determine the squawk. When I gave the answer, I was told I was not fast enough and should have the data immediately. I tried to explain that in the aircraft I would have the charts open to the current times and pick the squawks quickly. That was not acceptable to him. He asked a question concerning aircraft degradation and fuel consumption. The AC said he would compare the fuel flow with information in the performance manual to determine our capability. We were informed we did not know the answers to his questions and he would show us how to develop the data (we are still waiting).

We left wondering if we would be sent home or put on alert. This was one of our leaders who seemed to be intent on making the crews look bad in front of the local commander.

The following crew went through the same process with the same results. We were discussing what our options were with the second crew, when the third crew finished their briefing. The AC, who was one of the best, and a fair-haired boy in the wing, went directly to the phone and called Little Rock. When he got our squadron commander, he explained what was happening and asked him to get this guy off of the crew's backs. He did, at least for a while.

The crews at Greenham had not performed a successful moving exercise in several months. This information was repeated at each morning briefing and each time the vice commander spoke to us. The alert area was a series of hardstands with several B-47s on each, and a saw-toothed parking area to the left of the hard-stands as you faced the runway. The rule had been established that since we were in England, all traffic would yield to the left rather that to the right, as it is in the States. That meant the aircraft on the sawtooth had precedence.

A moving exercise at Greenham was critical. Our missile warning time was such that the first aircraft had to have a perfect start and cross the hold line with the following aircraft at 15-second intervals with no slack at the end of the stream. Any delay could jeopardize the survival of the aircraft on the ground. We all knew the drop-dead time, or to put it better, the time with which we would be declared ineffective if we did not cross the hold line before that time expired.

The weather was terrible. Freezing rain had fallen most of the day, and the temperature had remained below freezing into the night. Great Britain seemed to have a sheet of ice over it. The alert horn went off. The response brought memories of the Keystone Kops. People were falling on the ice; the vehicles were sliding off of the roads. The force should have been downgraded. The crews arrived at their aircraft and began the engine start when the message came over the radio indicating it was a moving exercise. The birds had a solid sheet of ice all over them. It was impossible to see through the windshield or canopy. The defrosting system was not up to the immediate removal of the ice, especially in our case.

The aircraft began to move carefully. No one wanted to take any chances with the birds full of gas, weapons and ATO. We did not have a clean start, and the AC had to open the canopy to scrape the windshield in order to see. It was an absolute hell for the crew chiefs. They could barely stand and had to move power carts, chocks, and then get into position to marshal the initial taxi from the parking spots. We arrived at the intersection with the sawtooth behind another bird and slid as we tried to stop. The aircraft ahead of us was yielding to the left. We cautiously followed, hoping not to slide off the paved area. Throughout this debacle, the vice commander was on the radio as a cheerleader, encouraging us to press on to make the exercise effective. We were the last to cross the hold line. We were late. When the force was polled for their timing, I reported the correct time.

The aircraft recovered and were recocked. This took an inordinate amount of time as the weather conditions had not improved. We were all informed all crews were to report to the briefing room when all actions were complete. The crews finally arrived and waited for the ax to fall. The wing representative was the only non crew member present. He reviewed the results of the exercise and asked each of the aircraft which had preceded us over the hold line, also late, why they had not met the timing. The AC explained that he was being correctly cautious since every briefing mentioned that safety was paramount, and when this was determined to be an exercise, he felt the prudent thing to do was to be careful. He also had to yield to the left.

The wing rep found little to argue with in reply. He then turned to my AC and asked him the same question. Mac replied he too was being cautious.

There was a slight pause and he looked at me and spoke to Mac. "Doesn't your copilot know how to figure timing?" The implication was that I could take the time the command post gave as the initiation time when they polled us and then I could adjust ours to fall within the effective range.

I looked back and said: "Colonel, if you want me to lie for you, I won't do it." There was a deathly silence; no one looked at me except my interrogator. I held his stare until he broke it and changed the subject. We then got a lecture on how to prepare our gear when we went to bed, to ensure a faster response time.

Our time off gave us opportunities to go to London and other parts of England. A group of us attended the Gran Prix race at Silverstone. We checked out a military vehicle and drove. We parked among Rolls Royce's, with people having lunch off the tailgate, and others whose vehicles caused us to wonder how they even got to the race. We had a good viewing point right next to the refreshment tent which served stout, ale and beer in vast quantities.

During one intermission there was an aerial demonstration. The pilot did outside loops and many other difficult maneuvers. The emcee ran on as only the English can, making it all so natural, as if it were commonplace. He explained how the pilot had lost his job as an airline pilot for looping an airliner . . . with passengers on board. He went on and on. As the demonstration ended, and almost as an afterthought, he mentioned the pilot was 71 years old.

The height of the day was the Gran Prix race. We saw one of the greatest drive a perfect race. Jim Clark. It was as if the car and driver were one. Everything was perfect. Naturally, when he won, it made it even better. I wished I had the ability to perform as well as he had.

The B-47 force was being reduced; wings were closing at an accelerated rate. A conflict in Southeast Asia was claiming volunteers and priorities were changing to support it. The 384th Bomb Wing closed in 1964. I was on my way to Pease AFB, New Hampshire, along with many other people.

Available housing at Pease was almost non-existent. Most of us arrived in mid June, at the beginning of the tourist season. The motels were full. I went from fifth to tenth on the housing list as others who outranked me signed in. It was a roller coaster and frustrating, for we had to work and could not pursue a place to live. This fell to the wives for the most part. Wendy finally found temporary housing, a beachhouse with a cancelled reservation normally rented for $120 a week. She talked the owner down to $90 and we moved in for three weeks. My housing allotment was $125 a month; cash became scarce. This did allow us time to eventually find a rental house. The kids loved it; they spent every day at the beach.

The 100th Bomb Wing pulled Reflex duty at Torrejon Air Force Base near Madrid, Spain. The schedule was three weeks in Spain, the first and last weeks on alert, and the middle week on CCRR. This came every six weeks. The six weeks at Pease contained at least two weeks of alert. It got old real quick. However, it was better than the 509th, also at Pease. Their cycle was three weeks Reflex, three weeks at home, and then three weeks Reflex, and three weeks at home, ad infinitum.

I found that many of the people in the squadron were Boston Red Sox fans. They even had some of the players attend some of our squadron parties. The major leaguers were kept in a small group and the rest of us had no access to them, even to say hello. It seemed everyone wore a Red Sox ball cap when we engaged in activities in the squadron. I stuck with my St. Louis Cardinal cap and wore it every chance I got. No one said anything, but it was obvious they did not appreciate it.

Shortly after I arrived at Pease I found it necessary to update my security file and records. My older sister and her family had accepted a position in Liberia, West Africa. She and her husband were employed by the Southern Baptist Convention at the Ricks institute in Monrovia, the capital. Basically, they were missionaries but performed other functions as well. Pat is a registered nurse and Robert is a CPA. Since I was a SAC crew member and had access to highly classified material, I wanted to make sure the Air Force was aware that members of my family were living in a foreign country. A disinterested lieutenant asked what he could do for me and I told him I wanted my records to indicate my sister's new address in Liberia.

He suddenly became very interested. He ignored me, grabbed the phone, called his supervisor, and informed him that he had a captain bomber pilot in his office who had a sister in Siberia. I was able to calm him down and carefully explained the difference between Liberia and Siberia. He finally caught on and corrected my records.

Shortly after the first of the year, 1965, we closed down the Reflex operations overseas. We were in Torrejon, closed down the operation, and returned the aircraft to the States. The only thing removed from the birds was the ATO rack. We were to ferry the weapons back to Pease. The aircraft gross weight was still about 220,000 pounds. This was stretching its performance at the altitude of Torrejon's runway without the use of ATO. We could not make the intersection immediately after takeoff at the altitude that traffic control wanted us to be at under normal redeployments, so we knew this would be touch and go.

The thirty bottles of ATO produced 30,000 pounds of thrust for about 15 seconds. It was planned to be fired at a predetermined speed following decision speed. The added thrust got the aircraft airborne and increased the speed to the flaps up speed. The rack was designed to be jettisoned immediately after burnout in order to reduce drag. ATO really smoothed out a takeoff. Of course, once fired, you were definitely committed; there was no way to un-fire it. However, since this was not an EWO mission, and the chance that the rack hanging up or not releasing at the right spot, plus we had nukes on board, it was not in the plan.

I figured the takeoff data and rechecked it several times. It was scary. The water injection system, which we needed and had planned for, normally lasted 75 seconds. Our takeoff roll usually lasted less than 60 seconds, with water burnout occurring shortly thereafter. The takeoff data indicated a takeoff roll of 82 seconds. This presented a problem. After a long discussion, we decided to hold the water injection until the 70 knot check. We hoped this would preclude the water burnout from occurring prior to or just as we unstuck. The hope was that the extended takeoff roll would not exceed the runway available. The best we could figure it would not.

Everything was normal the next day. We started our takeoff roll. As we checked our airspeed indicators at seventy knots, the pilot started the water injection. It worked as designed and the roll continued.

And continued.

And continued.

We finally reached unstick speed as we were about to enter the overrun. As soon as the gear came up, the pilot called for the flaps rather than wait for the normal 300 feet of altitude. The water burnt out as the flaps began retracting. The bird wallowed a bit and I lifted my feet off of the deck to help it along. We gradually gained altitude and airspeed. We were well below the required 6,000 feet at the intersection.

We arrived at Pease; after notifying approach control we were Left

Hand Flight, they worked us into the pattern to avoid overflight of populated areas. The before-landing checklist was run, and the switch for the approach chute was activated.

Nothing happened.

It was cycled several times with no success. I called the command post and advised them of the situation; we foresaw no difficulty and would proceed with the landing. They rogered.

Final approach was normal until the flare. Normally, final approach advises the pilot, as the aircraft reaches minimums, to take over visually and land the aircraft. He did this time as well, and just as the pilot flared, he added: "The command post advises to cut 1,2,5 and 6 upon landing." We were in the flare and it caused a small additional flare, but we touched down, deployed the brake chute and then decelerated as normal. We did not shut down the engines.

I learned about flying from that!!!

It was the spring of 1965 and we had stopped Reflex to European bases. However, we still had a commitment to keep about half of the force on nuclear alert. The location of Pease precluded parking half of the 100th and 509th aircraft on alert. It would have been impossible to get them all off the ground within the required timing criteria. Therefore, we began Reflex to Lockbourne AFB at Columbus, Ohio. So much for forward basing.

In late April we were at Lockbourne when we noticed an increase in activity with the C-130 unit. They began to load marines in combat gear and leave. The Dominican Republic was their destination. We did not increase our readiness.

The following is an example of the frustration of how being in the back seat can lead one to do things which are somewhat stupid.

I had an AC at the time who was not an instructor. Unless we had an instructor on board, I could not get any front seat time, but he had some sympathy for me. We were scheduled for a redeployment flight back to Pease with a training mission on the way when we came off of alert. We both knew the rules and the repercussions if we were caught, but I took off in the front seat. I had front seat time so it was not a big surprise. The takeoff was normal and everything went as planned . . . until we got to air refueling.

I pulled into the contact position and the boomer stuck us with the boom. No contact. He tried again, several times.

No luck. The AC was running the refueling panel procedures and we reran the checklist. No luck. A quick lesson in panel management from me had no results. Finally, he decided we should change seats and see if we could correct the problem. I asked him who would be in the seat while we changed since we had no fourth man on board. He said George, the autopilot, would fly it. I advised the tanker we would back out and check our equipment. I backed out to about a 100 feet, put it on autopilot, and the AC unstrapped and came forward. I then unstrapped and left the pilot seat. George had complete control as we exchanged seats. This was forbidden and we would have been in deep doo doo if the nav had told anyone. He did not. When I got squared away, we reran everything and still could not onload the fuel because of the malfunction. If the tanker had known what we were doing he would have been somewhat upset, I'm sure.

I learned about flying from that!!!

Throughout the summer we watched as the number of troops in Southeast Asia continued to grow. The requirement for aircrews to support it was also growing. We already knew we were to close the two wings at Pease at the end of the year. We had begun to lose people as well. It seemed if a pilot had even been on a base with a fighter, he got an assignment to them.

In early October, the 509th alert crews were called into the briefing room and told they would be shutting down alert force in just a few hours and assignments were on the way. We began to wonder what was in store for the 100th.

The 509th began to shut down and people began to leave. Airlift (C-124s and C-130s) claimed most of them. The shutdown was so rapid that assignments were not always in order. Some were sent to the wrong bases. Some were stopped by state police and told to call for a change in orders. We had begun to lose people in the 100th as well. 509th crews, who had not received assignments or were awaiting departure dates, were transferred to the 100th. We were still scheduled to close down at the end of the year and were told to expect our assignments in December. I was able to complete everything but my stan-eval ride for upgrading during this period.

We watched friends go, some to never see alive again. We knew we would all eventually end up in the war, but not in what capacity. The crews that were kept in SAC and supplemented us in the 100th were generally all about the same experience level and were my contemporaries. Most of them spent their whole career in SAC.

The assignments began to trickle into the base, at least most of them. Finally, in the middle of December, I got mine.

"Hooppaw, James D., Capt. FV3085050—KC-135, Clinton-Sherman AFB, Okla. Reporting dates to follow." It was a surprise. I had only requested something in which I would be the pilot (fighters or recon). At least it was not to the dreaded B-52. I do not think anyone wanted a B-52 assignment.

I was on alert to the end. We came down at 1000 hours on 1 January 1966. The last B-47s to pull nuke alert. The end of an era. While we realized it, we did not pay much attention because of the growing commitment in Southeast Asia. The squadron told us to go home; they would call us if we were needed. After two weeks, I went in just to get out of the house. Still no date for a class at Castle for KC-135 training. We spent the time ferrying aircraft to the boneyard at Davis-Monthan AFB at Tucson, Arizona, and flying for currency and pay. It was a time of great uncertainty.

I decided to learn as much as I could about my new assignment. I began to research Clinton-Sherman. No two references had it at the same place. It was listed at Clinton, Oklahoma. It was also listed at Braithwaite, Cordell, Bessie, Elk City, Foss, and Burns Flat. I found it was at Burns Flat when I arrived. Finally, in February, I received a date to report to the 4017th CCTS at Castle AFB, California, for KC-135 training in May.

I arranged for some leave, settled my affairs in New Hampshire, and we started the trek to Oklahoma via Illinois to see family and friends. Wendy drove the family car with Bret and the dog, and I drove the TR-3 with Jami. It was March and the weather was clear and cold. The heater in the TR-3 was great until the heat got to waist level . . . then it dissipated rapidly through the cloth top. We bundled up pretty well so it was not too bad.

We arrived at my parents' home and were enjoying a good leave with old friends and relatives. One afternoon the phone rang and Wendy answered. It was a telegram for Capt. James D. Hooppaw. It could not be good news. I motioned for her to take the message. She did. It read:

CAPTAIN JAMES D. HOOPAW, FV3085050, RFD NMB 3, CARBONDALE, ILL.

R 231516Z BPMASG-O 05988 MAR 66. YOUR TDY SCHOOL KC-135 HAS BEEN CHANGED TO B-52 CLASS 66-16-15C COMMENCING 23 MAY 66 GRADUATING 15 AUG 66. YOUR NEW UNIT OF ASSIGNMENT IS 70 BOMB WG CLINTON SHERMAN AFB, OKLA. THE NEW TDY SCHOOL WILL BE CONDUCTED AT 4017CCTS, CASTLE AFB CALIF. YOUR ORDERS ARE BEING AMENDED AND WILL BE FORWARDED TO YOU AT THE ABOVE ADDRESS UNDER SEPARATE COVER SHEET. ACKNOWLEDGE RECEIPT AND UNDERSTANDING OF THIS TELEGRAM BY RETURN COLLECT WIRE IMMEDIATELY.

I reluctantly acknowledged. (When I got the telegram in hand later, I thought I might have recourse since the name was misspelled. However, since most of my orders were misspelled, I gave up that line of reasoning.)

I was not too happy for I could see more time in the right seat. SAC still had majors in the right seat of B-52s, so the future looked bleak. We decided that I would go ahead to Clinton-Sherman, arrange for housing, and then return and pick up the family to make the move smoother.

I drove the TR-3 and passed through Clinton, Oklahoma, heading west. As I came up on Foss, I saw a sign which read: "Clinton-Sherman AFB, 8 miles" with an arrow pointing south. The base was actually at Burns Flat, and if you looked to the right toward the base, you missed Burns Flat. I checked into the 6th Bomb Squadron and began to learn what I could about the B-52 before going to Castle to begin training. I was eventually assigned a house and returned to Illinois, picked up the family, and returned to Western Oklahoma.

I got a few flights in the aircraft and then prepared to leave. We were expecting our third child and decided that it would be best if I went to Castle alone. In mid May, I packed the Triumph and set out to learn to fly the crate the B-47 was shipped in . . . the B-52, later to become known as the BUF.

Air Refueling

We contacted the tanker and began preparations for the air refueling. It was to be a short track, designed more for practice than for the fuel which was a nominal off-load. I kept the speed schedule, and at the ARCP was at 280 KIAS and one thousand feet below the tanker's altitude. I got a visual on the tanker, and we finished the checklist in preparation of transferring fuel. I started my climb to arrive aft of and slightly below the tanker. I then moved into the precontact position and notified the boomer.

"Maggie 11, stabilized, precontact."

He replied: "Maggie 11, roger. Cleared to the contact position."

A slight touch of power moved me forward and into the envelope. When my forward movement stopped, the boomer gently made the contact with the boom into our receptacle. I spent the next few minutes taking on fuel, and when that was accomplished, trying to show the tanker, also from Fairchild, and our crew that the old man still had the touch. This too was something that I would miss. This was easy compared to some of those in the past.

Clinton-Sherman By the Sea
(Garden spot of Western Oklahoma)

The bachelors were told there was a girl behind every tree. However, there were few trees. I got the family settled in housing—one of the best we had ever lived in on a base. We were expecting number three child about the time I was scheduled to complete training at Castle AFB, California. We decided that Wendy would stay at Clinton-Sherman and I would go to Castle alone. I hoped to be home before the baby arrived.

I left for Castle to begin the B-52 transition training with little to look forward to. I had flown a few flights in the aircraft and there were no big surprises. It was just a bigger bird, a bigger crew, and less work for the co-pilot. I was going as a copilot, and the future did not look too good for ever getting into the left seat. My original orders assigned me to a class date and class. My new orders kept the same starting date, which was Class 66-15.

I stopped at Edwards and visited Mac, a previous AC. We observed the practice for open house they were to have on Sunday. The flyby consisted of every bird except the B-70 and the SR-71. I also got to crawl around on all of the birds, including a tour of the B-70. This was before the aircraft was cut from the potential inventory. I must say it was impressive.

I checked into the 4017th CCTS on Sunday and met the rest of the class the next day. Most of them were old friends and, except for the guys just out of flying school, had come from B-47s. We met in the assigned room, somewhat small for the number of people. The instructor came in and informed us he would check the roster and then show us several movies to introduce us to the B-52.

He called the roll and looked up to see eight pilots with their hands in the air. Mine was one of them. The first one he called upon informed the instructor that his name had not been called. The other seven chimed in with the same. He initially asked if we were sure we were in the right place. Each of us handed him a set of orders assigning us to Class 66-15, to begin that day. It was obvious someone had made a mistake somewhere. The instructor told us to enjoy the movies and he would try to sort out the answers.

The group consisted of eight pilot/copilot teams, plus the eight of us who had questionable orders. A total of 24 in a class designed for 16, eight of whom were fresh out of flying school. To them, the assignment to the mainstay of the strategic nuclear bomber force was serious business. The rest of us had spent two to six years in SAC, where the rule of thumb was to measure it with a micrometer, mark it with chalk, and cut it with an axe. That's the way the mission worked; you plotted your target with the utmost precision, flew an aircraft with a non-precise bombing system, and nuked the target. Of course, we had been through the same type of introduction and were just a bit cynical.

The movie was started and the instructor left. The first movie was *MITO* (Minimum Interval Takeoff), the procedure used if launched off alert. The first aircraft took off as soon as possible and the rest would follow at 15-second intervals. It was designed to get the force off safely and quickly to ensure its survival. Each crew was required one annually. The way things normally worked out they got more.

This was sometimes as hairy as it sounds. The procedure came about when I was at Little Rock. Our crew's first turn came in an eight-ship MITO. We were number five. Number four crossed the hold line five seconds late and my AC decided to make up the difference, so we were only ten seconds behind. It gets real smoky and with little crosswind visibility can all but vanish. We lifted off in a left bank, I reached for the gear handle as the pilot's corrective action took effect. All I could see out the right side of the cockpit was the runway and center line when we rolled back.

This was not normal. We flew in that position for about 30 seconds before the pilot regained control enough to roll level. The observers on the ground told us later that they had written us off. The turbulence created by the preceding aircraft could make it very dicey for the last one in line.

The movie brought out some hoots and hollers from us. It had been filmed at McCoy AFB, Florida, several years earlier when first tested. The runway at McCoy is 500 feet wide and allows for aircraft to be offset from one another as they launch. Most runways for B-52s are 300 feet wide and do not allow for this luxury. B-47s were the aircraft in the movie. The reason for the noise was that most of us had done it already, and one of the pilots in the room had participated in the test and was thus in the film, although not identifiable. Having completed at least one a year since the inception, we felt somewhat experienced and were amused at the seriousness of the commentator. The brown bars (second lieutenants) were looking at us like we were crazy. In a way we were.

The second movie was *Why Low Level?*. It received the same results as the first, even though we had no participants present. The movies were used as an introduction tool to the mission. The sad thing was that in 1972 they were using the same movies with no updated material.

The instructor returned and informed us that we had been assigned to the wrong class. We had somehow figured that one out! He also asked us to attend the party at 1630 at the club. This event was held for each new class so the crews could meet each other, including the navs and EWs they would be crewed with during the training. SAC had been informed and had promised an answer by that time, and we would be told our fate. We began to think maybe we were not to fly the beast after all, but refused to get our hopes up; we had been in the Air Force too long for that.

The word was that someone in personnel had made an error and we were really assigned to Class 66-16 which was to begin in 12 days. We were told we could take leave and come back. Since most of us had not been gainfully employed for several months, we wanted to get on with it, not go on vacation. We were also drawing TDY pay, and as little as it was, it did help. They put us to work. I had two twenty-four shifts as aerodrome officer. Others inspected mess halls and performed other essential duties. By the time Class 66-16 was ready to start, it seemed everyone at Castle had heard of us and were not happy with us. We did not fit into the niche of students who did everything without question.

I got lucky. I received a note to report to the Commander of the 4017th. I went to his office and was told to go right in. I noticed that on the wall behind his desk was a very large picture of the YB-52, the first one to fly; more about that later. I was informed that I had been selected to the Regular component of the Air Force. I was asked to sign the paperwork changing me from a Reserve Officer to a Regular Officer. I eagerly took pen in hand and signed. I was congratulated by the Commander and Director of Academics.

The day finally arrived when our class was to start. I met the copilot I was to fly with. He was fresh out of flying school. Big and quiet. A real nice guy who became a good friend. We were able to get him assigned to the same apartment with me.

I had to go through the school as a copilot, but in every other sense, I was the aircraft commander, responsible for the rest of the crew and their actions. The flight instructor was very understanding of my situation and checked me out in the right seat the first flight. The duties were almost the same as I had been performing, just fewer of them. I flew left seat from then on until my check ride at the end of the course. It helped my copilot as well; he got more time in the seat than he would have otherwise. He was also assigned to Clinton-Sherman and was a bachelor. I assured him there was a girl behind every tree in Burns Flat!

We did get our come-uppance. Those of us who had come from B-47s asked why we had to sit through the Tactical Doctrine class since we had been using it for years. In the B-47, all crew members had to know all of the bold print items for all three positions. These items were like emergency procedure bold print items and were to be memorized. In the B-52, one had to memorize only those items which pertained to their specialty (P,CP,RN,N,EW,G), which we did not know. They rigged a test for us that set us up. While no one failed, they made the point that we needed some training.

The B-52 was big and flew like it. The B-47 did not take great effort to fly. The B-52 flew like a truck until the pilot learned to make it work for him instead of against him. The controls are heavy. The first surprise is turning. There is a slight delay before the aircraft responds to the initial input for a turn. The nose starts to pitch up, and once the turn is established, the nose drops. A coordinated turn requires turning the control column in the desired direction, applying forward pressure to hold the nose level, and then applying back pressure to maintain the altitude for level flight.

In the B-47 the throttles were never, never, advanced quickly if one desired to continue among the living. It was almost guaranteed that they would hang up in a stall. The B-52 engines could be advanced from idle to full open in two seconds without a stall. Still, it was something I had to work at; four years of careful throttle manipulation were not easily overcome.

Once accustomed to the aircraft's differences, it became much easier to fly and provided a very stable platform. One of the big advantages was the airbrakes. The B-47 did not have them; the aft gear were used instead. A special switch dropped the drag gear which acted as an airbrake during penetration. In the B-52 they are on the wing and have saved many a pilot from embarrassment.

I was sure that when I returned to Clinton-Sherman I would be on alert within six weeks. I returned the first of September and was not fully qualified until the end of November.

So much for prophecy.

I left Castle to return to Clinton-Sherman. I would have made it in two days easily, except for an overnight delay in Seligman, Arizona, to replace a front wheel bearing in the Triumph. I was eager to get back, for I had not seen Jill, my new daughter, who had been born several weeks earlier.

The squadron commander informed me I would replace a major copilot and would fly with an instructor to upgrade. I could have kissed him. I completed everything in my local qualification except a signoff in Terrain Avoidance. Every time I flew, the system failed or weather intervened. I was finally crewed with an instructor who had started flying two years after I was born. He taught me more than I can relate. After the first few missions, Hal would attend the initial morning briefing, turn the planning over to me, and show up for crew brief at the end of the day. I had to solve any problems that came up and make decisions he would have normally made. I must have done it right for I did upgrade. I also asked Hal to be my copilot for my checkride, just to be safe.

The radar-nav on the crew was the nav I had met at Benguerir in 1963. He had not changed and we became good friends, but more about Jack later.

Alert in the B-52 was almost the same as in the B-47; there were just more people in the aircraft. Two engines were started with cartridges in them for a faster response, and the engines did not have an overtemp problem.

Entertainment was the same. We had movies, television, card games of all kinds to include the almost continual poker game, a library, pool table and many games, plus anything anyone could think up to liven the place up a bit. There was even a small swimming pool for the summertime. All kinds of sports gear was available, even golf clubs.

We continued a game of golf I had learned during alert in B-47s. It was played on a pool table. The cue ball would be on a spot for the tee off and another was on the far spot. The idea was to sink the ball with the cueball in each of the holes in sequence around the table until eighteen holes have been played. After each hole the balls are respotted and play continued. It is not as easy as it sounds.

We had another variation. We used clubs and golf balls. We would start at one end of the hallway. The hole was the space between the center bars which extended from the top of the door to the floor of the exterior doors. We had straight shots, 90 degree shots around corners, and even went down the stairwells. It helped pass the time, although the real golfers thought we were crazy.

The gunners flew in the tail of the aircraft in their own compartment and provided an extra set of eyes. They enjoyed being in command of their own portion of the bird. In the later G and H models they were moved up in the front crew cabin. The copilot was responsible for reminding the crew to make station checks every 30 minutes and to check with the gunner every 15. A station check consisted of equipment, oxygen, and status report. It was not unusual to have to call the gunner several times when the flight was an all-nighter or involved an extended nav leg. There were times when he did not answer. When contact was lost under certain conditions it required a descent and a crew member would have to travel the length of the fuselage and check on the gunner. I was never on a crew when this was necessary. The AC would just push the rudder pedals back and forth a few times and the gunner would come up with his oxygen check and cabin altitude. The movement of the rudders bounced him around like a ping pong ball and never failed to wake him.

The missions in the B-52 were basically the same as in the B-47, with a few exceptions. We were flying the B-52E; it carried AGM-28 Hounddog missiles, one under each wing. I hated them for they were a pain in the butt. The crew had a gunner and the copilot did not have to worry about the guns. The copilot also did not have to worry about the ECM. There was an officer crew member who sat back in his cubbyhole surrounded by electronic equipment and protected the crew from the RBSes and ECMs. He also shot the sextant for celestial navigation legs. The nav read all the checklists to the radar for bombing. In short, the copilot had little to do compared to the B-47.

The Hounddogs were not flown on all missions, although most EWO missions had them. Their engines could be used on takeoff if extra thrust was required, but we always started them after takeoff. Sometimes they started; sometimes they didn't. The missile engines were normally put into idle for air refueling, but could be used at cruise power if they were needed for additional thrust—an engine out on the bird, or a heavyweight refueling at high altitude, for example. Their use could cause a problem on an evaluation ride. Air refueling checkrides always terminated with a practice breakaway from the tanker. This called for the pilot to put the throttles in idle and descend 1,000 feet below the tanker, while keeping the tanker in sight. The tanker would add power and climb. The idea was to get separation quickly. The copilot could get caught up monitoring the separation, forget to reduce the missile engines to idle, and flunk that portion of his checkride.

The Hounddog was also not the most accurate of weapons systems. Since they carried nukes, close was good enough in most cases. They had to be programmed on a navigational leg to the target coordinates. A simulated release was made similar to a bomb run. Some were so bad you could not even hit the ground with them.

The aircraft also carried the Quail missile on EWO missions. They were operated by the nav team and used as decoys.

Enough said!

The wing was assigned Chrome Dome duty in 1967. This was airborne alert. The mission was a predetermined route in the north country, always within striking distance of assigned targets. The aircraft were EWO configured, just like the alert birds. In fact, they were alert birds. They were in the air and each had a full complement of nuclear weapons and could respond with an attack on its targets.

The crew was often augmented with an extra pilot, normally a qualified B-52 pilot or copilot. It was often a KC-135 copilot intent on building up flying time rapidly—twenty-four hours at a whack. The extra pilot allowed the pilots to rotate and get some sleep while maintaining control of the aircraft in a safe manner. The other crew members rested alternately as the mission requirements allowed.

We had a flight with the DCM as our third pilot. He was qualified in the aircraft, we thought. I eventually found myself in the left seat and the DCM in the right. We had taken the aircraft with an inoperative valve 29 in the fuel system. It could not be closed. This required particular attention to the fuel sequences to maintain weight and balance. I found myself giving fuel panel lessons to the DCM, often reaching across the cockpit to set the switch when I could. He could not find them, even though they are all well numbered. As we made subsequent seat changes, we made sure he was in the left seat where he could have less impact.

The flights had at least two heavyweight refuelings, always at night over the most desolate terrain on the continent or open sea. Hal liked to have me control the throttles while he flew the control column. He did not need me. He was one of the best pilots I have ever flown with. One night he had about two-thirds of the fuel, but he asked me to take the aircraft. I complied and asked what was wrong. He replied that his glasses had fogged up so badly he could no longer see the tanker. He also had a pair of glasses for instrument flying; he seldom got the wrong ones.

Chrome Dome flights could get long. The normal training activity was not present; mainly we just bored holes in the sky. The longest flight I had had before this was a 14 hour flight in the B-47. At least in the B-52 it was possible to move around a little and actually stand up at the ladder. Unless you were extremely short, this is the only place to stand erect. There is not much room in these birds. Boring holes in the sky is always tedious, but on Chrome Dome, with the seriousness of the mission and the restrictions because of the weapons load, it was even more so—especially when the northern lights are not out or it is so dark the ground cannot be seen. Sleep comes easily unless one is trying to sleep. It is difficult to stay awake with no activity, sitting in the seat anxiously awaiting the next position report for something to do. A lot of coffee gets processed at these times. Of course, flying hours pile up rapidly if you need them.

The pilot could spend the long hours perfecting the operation of the firelight test switch. This switch was on the instrument panel behind the control column. It was used during preflight to check the electrical continuity of the engine fire warning system. A turn to the right and all eight engine fire warning lights would illuminate, indicating the system was operating correctly. It was common when someone who was not familiar with the aircraft was along to brief them on the different items in the cockpit and their functions. One of these items was the engine fire warning lights. The pilot would explain the operation and severity of the situation if one illuminated. Later in flight, hopefully at night, when all was quiet and nothing in particular was occurring, the pilot could put his left foot on the test switch and move it slightly to the right. This, if done gently, would cause one of the fire warning lights to come on. It did not take as long for the extra man to see it as it took to calm him down afterward. And we wonder how crew members get bad reputations!

The most memorable Chrome Dome I flew was in the winter of 1967. The western part of Oklahoma was covered with a sheet of ice and had been for several days. This caused the airborne alert missions to be cancelled for those days and the wing was getting a lot of heat from 2nd AF to try and get a mission off the ground. It was our turn to fly. We met at the alert facility, knowing we would not even attempt a takeoff. It was all we could do to safely negotiate the trip to the alert facility in our vehicles. We had our breakfast and talked about what we were going to do the rest of the day. The preflight crew came in and told us the aircraft was mechanically in condition, but maintenance was trying to remove the ice from the wings and fuselage.

We arrived at the aircraft and began to load our gear, expecting at any minute to be informed we were cancelled. Maintenance was frantically trying to remove the ice and snow, with little luck. We were told to go ahead and start engines. With ice over everything including the ramp, we did not even want to taxi, but the wing staff was pressuring the pilot to at least attempt to get to the end of the runway. We cautiously crept to the taxiway and then to the hold line. The wing commander and DCO were asking what we thought every few minutes. The pilot kept replying he was not too confident in the condition of the runway.

We stopped at the hold line and computed our takeoff data again, several times to be sure. We had reduced our decision speed point back from 5,000 to 3,000 feet and came up with 90 knots for a decision speed. The pilot and I decided we could give it a go, but did not expect to reach the speed because of runway conditions. The book said we had enough runway to accelerate to that speed and still stop within its confines. We could abort and that would be that. We would have tried, the wing would look good, and still take a weather cancellation. Takeoff time was approaching and the wing king was waiting for an answer. The pilot said we would try.

The safety office, being forewarned, had set up a video camera at midfield to capture this memorable event. We found out later they forgot to put tape in it. I wish they hadn't. The entire alert force and most of the maintenance people stopped to observe the attempt. They were laying bets that we would end up off the end of the runway in a large black and red fireball. We tried not to think of that possibility.

We took the runway and the pilot advanced the power. I checked the gauges and paid special attention to the 70 knot check. The nav started the timing; as he called out its expiration, we had 91 knots. The pilot called committed and we pressed on. It was a long takeoff and, but for a slight skid at decision speed, very smooth. The observers told us we disappeared in a cloud of ice and snow which blew off the aircraft as we lifted off and began our departure for a twenty- five-hour flight. Our gross weight was at the maximum for takeoff. The ice must have added several thousand pounds at the least.

An airborne alert bird from another wing flying the Thule monitor developed a fire in the cockpit and the crew bailed out. They were almost over Thule AFB, Greenland. Those that survived were picked up quickly. However, this was winter and the problems the crew encountered became a big issue, requiring additional survival training at each SAC base. The crew had trouble finding their survival gear, and since it was nighttime, could not identify items which could have aided them—in particular, gloves and wool caps.

The result was that each base conducted special training for each crew member. It was set up in a large building, which allowed a parachute harness to be attached to a set of ropes from rafters and raised above the floor. Each crew member was hooked up in the harness, blindfolded and lifted several feet above the floor. He was then lowered to the floor. He was expected to get out of the parachute harness, find the survival kit, open it, find a ski mask and gloves, and don them, all within two minutes. The object was to get the items before the cold precluded the use of the hands. Once this was accomplished, an item by item inventory and blindfolded identification had to be made of the survival kit contents. It was a good learning process and provided a lot of entertainment for the observers, until their turn came!

It was about this time that we began to hear the nickname which was to adequately describe the B-52. *Stratofortress* was somewhat over serious, and like the C-47, which became the *Gooney Bird* versus the *Dakota*, the B-52 received a fitting name. We first heard it from the tanker troops returning from YOUNG TIGER tours in Southeast Asia. The name was the BUF. The acronym was used in lieu of the words Big Ugly Fucker. When questioned by others such as newsmen and members of the gentler sex, it was changed to Big Ugly Fellow. It loses something in the alteration. The name was first offensive to us, but later became one of affection, used by all those who flew it.

We could tell things were about to change for us. Amarillo AFB, Texas, closed, and we received personnel from the bomb unit that had been stationed there. The crew members who came in had returned recently from ARC LIGHT, the code name for the B-52 mission in Southeast Asia. The rumors that we would be sent soon were looking more and more like they were true. It became even more evident when we began to phase out the E models and receive the black-bellied D models.

Our first augmentation (volunteer) crews were sent for a three-month tour. The KC-135 crews had been participating for some time in YOUNG TIGER, which was the SAC deployment of tankers to support the war. It was just a matter of time.

I had completed my upgrade but had not been assigned a crew. The squadron commander had given me my pre-stan-eval ride, and at my debrief, after passing the subsequent stan-eval, had commented to the wing commander that he thought I would be a strong AC. I had the experience to draw from, for I had flown with a wide variety of pilots and crews. I knew I would use a little bit of something from each pilot I had flown with to run my crew, if I ever got one. The senior copilots that had come in from Amarillo had been qualified and were waiting for a crew as well, so the competition was strong. The squadron commander called us all in and explained that he would assign crews by seniority. He identified me as number one in line. That made me feel better, but time passed with no action.

I was on alert with Wiles Lovable, who had replaced Hal as my AC, when I got a phone call from the squadron commander. He informed me that effective the following Monday, I would be the AC of crew E-13. Even the number did not detract from my elation. E-13 was also on alert with us. I immediately began to get to know the crew better. I knew all of them but had never flown with any of them, and I checked around for more information. The news was good. The nav team was one of the best. The copilot and EW were fairly new, but no one had any negatives about them. The gunner was experienced and well respected.

The next week the unit began training in conventional bombing and ARC LIGHT procedures in earnest. The chickens had come home to roost. I remembered in 1964 we were told if we voted for Goldwater we would go to war. I did and we did. It is an old joke but very true. I knew we would be on our way soon, but at least I would go as an AC, which meant a lot in many ways.

We had started changing over to D models, were switching out our E models with other units, and also delivering C models which were used for training. We were scheduled with another crew to swap out a couple aircraft with the unit at March AFB, California. We spent the night. We rented a car and went to L.A.; the RN visited relatives. I took everyone to the Playboy Club; we spent some time in other spots as well and then returned to the BOQ at March.

The next day we had a mission in a two-ship cell for fighter intercepts, some bombing activity, and then back home. The runway to the north at March has a mountain several miles off the end; a turn to the left is required to clear it. After takeoff, when the copilot called to reduce power on number two nacelle to activate the air-conditioning system, I asked him to wait and flag the item so we would not forget it. It was hot and turbulent and I wanted all engines up for better control during the turn. We rolled out and continued our climb. Our level off altitude was 24,000 feet and as we approached 20,000, I began to feel like I had an upset stomach. I just supposed it was the bad limes with the tonic water and malarial medicine taken the night before. Then the nav asked if anyone else felt bad. The copilot and EW said they did, so I called for a station check. The copilot replied that the cabin pressure was 20,000 feet. I got everyone to check in on 100% oxygen and called center for an immediate level off.

The radar, who had not been with us the night before, asked the copilot to check the air-conditioning master switch. He did; it was still in RAM, which meant we had ambient air in the cabin. He moved it to 7.45 and the cabin pressure began to fall. Everyone reported they were feeling better, while I berated myself silently for being so stupid and not remembering the switch when we finished our turn.

I really learned about flying from that!!!

Everyone needed water survival training. This caused the wing a problem, for there were no facilities available. It was also the middle of February. The problem was solved by building a plywood structure around the deep section of the L shaped pool at the O Club. Several flight line heating units were rolled in for heat and the training began. The water was not heated.

The training consisted of being strapped into a parachute harness and dropped into the pool. The crew member had to disconnect the harness, inflate the Mae West flotation device, swim to and get into the one-man life raft. An explanation of water survival gear also had to be rendered. Needless to say, the water temperature provided an incentive to accomplish the above procedure as quickly as possible. Once completed, a towel was provided and the flight suit was replaced with warm dry clothes. Although the enclosure was not airtight, the exhaust from the heating units helped keep the pace of training up.

The following year we were scheduled to go to American Airlines water survival in Oklahoma City. It was much more enjoyable, even though we had to furnish our own transportation for the 110-mile trip.

We had received some assignments for people, but generally the unit had been kept intact. The ones who left were, for the most part, young copilots who left to become forward air controllers. Some friends were lost forever; they left and did not return. The new guys from Amarillo helped train the rest of us. Some were much better than others. We practiced cell formation, conventional bombing (this term is used to differentiate the type of bombs and bombing, as well as the tactics used versus the nuclear weapons and delivery tactics), low-level conventional tactics, as well as the ECM and gunnery tactics. My confidence in my crew and our capabilities grew accordingly, and I can only assume their confidence in me as the AC did as well.

We received the word that the unit would indeed go to Southeast Asia for a TDY of up to 189 days; any more than that became a permanent assignment. We were to join other units, which were also TDY, and replace units redeploying to the States. The departure dates were staggered, and the lucky crews flew aircraft to Andersen AFB, Guam. The rest of us made the trip in KC-135 tankers loaded to the max. Our deploy date was 13 April 1968.

BOMB RUNS

We entered the low-level route and ran our terrain avoidance check. It was clear and I descended to the minimum altitude as we passed the surrounding terrain at 280 KIAS. The crew worked with precision through the navigation legs, ran checklists, and prepared for our first bomb run. I just enjoyed flying. We reviewed the bomb run, which would be a simulated release of two weapons on two targets. We reviewed the timing points and times to each target. As we approached the IP, the copilot contacted the RBS site and passed the information for the bomb run. He also informed them we would have two racetracks following the first release. This meant after the release and at the end of that leg, we would fly a route back to the IP and make two more runs of the targets and then depart. The flight pattern resembled an oval racetrack. I had spent a good portion of my flying time in this activity. After all, it was a bomber.

I concentrated on maintaining airspeed and altitude while keeping the Flight Control Indicator centered. The countdown began as the bombing system automatically gave me time and heading to the release point. The scoring tone came on at twenty seconds to go. As the time expired, the bomb doors opened and a simulated release was made by tone termination. I turned to the heading to the second target and the whole process began again, but in a much shorter time frame. After the second release we entered the racetrack pattern for the second bomb run and awaited our scores from the bomb plot.

The ARC LIGHT missions were slightly different as they were all at high altitude, but the basics were the same.

ARC LIGHT missions were flown in cell formation with color call signs. A transmission would sound like this:

"Red right 240."

"Red two."

"Red three."

Most transmissions were short and to the point with the trailing aircraft responding by call sign. One day we were working our frequency, which was supposed to be only for us. After several calls we heard the following:

"Knock off that red and blue shit. We're trying to fight a war down here."

That pretty well sums it up and brings back many memories.

April 1968

The alert facility was no longer in use for alert duty. The wing had been alerted and training had been completed in the D model. We had received leave, if it fit schedule, and were prepared for a 189 day TDY to Southeast Asia. We had been briefed, rebriefed, trained and tested, and flown for the past four months in preparation. We felt we were ready, but the real test was yet to come. We hoped we would be equal to the task. Many of us had been in B-47s and had participated in lengthy TDYs, but not of this nature. There were many who had never been out of the country. There were World War II veterans (three of whom had been prisoners of war), and Korean War vets. The largest number of us had never dropped a bomb in anger, much less faced the potential of someone shooting back.

The final processing was to be done in the alert facility. The aircraft we were to depart upon was a 70th Bomb Wing KC-135, crewed by our own people. Most of the B-52s had already departed. Since, out of necessity, there were always more crews than airplanes, the rest of us rode on tankers. I always imagined going to war in my own airplane, but I would get that chance later. In addition to the processing, the facility had been set up for the families who were present to send us off. Aircrews and maintenance crews would travel together.

The facility was quiet for the number of people gathered there. Even the children were subdued, as if they completely understood what was happening. Good-byes had already been said in private in most cases, but that last touch had yet to occur. The time passed painfully slow, but altogether too rapidly. Finally, the word was passed to begin loading the aircraft. A last hug, a last kiss, and sixty misty eyed men descended the rampway enroute to the aircraft, and looking forward to six months together and strangely alone as well.

The KC-135 had been loaded with our baggage and cargo, including an aircraft engine. These were strapped down along the aircraft centerline leaving a few airline-type seats in front, and troop seats along the fuselage of the aircraft. A troop seat is canvas stretched over a tubular frame attached to the aircraft for support. A frequent flyer on a tanker knew which were the most comfortable and fought to get them. The airline seats, when installed, were for officers and/or crew members. As in any aircraft, the best seats are in the cockpit, especially if you are a pilot.

Our flight was scheduled to fly direct to Hickam AFB, Hawaii. Our departure was near midnight, and we arrived in Hickam about 0200 Hickam time. We passengers were sent off to base operations/passenger terminal while the aircraft was refueled for the second leg of the journey which would terminate at Andersen AFB, Guam. Those who wished, refueled themselves at the snack bar. Those who had made these trips before were less inclined to partake of large amounts of fluid. It took about two and one half hours to prepare the aircraft, and we were bused back and uploaded.

The trip into Guam was longer. At least it appeared as if it lasted forever. We slept, we read, and when possible, moved around a bit to keep from growing roots. A KC-135 with sixty passengers and an engine does not leave much space to move in. The aircraft had two urinals in the rear and one up front. Those of us who had made similar trips before had anticipated them filling up, but not as rapidly as they did. They were overflowing at an hour prior to landing. The last hour was not a comfortable one at all. Fortunately, some unique receptacles were found and used!

We arrived at Andersen just after midday and were met by a representative from our wing. Our gear was loaded on the bus and we were taken to in-processing. Each crew was given a schedule for the activities of the next few days and then taken to Crew Control to arrange for quarters.

The gunners lived in trailers about a half mile from the operations building. The rest of the crew were all quartered together in one room about thirty feet by thirty feet in what had been the alert facility. The facility was a three-story building with two wings connected by a shorter wing which housed the Crew Control office, storage area, lounge area and maids' laundry.

Crew Control advised us they had only one room and there were two crews. Since I was the lower ranking pilot, we were assigned to a non air-conditioned room about half the normal size. We found this out after we had unloaded our gear. I reported this to our operations officer, and he assisted us until we were assigned to the BOQ. It was about a mile away, but bigger and air-conditioned. It was also on the third floor. We got plenty of exercise moving baggage that day. I believe the only times we got a first floor room was when we spent less than a week on Guam. Most of that time was spent in the air.

The rooms were close for five people. Most of us had spent a lot of time in alert facilities and had become accustomed to crowded quarters. We had some leeway in moving the beds and lockers around to provide a little privacy, but there is only so much that can be done in a small room. I maintained that since I was the pilot and senior man, I got my choice of beds each time we moved. The crew selected theirs in the same manner. No one ever seemed unduly upset about this arrangement. I always selected the same corner area. Maybe it was superstition, or maybe it gave me a feeling of permanence in some way. The crew pretty much stuck to the same positions as well. Each had his own way to find that necessary time to get away from the others. My method was to rise early and go walking. It worked pretty well.

Our first scheduled duty was the next day at Scat School to bring us up to date in current operation, reviewing the mission profiles and paperwork generated for each mission, and the paperwork we would be expected to complete and turn in. This took two days.

One of the things that was stressed was the way the coral, of which the runways and taxiways were constructed, was slick as greased owl shit (their term). At the time I could not comprehend how slick that was. I knew from experience a B-47 did not stop easily on ice; then one rainy day I tried to stop a BUF on it. The aircraft took on a life of its own, but eventually stopped just short of leaving the taxiway. I used more caution after that, but sitting in that big bird with absolutely no control showed me how slick greased owl shit is!

Our first flight appeared on the schedule the next day. We would fly the Black/Brown mission as Brown Three. Brown Three was the third ship in the second cell of a wave of six ships. The missions that are recalled the most are the Black/Brown out of Andersen or the Ivory/Walnut out of UT. The reason they are memorable is the takeoff times. 0000-0200 in the morning. We had an extra pilot and radar with ARC LIGHT experience flying an over-the-shoulder with us. Their duty was to see if we knew what we were doing and could do it safely. We must have, for he signed us off and we were on our own from that time forward.

Baggage. It was a pain in the ass. Each person was required to take his own professional equipment. Sometimes we flew as a spare with other crews and needed to ensure we had what we needed to get by. A list of needed items and suggestions for personal items was provided before we deployed. It could have been shorter. The biggest problem was that while we were assigned quarters, we did not keep them when we deployed forward. Any excess items had to be stored until we returned to Guam. Since baggage movement became a crew effort, the total stored increased for each subsequent deployment. We rapidly learned what we really needed and stored the rest. Baggage on subsequent ARC LIGHT tours was drastically reduced. The following is an example of what was required and what was actually used. It is divided into professional and personal gear.

Professional gear:

·Flying suits, summer weight. Each crew member was issued four. They were all needed; by the end of the tour the gray/green color was washed out to a whitish gray. If you had more you took them. One flight was all you could get between washings. Stretching it to two flights caused social isolation.
·Jacket, summer
·Boots. Insulated quick donning and regular combat boots
·Helmet, flying, with attached oxygen mask and bag to carry it in

·Headset, flying, to be used when permitted, especially during preflight to keep from baking the brains with the helmet on

·Gloves

·Full set of winter gear. The reason was that we still had our EWO commitment and might have to use it for that purpose. It made sense; on return to Andersen, if pressurization or heat was lost, the temperature at 40,000 plus feet dropped dramatically inside the aircraft. Descent to a warmer altitude was possible, but with a great degradation in fuel consumption. Therefore, with the gear on board, the crew could don it to keep close to warm. I insisted we put the minimum together in a duffel bag my brother had used throughout his tour in Korea fifteen years earlier, and we dutifully carried it on each trip out of Andersen. We grew to hate it. We never had to use it, although others did lose heat, but we were prepared. I felt a little inconvenience was desired over trying to explain frostbite received by not following directions. I doubt if the crew has ever forgiven me for lugging that bag around.

·Briefcase—with Dash 1, appropriate regulations, manuals and checklists

·Class A uniform with blouse (blues)—in case one had to return to the States or meet a court-martial, or so on and so on. I never used it.

·Summer 1505s—slacks and short sleeve uniform shirts—enough for the few times a flight suit was not appropriate. If one were grounded for any reason, duties could still be performed in the appropriate attire.

·Socks, underwear and shoes—proper colored

Personal gear:

·Enough civilian clothes for a six month tour with accessories

·Personal items for health and welfare—shaving kits, tape players, radios, alarm clocks, cameras, golf bags, tennis racquets, etc.—generally items to help pass the free time. What a way to go to war! I always carried a good supply of books to read.

It did not take long to learn what was necessary and how to cut down without coming up short on requirements. For example, we learned to cut

down on the number of uniforms and civilian clothes; we could purchase items if needed. We should have known but took the list we were given as re-quirements. The subsequent tours were much lighter in the baggage . . . going.

You can not imagine the stuff that was brought back, legal stuff, just a great amount.

The crew learned after our first *bag drag* to reduce what gear we carried when we flew. Other than when we deployed, I only had the flying clothes I wore, my helmet bag with the helmet, headset and checklists. I carried a small briefcase with my emergency procedures, a few appropriate regulation and hot tips in a small folder. (Hot tips were actions which had solved air-craft problems in the past and might be applied again). There were others, not official, not always proscribed or condoned by Boeing or SAC. For ex-ample, the pilots had a procedure to dump an additional twenty thousand pounds of fuel per hour if weight reduction was needed. Dumping fuel is supposedly not possible in the B-52. It involved fooling the float valves in the drop tanks. I also stuck in a change of underwear, socks, slacks and shirt, just in case we landed somewhere else. It came in handy several times. The copilot had a complete Dash 1 and his flight gear. The nav team combined their manuals to just one set in one bag. In addition, we had the mission bag, chapkit box, and a cooler for food and drink.

We had to abort into U-Tapao once and the extra set of clothes came in handy. At the club that evening, the nav and radar decided to go into town with some friends. Rules stated that only long pants could be worn off base. The nav, who was six foot three, had only brought a pair of Bermuda shorts. Since I did not care to go, we went into the men's room and switched pants. While we had the same waist size, the inseam was different. He left with a six inch gap between the pants and his shoes; I stayed behind wearing a pair of shorts which hung well below my knees!

TYPICAL MISSION

There were three basic missions. The only real difference was that we only took on a nominal amount of fuel out of Kadena for a mission of about eight hours, and no refueling out of U-Tapao with flight time average of four hours. The most memorable were out of Andersen. They are memorable because of their length and the crew duty day. The flight itself varied in length depending where the target was located, but generally was 10 to 12 hours long. However, the day actually started four to five hours prior to takeoff. The mundane things had to be taken care of—shower, shave, dress and eat. The meal might or might not be available depending upon takeoff time.

Duty actually began with the gathering of the gear for flight and proceeding across the compound to the operations building for the eventual mission briefing. The main briefing was preceded by specialty briefings. The radar and navigator went to target study, the EW and gunner to defensive updates, and the pilot and copilot reviewed the mission package. I would check and sign the flight clearance Form 175 while the copilot completed the weight and balance form. We would review the mission route, target, defenses, air refueling, fuel requirements and reserves, and weapons load, and then check the flight orders for additional people—in my case, that my name was spelled correctly.

Extra crew members would appear at this time, and I would cover anything I felt they should be aware of and brief them of what I expected during the flight. I would also give them a quick reminder when we finished our preflight of the aircraft. The rest of the crew would gradually drift in, and items of particular interest about the mission would be reviewed.

The crews would take their seats, arranged by wave, cell and crew position. Extra crew members, staff, and horse holders would sit behind the crews, with the first row saved for the commanders and senior staff. The general crew briefing would begin at the specified time. The first item was always the time hack to set everyone's watch at the same time. This was always zulu time (Greenwich mean time); from then on all references to time were in zulu time. The rest of the briefing contained target and route data, intelligence, air refueling information, weapons load, fuel reserves, weather, emergency data particular to the mission, search and rescue procedures and updates, a prayer from the chaplain, and finally words from the commander.

This was a very formal briefing, and except for the occasional joke by the chaplain, held little humor. We were going to war after all. The fact that the commander had three stars also had something to do with it, I believe.

After turning in our paperwork, we would gather the items which had not been loaded on the bus and, along with at least another crew, board the bus. We went by base ops to file, and if there was time, stopped at the snack bar.

We arrived at the aircraft one-and-one-half to two hours prior to scheduled takeoff. The first crew would get a quick brief from the crew chief on aircraft status and offload their gear. The other crew would then ride to their aircraft. The crew chief presented the pilot with the Form 781 to review and answer any questions he could about the aircraft. The crew would then disembark and start the exterior preflight. The nav team checked the bombs, and the pilots did the walkaround and then did the interior. If everything went well, a few minutes were usually available prior to engine start to allow for a smoke, stretch of the muscles, relief, etc. This was the time I briefed any extra crew members that I expected them to be on oxygen and interphone, strapped in the chute for takeoff through the 12,000 foot check, during air refueling, in country, penetration and landing and any other time that I felt was necessary. I explained that I expected them to stay on interphone with oxygen immediately available and not to speak on the bomb run or other critical phase unless absolutely necessary. I would also review emergency procedures and explain that if I told them to go downstairs and prepare to bail out, I would wait until the RN told me they were gone. If they delayed too long, or failed to follow directions, I would order the RN to go and they would inherit command of the aircraft, for I would be gone right after the RN!

The mission was made up of a wave, two cells which were made up of three aircraft each. The cells were separated by 12 to 20 minutes. This changed later on in the war when operations were out of UT alone and a cell was considered a wave.

Each crew would preflight their assigned aircraft. A spare crew would preflight an aircraft which was designated the "manned spare." This crew would start engines and be prepared to fill any position which might become vacant due to mechanical problems. It also taxied to the runway and was available within certain time frames to fill in if any airborne aircraft aborted. There was also an unmanned spare which would be preflighted and cocked in case the spare was used and another bird fell out of the launch. Sometimes this occurred before the first aircraft started engines, which was not too bad. Occasionally, it occurred at a time when the response became a goat rope. This resulted in a *bag drag*.

No one liked a bag drag. Things could get lost easily, temporarily, or forever.

Bag drags had been used for many years, but not with the urgency of an ARC LIGHT mission. They became an art form. In reality, they were simple. The crew scheduled to fly one aircraft with a specific takeoff time would preflight the assigned aircraft, and if everyone checked out, start engines and fly the mission. Everything did not always check out and the mission would be delayed or cancelled. The only thing the crew missed in most cases was a training flight. Normally there was not a backup aircraft the crew could go to at the last minute and continue.

ARC LIGHT was an exception. We had a manned spare which could replace any aircraft that fell out of the lineup. This aircraft would have engines running and be positioned to be able to fill in at any point in the stream without delaying it unduly. We also had an unmanned spare, preflighted and cocked for engine start if needed.

When, in the course of human events, something went wrong or an aircraft aborted, the crew, if directed, would bag drag to the spare. This consisted of gathering all equipment the crew had loaded on the original aircraft. This would be put on a maintenance truck (hopefully just one) with the crew and driven to the spare. This could get hectic when a launch was in progress, and it never seemed to occur at any other time. If engines had been started, it involved shutting them down, gathering the professional gear, secrets box, cooler, chapkit box, lunches and anything else the crew had on board, and racing to the spare. Upon arrival at the spare the pilots would start the engines while the rest of the crew onloaded all of the equipment. It was difficult not to miss at least one thing. The crew was racing the clock to meet a takeoff which would keep them in the cell to which they were assigned, or be able to launch and fill in at the end of the stream within the time constraints of the mission. Time on target was the critical factor.

The crew knew of the possibility, but until we had run the drill we did not really plan ahead. After our first bag drag, we did things a little differently. We consolidated as much as we could to reduce the number of items. We did not get comfortable and spread out until we were airborne and on our way.

There were few bag drags when a crew was deploying from UT or Kadena. In addition to the normal complement of gear, we had personal gear and anything we'd purchased. Depending upon the departure base, this could include extensive stereo equipment, china, bronzeware, etc. Naturally, this would not fit into the crew compartment, and the bomb bay was already filled, so it was loaded into the 47 section, an open compartment in the fuselage, aft of the bomb bay. It contained little but electrical equipment. Unless it occurred early, a complete bag drag was almost impossible. Items left might never be seen again. We took birds which, under other conditions, would have stayed on the ramp.

We were introduced to the bag drag our second mission. We were the spare crew and would start engines and taxi across the runway and wait, ready to fill any hole that developed. Everything went as scheduled. We went through our preflight. Then, Charlie called to tell us that number two in the first cell had a broken airplane. They would take the spare we had just preflighted and we would move to the unmanned spare. This move was reasonably smooth. The maintenance troops transferred us to the spare. It was time to start engines when we arrived at the unmanned spare. The copilot and I were in the process, while the crew loaded the gear. Charlie called us and advised us number three in the second cell had a broken bird and would arrive to take the one we were in.

The crew gathered the gear and loaded it on maintenance vehicles while I sat on the brakes with the engines running and waited for the other crew to appear. They arrived and the pilot team replaced me. We were transported to the original number two which had been declared back in service and ready to fly. We ran a quick check, started engines, and taxied to arrive at the end of the runway just as the last aircraft in the second cell started his takeoff roll.

We paused to recheck those items we had rushed through and began to relax as everything started to fall into place. The copilot and I were the only ones strapped in with helmet and parachutes connected. The rest of the crew were on headsets and just strapped in with the seat belt, for we knew we would not possibly be flying today. Thirty seconds prior to the expiration of our launch envelope the nav advised me: "Pilot, time is almost up. We can relax and get clearance to return to parking." These words were no sooner out of his mouth when Charlie called.

"Spare. We've had an airborne abort. You are cleared for takeoff."

I replied: "Roger, spare copies and rolling. Advise tower that I will be turning left immediately after liftoff. Will call airborne." I was adding power to move into position as I told the crew to strap in and check in. They were ready and checked in by position before I was lined up. The takeoff was normal—the aircraft unstuck and I attained about 200 feet, raised the gear and broke left across the parallel runway. This maneuver saved us many minutes on our departure; we could now raise our flaps on departure heading and not wait to turn until they were up.

I checked in with Charlie, and he advised us we would be number three in the second cell, as the other aircraft had moved up to fill the position left by the aborting aircraft. If we could catch up prior to A/R, we would get the scheduled offload. The nav team got busy and we set out for the intercept.

Several hours later as the second aircraft in the cell rolled out of his turn into the ARIP, I pulled in behind him and reported in the number three position. The mission was normal from there on until we started home; since we had burned a lot of fuel to catch up, we had a tanker waiting for us on the return trip to Andersen. We broke off from the cell, hit the tanker and returned to Andersen alone. From that time forward the nav was forbidden to comment on the possibility of launching when we pulled spare duty. All in all, it was a good experience for we reevaluated the amount of baggage we carried on future flights!

A word about Charlie probably needs to be said. In the States when we were flying, the supervisor of flying was required to monitor the launch and generally cover the ramp to aid crews if they needed it. Other than that, the crew worked through the command post. ARC LIGHT demanded alterations. The command post had other responsibilities, was not in a position to visually monitor the situation, and the crews needed immediate responses when problems arose. Command post controllers were not necessarily qualified in the aircraft. Therefore, a highly qualified instructor was assigned the duty of Charlie. Each base had several to share the duty. They worked in a tower, lower than the airfield tower, but high enough to monitor the parking area. His responsibilities were to coordinate the needs of the mission with maintenance and other agencies. He also was an immediate store of knowledge when the crew had problems. Sometimes he was a big brother and bolstered confidence when things were rapidly deteriorating around the crew. He, more than anyone on the base, had a working knowledge of the different crews and their capabilities. The bases that had tankers had a similar setup. Maintenance also has an equivalent representative at Charlie's side.

When I flew out of Kadena in 1969, two of my previous AC's were Charlies. I always felt they were looking over my shoulder. I know they held the launch several times so I could be repaired and keep the lead. Charlies were some of the good guys.

Engine start was always interesting and sometimes eerie. No radio transmissions were made unless problems arose; each aircraft silently taxiing, in order, to their place at the end of the runway. Of course, one had to know the position of the other birds; we were never parked adjacent to each other. It was a sight when no one had trouble and the birds just started and began to move. At the scheduled takeoff time the first aircraft would cross the hold line and the others would follow, at one minute intervals, with no request for takeoff clearance. At other times, the radio would be alive with continuous calls for maintenance assistance up to and through the launch, including mission aircraft, spare aircraft, and aircraft that had launched but were encountering difficulties.

Departure was usually smooth out of Andersen if everyone got off on time. The birds were at maximum gross weight and took a long time to get to altitude. During this period the trailing aircraft attempted to slowly close the gap in order to be near their cell positions at level off. Out of UT it was much more critical to be in position by level off. The pilot would clear the crew off of oxygen at 12,000 feet and everyone would begin to get comfortable. This meant if the pressurization was working properly with no fumes noted, the crewmember would remove his mask and let it dangle beside his face, immediately available if needed. If he desired to smoke or remove his helmet and put on the headset, or even unstrap and really get comfortable, he would request to do so and normally be cleared by the pilot. The radar-nav would advise the pilot of his distance from the lead or number two, depending upon cell position. Obviously, if we were in the lead, that would not be necessary. Additionally, the terrain avoidance system would be activated allowing the pilot to monitor his position in relation to anyone ahead. This was also the time for checking various types of equipment. If problems arose, assistance could be obtained from Andersen while in UHF radio range. If serious problems developed out of UHF range, contact could be made on HF radio.

Air refueling occurred three to four hours after takeoff. The onload varied depending upon the mission and target location. It was usually between 85,000 to 100,000 pounds. This activity was usually conducted in radio silence unless something happened necessitating communication. It was easy to recognize a new boomer. He would give the pilot directions as he approached the envelope. These directions would be, "Forward one— Up one" and so on until the receiver pilot would tell him in no uncertain terms to, "Stick in the goddam boom!" The track was limited with little time for disconnects. In other words, the tanker needed to constantly be passing gas to ensure the scheduled offload was given and preclude a post-target refueling. Pilot pride also kept them on the boom sometimes when skill seemed to have departed. If you were in the envelope, you expected to receive fuel.

This could get dicey with weather, turbulence, or an engine shutdown. It could really get interesting if you had all three. With an engine shutdown, it was possible to lose hydraulic pumps and thus reduce the lateral control. The one thing the pilot dreaded was a breakaway, not only for the time consumed but for the supposed embarrassment of having everyone in the cell know you had it called. After A/R, the cell would rejoin and continue to their common point and then on to the pre-IP and targets.

A clear blue sky over a blue green ocean provides the pathway to a nation in conflict. From 30,000 feet, the approach gives little indication of the turmoil below. The beaches look calm and white. The many concrete runways, visible along the coast, belie the devastation their inhabitants wreak in the countryside. The ground appears lush, green and peaceful. A tinge of purple covers the mountains, often surrounded by cumulus clouds. It was difficult to believe what occurred on the ground. There are many aspects of the war. Ours is only one . . . a detached one at best, seldom challenged until 1972. At night it changes; it was then possible to observe the firefights outlining the struggle below.

Radio contact would be made to the appropriate agencies prior to coasting in, information updated if required and final checklists run up to bomb release. This was also a time when communications were held to a minimum. Each crew member became engrossed in conducting his assigned duties. The most critical coordination within the aircraft was between the pilot and radar-nav. Number two and three had to be in position for their bombs to fall in the correct position in the target box. After bomb release, the aircraft would make a post-target break and the cell would rejoin and start the climb for recovery back to Andersen, or UT, or Kadena if scheduled to deploy.

The most boring part of the flight began. At level off, it was usually time to eat. We carried frozen dinners which could be put in the oven. From level off, after bomb release, until final penetration and landing, very little happened. Paperwork was completed, meals consumed, naps taken, letters written, and an extreme effort made to stay awake, especially if it was the middle of the night. If the crew had planned well, the EW would put a tape on the recorder and the crew's choice of music could be heard on private interphone. This provided a good background to pass the time. The rest of the flight was about four hours of boring holes in the sky until arriving at Andersen. Many times while trying to stay awake, I wished I had been able to fulfill the dream of playing second base for the St. Louis Cardinals. Instead of an exciting life in the big leagues, here I was boring holes in the sky over a never ending ocean. Of course, I had realized very early the only thing which kept me from playing was talent.

The night flights were the most difficult. Regardless of the crew rest taken prior to flight, the body wants to rest. The activity of flight itself can be tiring, both mentally and physically. Add to that the restriction of the parachute, helmet, oxygen mask, and an ejection seat allowing little movement. Fatigue slowly takes its toll. The easiest time to fall asleep in an ejection seat, which by definition is not comfortable, is when the aircraft is on an eastbound heading with the sun beginning its spectacular rise above the horizon. It is almost impossible to keep from nodding. There must have been millions of gallons of coffee consumed by thousands of pilots over the years to combat it. Although I do not know of any case personally, I am sure, with all the missions flown, there were times when everyone on the aircraft was asleep at the same time. I don't think anyone ever flew on past the penetration point for landing at Guam.

The cell would begin their spacing for landing as they approached the penetration point about a hundred miles out of Andersen; unless something went wrong, as one turned off of the runway, the next aircraft was touching down. This was far from the end of the mission. The bus would pick up the crew and take us to debriefing, where we were interrogated by operations, intelligence, weather and maintenance. Once this was complete, the crew was then free to leave. This usually included a stop at

Gilligan's Island.

Gilligan's Island was an open structure with tables and benches . . . a place to unwind. Snacks and cold drinks were available. Most of the time a representative of the flight surgeon was there with a bottle of Old Overholt (combat whiskey). Anyone who felt they needed it could get a free shot. After trying it once, I knew why it was free and why only one shot was given.

The usual fare was chili dogs and beer or pop. Maybe it was the weather, indifference or incompetence, but the standing joke always referred to having a cold chili dog and a hot beer. Hunger and thirst satisfied, the crew would then gather the gear and return to quarters and a welcome bed.

Normally the crew was kept on a schedule which allowed for the body to recover. However, at times when crew availability or experience was low, it was not uncommon to find oneself in a cycle that seemed to never allow for any rest. The duty day would be such that each day was beginning at a different time. It was hard to tell what time it was, much less what day it was.

One period when a cadre unit was being replaced with one from the States, we seemed to receive a large number of RTU crews. The experienced crews were primarily at UT and Kadena. The instructors were flying over-the-shoulder rides with the new crews, and it fell to the rest of us on Guam to fly the lead as often as we could be scheduled. According to regulations, 12 hours of crew rest are required prior to reporting for duty to fly again. It started one hour after landing. We were put on a schedule during this period where we would fly 10 to 12 hour flights, go into crew rest one hour after landing, and be lifting off the runway eighteen hours later. The body's circadian rhythm was all screwed up. We stayed on that schedule until we approached our monthly allowable flying hours and then deployed to UT, our place taken by a newly arrived crew from UT or Kadena.

The days became nights and the nights became days. However, it was, by far, better than what the troops on the ground in-country had to live through.

MISSION ONE

Our first mission was a Black/Brown. We were Brown Three. As previously mentioned, we had an over-the-shoulder team ride with an ARC

LIGHT experienced pilot and radar-nav along to ensure we did it right. Apparently, we did. We were signed off to go solo as a crew thereafter. Black/Brown was the midnight special. Takeoff was in the 0000 to 0200 local time, and landing was somewhere around noon that day.

The biggest question in my mind, and I think in the rest of the crew's as well, was whether we could complete the mission as planned with no problems. The fact that it was a late- night takeoff seemed to add pressure, at least to me, for I knew the air refueling would be at night and the onload in the 100,000 pound range. I had confidence in my ability, but the thought of failing to get the gas was always in the back of my mind. This was one of the unwritten measurements of pilots in the BUF. The ability to get the gas was needed in order to complete the rest of the mission. Each of us has his own level of conceit, and to some extent, thinks he is one of the best. Failure to live up to one's own expectations can be devastating. The word gets out as well. We all knew pilots who failed to make the grade in some way. It was always disconcerting to have someone who could not hack the job making policy and decisions concerning the crew force, when it was known he had never even been an AC, instructor, flown a similar mission, or even had the responsibility for the results. Believe me, they are out there. Regardless, the need to have the respect of your peers can help overcome many obstacles, including the fear of failure.

The mission day, or night in actuality, eventually came. I admit my crew rest did not involve uninterrupted sleep. There had been two early mishaps when the programs started; I did not want to be in another. I thought long and hard about the coming flight and apparently did not display too much outward anxiety, for the crew all seemed to have confidence. The mission briefing, preflight and engine start were all as they should be, quiet and with no difficulties. Then, it was our turn to take the runway.

I did not call for clearance. The tower had our takeoff time and we were expected to make it or advise Charlie. I cannot recall a delay for the bulk of the wave at any time. Lead would just add power, take the runway, and the rest would follow at one-minute intervals. The second cell would follow at a given time and the wave would be enroute. There was a Soviet trawler in the vicinity, and although I doubt we fooled them, at least they had to work for any information they gathered.

I added power after Brown Two had started his takeoff roll and moved into position. The smoke from the water injection and engines still lingered on the runway; the centerline was visible and the runway lights were at full intensity as I lined up and moved the steering ratio selector to the takeoff and land position, pushed the throttles to full power and checked the water injection lights off. The engine instruments were all in the green and I called the 70 knots check. The nav started his stopwatch and we pressed on. The first 3,000 to 4,000 feet of runway 06 is slightly downhill; the airspeed tends to increase rather quickly, so we reached our S1 (decision speed) accordingly.

The nav called: "Now."

I checked my airspeed and we had a few knots to spare.

I replied: "Committed!"

If we attempted to abort now, the chances of stopping on the runway was almost zero. The runway was now an upgrade and the airspeed did not increase as rapidly. The end of the runway was approaching much more rapidly than the arrival of takeoff speed. At last, the aircraft reached unstick speed and I held the control column back. We lifted off with some room to spare and immediately left the lighted runway environment. I was now on instruments, for there were no ground references at all.

The end of the runway sits atop a six hundred foot cliff and altitude is gained immediately upon becoming airborne. This is good in a D model at 450,000 pounds. There are no lights to see, as one is now over the ocean. It's like being shoved six feet up a cow's ass! You can't see anything. The only references are the flight instruments. It takes a few missions to get accustomed to the feeling.

The departure is straight ahead until the flaps are up; then a turn to the west. The climb to altitude takes about an hour because the external racks with weapons add a lot of drag. The over-the-shoulder pilot explained things as they occurred and demonstrated how to monitor the cell position with the terrain avoidance equipment. He was good and helped our confidence without ever getting in the seat or directing any actions.

As we came closer to the A/R, I began to hope I would be able to perform as I wished and as expected. I recalled I had never had a solo heavyweight A/R. As we departed altitude at the descent point, the extra pilot suggested I let the airspeed build to 310KIAS and ignore the normal speed schedule. I held that until one mile behind the tanker and let it bleed off in the climb to precontact position. This was not according to the book, but since time was critical, the longer we had to get the gas, the better.

I found his advice sound and all the other birds had done the same. Much to my relief the A/R went very well and we were on our way shortly thereafter.

The cell rejoined and flew to an entry point where we turned toward the coast of South Vietnam. We paid close attention as the lead made the radio contacts and received the information from the ground control agencies. The cell then proceeded to the pre IP and prepared for the bomb run. We flew in trail, above and behind, with one mile separation between aircraft. This changed later with the trailing aircraft offset to the right and left to get better coverage in the bombing box. The box was a predetermined area, and each one was of a different size depending upon the target objective.

Bomb release was made in two ways. The first, synchronous, was not used often, although it was the method we were most familiar with. It paralleled the method we used for EWO. This method used radar identifiable points, within range of the target, and were referred to as "offset aiming points," since many targets were not identifiable with radar. Premeasured distances from the aiming point to the target were fed into the bombing system, and the system released the weapons automatically. There were not too many of these points in South Vietnam which could readily be used. Therefore, most drops were controlled by the ground agencies.

The radar site would pick up the lead aircraft on radar and guide it to the release point by giving headings and time to release. Example: "Red one, right 234, 120 seconds." Red one would acknowledge with the heading and his call sign. Once inside sixty seconds to release, he would acknowledge only with his call sign. The site would count down to zero which was expressed as "hack." The lead bomber would then start his bomb train so that it would fall within the limits of the box. Number two and three radar-navs were advising the pilots of the distance to maintain, and the nav was computing the time from the hack to start their release. Our first mission was this type of release (MSQ) and went as planned. Fifteen seconds after the last bomb was gone I broke to the left at 55 degrees of bank. We began to prepare our strike report as we rejoined. The report contained our fuel state. If anyone was below a predetermined amount which would put him back over Andersen with less than 30,000 pounds of fuel, a post-target tanker was called. In some situations, the aircraft could abort into U-Tapao, Thailand. Landing in-country was not considered except in extreme emergencies. There were few airfields capable of accepting a BUF. Previous attempts had not been completed successfully, and the base commanders did not want the additional mortar magnet on their ramp.

It may sound as if the bombs were released with little regard to the results, or in other words, "carpet bombing." While we did "carpet" the assigned box, the boxes were a given size and woe be to the crew that dropped outside of them. Bomb damage assessment film showed the box outlined on the film with the actual bomb trains. We had plenty of restrictions. If certain code words were heard on the radio, the weapons were not released. If the nav team did not hear the countdown and/or the word "hack," they did not drop. If the radios malfunctioned and the above was not possible, no drop was made. The worst situation for a crew, accustomed to flying in the lead position, now flying as two or three, was dropping on the hack rather than the expiration of timing. This did not occur often. There were other restrictions as well, and some will be mentioned later.

The SAC manual which provided the rules under which we flew our missions was about an inch thick and contained as many don'ts as do's.

The return was uneventful and lengthy. The sun began to rise as we passed the Philippines. The over-the-shoulder pilot emphasized that at our recovery altitudes, above 40,000 feet, we should use extra caution with throttle movement to preclude engine stalls. Although it never happened to me, I listened to a crew who had to descend many thousands of feet before the engines could be brought back to full power. We arrived back at Andersen and landed with eleven hours and forty minutes of flying time.

THE WAY IT WAS

It is difficult to explain to someone who has never been in the cockpit of a BUF how cramped the space is; they look at the aircraft and immediately think because of the size it has plenty of room inside. There are two levels in all models. The layout is different in the G and H, where the gunner is up front with the EW. Otherwise, they are basically the same. The radar nav and nav are on the lower level in the D model. The entrance hatch is actually between their ejection seats, which fire downward when used. This level contains a door where one can pass through to the alternator deck and forward wheel well, into the bomb bay, through the 47 section and into the gunner's compartment. It also contains the relief facilities, an area for water and coffee jugs, and a seat for an instructor nav or additional crew member. The crew enters facing aft; on the left on the side of the fuselage is a ladder to the upper deck. At the top of the ladder, to the aft, is the electronic warfare officer's station. It is a small compartment with an upward ejection seat facing forward.

Forward of the ladder is a flat area referred to as the bunk, although no bed is actually there. Moving forward, the instructor pilot seat is positioned aft and between the pilot seat on the left and the copilot seat on the right. It also faces forward. The gunner has his own compartment 150 feet aft in the tail. A person of normal height cannot stand erect on the upper deck.

The pilot's seat is an upward ejection seat and not very comfortable. If the pilot were designed to fit the aircraft, he would be short of stature with very long arms. I am five eight; I was cramped. The seat contained a survival kit topped with a cushion which the pilot sat on. A backpack parachute was attached and fit into a recess in the seat back. These stayed in the aircraft and were inspected at given intervals, and by the crew prior to each flight.

The Mae West was fitted and donned prior to the parachute. It was not the old style with bladders across the chest. The new model was two small inflatable bladders on a harness, one under each arm. These fit through a gap in the parachute harness. The pilot fit the chute to his body and strapped into it. He would then connect the seat belt to the shoulder straps and quick opening device on the parachute. The helmet is donned and the oxygen and radio connections are made. This further restricts movement. The pilot must then position the seat so that he can reach everything and have full throw on all flight controls. During ARC LIGHT we also wore chapkits, which held additional survival gear particular to the area.

The original chapkits were similar to a set of chaps, worn around the waist with the pockets full of equipment around the legs. Once donned, they provided little movement to the legs. Most crew members did not put them on until just prior to entering the theater of operations.

The later model chapkits were more comfortable and could be donned at takeoff for shorter missions such as those out of UT. The nylon net vest had pockets which contained radios, flares, shark repellant, a holster with a .38 Combat Masterpiece revolver and many other items.

The aircraft has limited, but adequate, visibility for the pilots. There are windscreens, side windows which can be opened, and several small overhead windows, one of which is in the ejection hatch.

We had been on Guam for what seemed like forever as we watched other crews deploy for Kadena and U-Tapao. We began to think we would never deploy. Finally, on our ninth mission, we deployed to U-Tapao where we flew with crews from Pease AFB (now a BUF unit) and Fairchild AFB.

Our original mission nine resulted in an air abort. Shortly after takeoff we had a fire warning light on number two engine and shut it down. A fire warning light on number one illuminated soon after; we shut it down as well. We had a full load of weapons and fuel. Two engines out at this point meant we could not continue. Six engine A/R is not authorized except in emergencies. There was also time to launch the spare to replace us, so nothing was lost. We ran the checklists and set the aircraft systems to compensate as best we could. The indications were an air bleed leak, and there was little we could do to correct it once we had it isolated. Air bleed leaks, if allowed to continue, can be disastrous. I raised the airbrakes and lowered the flaps to increase the fuel flow and allow an earlier landing. As the aircraft weight approached 325,000 pounds, I requested and was cleared to the pattern for a landing. We had reviewed the landing with two engines out on the same side. The aircraft was handling well so I had little trepidation about the event, although we still had all the weapons on board. The weight had been reduced to near 300,000 pounds by the time we touched down. The aircraft pulled to the left. I then remembered to center the trim which the copilot was supposed to have done just prior to touchdown. The surrounding taxiways were filled with fire trucks, meat wagons, maintenance vehicles, and what appeared to be every blue vehicle with a rotating beacon. All the red lights on them were flashing. The landing was anticlimactic.

We logged four hours and forty minutes.

The next day we departed for Thailand. The missions out of UT were everyone's favorite. They were short. Most were less than four hours, with the average about three hours and forty minutes with no A/R. The shorter missions allowed us to fly almost every day. We attended the FNG briefings and flew our second mission the second day.

The arrival at UT was the first time most of the crew had been outside the U.S. or one of its possessions. The base was still being enlarged and the parking area had not been completed. We were assigned quarters with no air-conditioning. We spent two days in there until a trailer opened up for us. It was a concrete structure with louvered windows that did not provide much cooling. The humidity was about 120 percent; sleep was almost impossible.

The trailers, two rooms divided in the center by a bathroom, were the normal crew facilities. Each end held two crewmembers. The pilot and copilot shared one end and the nav team the other. The EW shared a room in another trailer with another EW. After more construction was completed, the pilot got a room to himself and the copilot moved in with the EW. On the last trip I made, two pilots shared a trailer, one at each end. This was a good arrangement. The rest of the crew still shared accommodations. Another good reason for being the pilot.

The rooms were about eight by twelve. They all contained a two-tiered bunk, two metal lockers, a desk and a refrigerator. The air-conditioning ran continually.

The climate at UT was even more humid than Guam, if that is possible. It was hot . . . day and night. The humidity hovered around 95-100% all the time. The base itself had been built on the shore of the Gulf of Siam. Cut out of the jungle, the vegetation surrounding the base was thick and green. The top of a nearby mountain had been removed to provide fill for the runway. When it rained, the heavens opened and it dropped like a waterfall. The sun came out and it was a steam bath.

The briefings at UT were nowhere near as formal as they were at Andersen. The briefers had more latitude, and it came out in the form of humor, sometimes caustic, but generally accepted as it was given. The slides with the mission data were interspersed with cartoons, which by all standards bordered on the gross and were always bawdy.

The favorite was a legion of Roman soldiers, all decked out in combat gear. In the foreground, a crusty-looking warrior in armor, holding a sword in one hand and the SAC lightning and palm leaves in the other is saying: "Men, we are going to war . . . but first a few written exams!" (The cartoonist is Col. [Ret.] Jerry Thompson). The staff was not as distant, and the crew attitude reflected it as well. The format was the same, just as detailed, but with the occasional icebreaker to show we were all in it together.

The room was always called to attention for the senior staff when they arrived. The next item was always the time hack. The briefer would give the time and the countdown to the hack, so all watches would be set at the same time. This required each of us to look down at our watch in preparation of restarting it at the hack. The countdown started at 60, then 30, and 15 second warnings. The last ten like space launches, 10,9,8,7,6,5,4,3,2,1, hack!

One night we were all seated with the countdown in progress. Instead of the hack, the briefer fired a blank round from a pistol. We all just about shit. The unexpected was always what we got at UT. We kept one eye on the briefer after that!

The missions began to blur together. We were flying every day. The short flights put little demand on us physically, unlike those out of Andersen. We were doing what we had been trained to do. Fly missions and do it often with none of the extra duties. It was good duty. We seldom flew into North Vietnam, and then only just across the border. These flights were much quieter.

The flights that stand out are the night flights. The book called for the anti-collision lights to be off on certain missions. Wise cells left the upper ones on so the other aircraft could be seen. There had been two too many mid-airs. Even with the radar giving the pilot distances it could close up real fast. A little of the mystery of it was taken out after I had identified civilian airliners in the area and other aircraft with all their lights flashing like downtown Las Vegas. We flew above most of the traffic at all times. On clear nights when the ground was visible, it was possible to follow a firefight with the flares in the air and tracer fire into and out of a defended area. It made me feel quite safe where I was.

UT also had a Gilligan's Island providing refreshments before and after flight. The fare consisted of banana, fresh pineapple, peanuts, hot dogs (questionable), pop, and beer. The first few flights I had bought a round for the crew. I rapidly calculated how this would mount up over a six-month period, so I had to come up with a better device. I finally hit upon the tire marking. Before each flight the radar-nav selected a main gear tire and, using chalk, marked it off in six equal parts: P,CP,RN,N,EW and G. The idea was that when the aircraft was parked after flight, the crew position on the bottom of the tire was obligated to purchase the first round. If it stopped on a line separating two positions, they both had to ante up a round. This helped reduce the cost, although a run of bad luck could be expensive. In the months to come, as we flew other aircraft, the tires were marked and other crews were doing the same. Most of the tires on the front trucks were always marked. As the crew chiefs became aware of what we were doing, they would watch the tire and thus select who they thought should buy. It behooved one to treat them with the respect they deserved for doing their jobs, for when you did not, they could spend your money for you and you never knew it.

The BUFs got preferential treatment. The time required to turn the aircraft after landing was critical to the next mission. The aircraft had to be repaired, if broken, refueled, and bombs uploaded. We were considered priority traffic when we returned to the field. The only aircraft with higher priority were emergencies and medical evacuation. I returned one night with over 90,000 pounds of fuel and heard a tanker inbound with low fuel. He was held for us to land first. Sometimes the tankers were so short on fuel they would land at U-Dorn, NKP, or Don Muang. It did not seem fair, but we had no choice in the matter. Best of all, we lost no one in the delays.

We had our first break after eleven days of flying. It was welcome. We came back refreshed and ready to continue. The second day we were number two in the launch. It was the copilot's turn to take off. Everything went well as we began our roll and the bird lifted off easily. At about 50 feet in the air, the fire warning light for number one engine illuminated. I told the copilot to continue to fly the aircraft and I retracted the gear. Normally, I would have retarded the throttle until the light went out in order to continue to get some thrust out of it until we gained some altitude. Since the EGT was high, I put it in cutoff immediately, pulled the firewall shutoff switch and trimmed the rudder. The copilot still had control and continued the climb. The nav had the engine shutdown checklist and read it for me to ensure we got everything. Once we had some altitude and the problem solved, I called Charlie and lead, advised them of our problem and that we would continue since all appeared normal now, but we would be slower getting into formation. The rest of the mission was normal and we recovered three hours and fifty five minutes later. Although it was the copilot's turn, I made the landing since we had an engine out.

We deplaned and went out to see if there was any visible damage to the engine. The outboard side of the number one engine had a hole about twelve inches in diameter in the cowling, and it was obvious there had been a good explosion in the engine. If I had not shut it down when I did, things could have gotten serious quickly. To this day, I cannot say what made me shut it down as quickly as I did. At that time, a fire warning light was not that uncommon and did not necessarily call for an engine to be shut down. If, when the throttle was retarded and the light went out with no other indications of an overheat or fire, then the throttle could be advanced to a lower power setting, and the engine allowed to run. Air bleed leaks are serious. The heat, if not checked, can eventually cause a fire, and fire is an enemy of airplane people.

I learned about flying from that!!!

Two days later we redeployed to Andersen where we flew three missions and then deployed to Kadena AFB, Okinawa.

We packed our gear, minus many unessential items, and went to mission briefing. We had heard so much about Kadena we were eager to go. We were number three in the cell, and on the return would break off and proceed to Kadena. I flew a lot of number two and three the first year, and the birds I got were not always in the same condition as the lead aircraft. It was a good experience. I flew a lot of bad BUFs and learned to cope with a lot of problems I had never seen before.

The copilot had the takeoff. The aircraft reached S1 speed and we were committed. The liftoff was smooth, and as I reached for the gear handle, we passed over the edge of the cliff, gaining some automatic altitude. The fire warning light of number five engine came on. I retarded it slightly and it went out. The instruments were normal, and I advanced it to just below its original setting and turned my attention to number three engine which had a fire warning light as well. I did the same as with number five and continued the same action with number two and number six. The copilot continued to fly the aircraft as I played musical throttles. He then called for the flaps. I started retraction and prayed for no more lights. It worked. I advised Charlie of the situation and that we were pressing on since the lights were out. He rogered and wished us well.

We met our tankers, and since we were going to Kadena, we had a smaller onload. I had received most of the fuel when I got a disconnect. Since I had been in the green, I asked the boomer why, and he said it was a pressure disconnect. This did not make sense as we were not getting a heavyweight refueling. I asked the copilot how the fuel panel looked, and he told me number one main tank was not taking fuel and he closed all the others to try and force the valve open. I replied that he should open them up before I forced something of his open. He did. I moved in and the boomer hit me again. As I started taking fuel, I asked how much I had to go for my complete offload. The pilot said 5,000 pounds and asked why. I told him I had a fire warning light on number eight. He immediately said I had my scheduled off-load, initiated a disconnect, and started a climb. Just because I had a full load of bombs, a lot of fuel, and a potential fire, I guess he decided he needed some space.

Once the tanker was clear I retarded the throttle on number eight to check the instruments. It also looked good, so I advanced it and we pressed on. The rest of the mission was normal, except the debrief when maintenance moaned and groaned because they had five engines on one aircraft to check. We were just glad to be in Kadena.

The facilities at Kadena were better than the other bases, and the duty was pretty good as well. The Clinton-Sherman wing staff filled the positions required of a cadre unit move to the wing at Kadena. This was not a problem, but for the previous months we had been away from them, flying with crews from other units, occasionally seeing our wing crews. Kadena was a lot like home. The island seemed to be one continuous military base from Kadena to Naha at the southern tip of the island. The shopping was terrific. The lack of funds was the only reason we did not buy more.

We had flown several missions and were on a break. I was facing a problem. My gunner had decided to leave the Air Force and would be returning to Clinton-Sherman when we returned to Andersen. I could not find out who his replacement would be although our wing staff was present. This was frustrating, for we had all learned the mission together and felt he was an integral part of the crew.

We went out as a crew for dinner and ended up at the O Club at a Marine base. The bar had a piano and a young lady played customer requests. She was a very nice lady and tipped the scales at 200 plus. The company was good, time passed, and eventually the story of the ham and the oven was told. It went over well. Before we knew it, the last call had passed and the club was closing. We left and tried to get a cab to return to Kadena. There were none available.

As we discussed what action to take, the piano player came out of the club and offered us a ride we obviously needed. We accepted, for the walk home was a long one. The gunner and I were about the same size: 155 pounds and five foot eight. The rest of the crew was larger. The lady was driving a Fiat 600. Somehow, we all were able to get into the car. The acceleration was almost nil.

The chassis must have been as low as it could be as we left the base, went down the hill, and started along the coast road. At the intersection of another main road, a Military Police vehicle pulled in behind us and the bubble machine came on. We pulled over and hoped for the best. The MP's first question was: "Don't you think you are a little overloaded?" The lady agreed, but explained our inability to get other transportation and we needed to get back for crew rest to fly the next day. She was only helping out. He hesitated and then advised her to be extremely careful and not to do it again. We thanked him. He stayed behind us most of the way to the gate.

We decided that we would not be lucky twice, and so all but one of us got out before we got to the gate. We walked through, they met us on the other side, and we were delivered to our quarters. I have since looked closely at a Fiat 600, and I do not know how the crew got in, especially with the driver.

Several days later, we redeployed to Andersen via South Vietnam. The 47 section and the forward cabin were full of the spoils (?) of war. There were tape decks, china and camera equipment. It would have taken a large problem with the aircraft before we bag dragged this one.

We landed at Andersen at 0440 Monday morning. At 0725 Wednesday we deployed to U-Tapao. Although it was a quick turnaround, we did not complain. UT, as previously mentioned, was a good tour. We were scheduled to have an L/C stationed at UT to return with us as an extra man. This was normal; unless the extra man was a senior staff officer (colonel or above), he was required to attend the briefing. If he did not, he was not supposed to fly. He did not show. We had completed the preflight, were ready to start engines, when the RN advised me our extra man had appeared. I told him to inform him that since he had missed the briefing, he was not going on my bird. The RN said the man wanted to talk to me; I relented. I could smell him before he got to the IP seat; the alcohol fumes were overwhelming. We had a long discussion about the requirements and rules about flying in his condition. He agreed with me completely but insisted he had to get back to UT or he would be in deep trouble. He actually was kneeling between the seats and was begging me to allow him to go. I did not want to be a complete horse's ass, but I also did not want to be responsible for him. He was also quite senior to me in rank. Finally, I told him that he could go if he got into the bunk after takeoff and stayed there until landing. He agreed; we heard nothing from him until the aircraft landed at UT. He promised me I would never be sorry. He was right.

UT was in the process of upgrading all of the facilities. The old club was still in use with its outside dining and bar area. We had learned the first trip that few people ever ate inside unless it was raining. It was not air-conditioned. The club also had free drinks for a couple of hours at least once a week. We had been advised of the possibility of contracting malaria. Quinine tablets were available. Most of us took our quinine with ice and a touch of gin.

The entertainment was also held outside on a wooden stage at the corner of the fenced-in patio area. This consisted primarily of music, mostly highly amplified. The bands played current music to which they knew all the words, even though they could not speak English.

UT had an open-air theater on the beach. We only attended it once. It was located several hundred yards west of the end of the primary runway. Every aircraft launch drowned out the sound for several minutes. The BUF launches were the worst for they seemed to last forever.

The tour at UT went well. The time passed swiftly and we redeployed to Andersen. One thing about returning from UT was that it gave us a chance to use the washers and dryers. The drill at UT involved hiring the housegirl, who kept the trailers clean, to wash the clothes. This took some bartering until a price was established, always one dollar a week and the purchase of a large box of Tide. Her responsibility was to wash, dry and fold the clothes. The clothes were washed in large dishpans with enough detergent added to wash the clothes of a family of four for a week. They were rubbed on the sidewalk, when there was one, to remove stains and dirt, and then dried. The normal tour was two to three weeks long.

I would take my flying suits and other clothes to the laundry room at Andersen and put them into the washer without adding soap. There was always enough residual soap in the clothes to wash them. I've had the machines run over with suds. A tour at Andersen was always good for something.

Our first flight out of Andersen was an early morning takeoff with a recovery just after dark. We were number three in the second cell. We were so good at that position that we kept flying it. The target was just north of the DMZ, and the radar bombing system of the aircraft would be used for a synchronous release. The number two aircraft developed radar problems during departure. I lost oil pressure on number two engine and shut it down after level off. We came off of the tankers; shortly after, that number one aircraft lost his radar completely and moved to the number two position. We moved up to the lead and advised the ABC in the first cell.

We had a good radar and could accomplish a Bonus Deal with the gunner directing the aircraft with no bombing radar system. He did this by giving distance and center line information from his gunnery radar to the trailing aircraft. They in turn established their drop timing and thus released the bombs.

The bomb runs in this area usually had little radio traffic. This was no exception. We hit our target and the gunner directed number two for his release. Number three was able to release by positioning off of us. We were above the altitude we normally flew in South Vietnam. It was a slow climb with one engine out. The subsequent climb to recovery altitude was even slower although we were more than 60,000 pounds lighter. I set my engine EPRs to give me 450 knots of true airspeed. We ate our dinner and filled out the paperwork. The copilot set the fuel panel and laid down in the bunk for a rest.

We were about an hour and a half from our penetration point and I was putting write-ups in the 781.

There was an explosion on the right wing. I tossed the forms into the copilot's seat; his butt reached the seat a microsecond later. The fire warning light on number six was bright red and the engine instruments were dancing around their dials. I immediately cut the throttle and pulled the firewall shutoff switch. We ran the checklist and I noticed number five had a vibration above 80 percent RPM. I kept it pulled back. I ordered everyone into their seats, strapped in and helmets on. I told them to stay in that configuration until we landed.

Once the situation was back to a semblance of normality I called the wave lead and ABC, advised them of the situation, and that I was reducing speed in order not to overtemp the remaining engines. He concurred and said he would advise the command post upon initial UHF contact. I spent the next hour reviewing "Landing with two or more engines out" procedures ensuring the crew knew what was expected and alert for any additional problems.

I would like to have had a daylight landing but had no choice in the matter. The night was lit up with the airfield lights and the numerous emergency vehicles with their flashing lights and rotating beacons spread down the taxiways awaiting our approach and landing. Actually, it was a very easy landing and rollout. Concentration on the objective can do wonders.

I learned about flying from that!!!

We deployed to Kadena a week later.

We had developed certain actions when we arrived at Andersen. The first chance we got, the RN and I would go to the store and buy a case of soft drinks and a case of beer. It was all the same price, 10 cents a can. We put it into the refrigerator with a small box. If anyone, including the RN and me, wanted one he paid twenty five cents. When the box contained enough, we took our initial investment out; from then on the box ran itself. The RN was in charge of the box and kept the supply adequate. Additionally, the officers added a dollar a mission and the gunner fifty cents. The box was a money maker. The second time we went to Kadena there was enough to treat the whole crew to an evening of fine dining. At the end of the tour we would all go to Kenny's, the best restaurant in the vicinity of Andersen, and treat ourselves to a steak and shrimp dinner with all the extras until the contents of the box had been used.

The tour at Kadena was easy. We flew only five times in eleven days. The quarters we were in were great. The nav and RN shared a room and the copilot and EW shared a room. The gunners were in a separate area. I, as the AC, got a small suite with a living/dining/kitchen area, a separate bedroom and large bath. It was great to discover privacy again.

I was in no hurry to return to Andersen, but we did.

It was now the middle of August. Those of us who were senior captains were waiting for the promotion list to major to be released. I did not think I had much of a chance, since I had been a copilot for what seemed forever. I found out later my top OER (Officer Effectiveness Report) was a 7/3, not considered too great. A 9/4 was optimal. It was written by a squadron commander who had the squadron long enough to write a 90 day OER on all of the pilots. Most got the same, a 7/3. If I had known it before the promotion board met, I would have really been worried.

We were back flying out of Andersen. At the briefing which occurred about 2200, we were told the list would be released the next day. We were also told that since some of us flyers had an interest, if we called in on our return leg we would be given the names of the lucky ones. Although there was nothing we could do about it, it was on everyone's mind for most of the mission. Naturally, the word was not passed and we landed, still in the dark, although it was mid afternoon.

The aircraft had some problems and we went directly to debriefing. For the moment I had forgotten the list was to be released. As I came out of maintenance debriefing I saw my crew, who had left before me. They had big grins on their faces, and one of the other pilots yelled: "Congratulations." It did not immediately sink in. Then it dawned on me and I was told the list was in the briefing room. I reviewed and felt good, not only for myself, but for the other good friends who had made the cut. We retired to Gilligan's Island and I bought a round for the crew. Since we had been up all night, we did not celebrate too long. I still had difficulty believing it. We went to bed soon after that.

I did not sleep too well and got up before the rest of the crew. I had to tell someone. That someone was in Clinton-Sherman, Oklahoma! The cost of a three-minute telephone call was $25.00. My pay was to go up in the near future, so I made the call. I identified myself, and before I could tell the good news, Wendy asked me if I had gotten the word about the promotion. She was told the night before. The cost was worth it anyway; it was the first time we had spoken to each other since March.

We went to the club for dinner and met other newly promoted captains who were still celebrating. There were five of us, and we had four or five bottles of Mateus with our meal. The long night before and little sleep began to take its toll. I started back to the room with the nav and EW. The RN and copilot came in later.

I woke the next morning to the copilot calling the EW. He got no response. I got up and went to see what he wanted. He told me he had to go to the bathroom, but the pain in his neck was so bad he could not move. I asked several questions and he assured me he could not move without great pain. I told him to stay put and woke up the rest of the crew. I then went down to the telephone and called the hospital, explained the problem, and asked for a doctor. They told me someone would be right there. I returned to the room and the crew was up and trying to determine what the problem was. Tom did mention that he had fallen the night before.

The ambulance eventually came and someone came up to the room. Naturally, we were on the third floor. He came in, walked over to the bed and asked what was wrong. Tom explained and was told to get out of bed. He replied that he could not. He suggested we move him to the ambulance. I asked if he was a doctor and he said no. I then told him to get a doctor, for, with the indications, he was not going to move him except under a doctor's direction. He said he could not, and I told him he could tell that to the DCO for that was whom I was calling. He relented and called the hospital.

The doctor arrived and seemed more interested in chewing me out than seeing to the patient. Since we were both captains, that did not go over too well. He told Tom to get up. Tom replied that if he could do that he would have gone to the bathroom hours earlier. The doctor continued to question him and appeared to me to be accusing him of malingering. He finally determined there was a problem and sent his corpsman for a stretcher. I tried to calm the crew but my anger was also at the boiling point.

When the stretcher arrived, the doctor told Tom to get onto it. I suggested he might need some help under the circumstances, and the doctor reluctantly assisted him with the help of the corpsman. He put his hand under Tom's neck and made him do most of the moving. Once on the stretcher, Tom said, with gritted teeth, the pain was terrible. We finally convinced the doctor to roll up a towel and put it under his neck for support. This seemed to help. Since Tom was in his underwear, I asked if they had a cover for the stretcher and was told no. I suggested rather strongly that they had the choice of any sheet or blanket in the room.

They covered him with a sheet and rolled the stretcher out. As they descended the staircase, I asked if it would not be better to take him down feet first since he seemed to have a neck injury. I got no reply, but they did turn him around on the second floor. I told Tom I would get cleaned up and come to the hospital as soon as I could.

I went back to the room, cleaned up and put on a uniform. I explained that when I returned I needed to know what had occurred the night before and left for the hospital. I was in the hallway of the hospital when I met the doctor who immediately began to berate me for giving his airman a hard time. I told him I obviously was not a doctor but could tell when someone was injured. I felt a doctor should make decisions. He told me his airman had been on duty all night. I heatedly explained that when you are on duty you are required to do things. The argument deteriorated from there, as we went round and round like the knob on an outhouse door. The people passing were giving us odd looks, for our voices had risen above conversation level. A door opened and another doctor came out and informed us the patient had a broken neck. The first doctor's attitude changed drastically. We had a calmer discussion as to what should be done. It was decided he would be taken to the Navy Hospital immediately,

Tom told us later that when he was rolled into the hospital he was not treated too gently until they saw the x-rays. They then slowed the gurney to go over seams in the floor. He also told us the injury was the same as when someone was hanged. He had four hours after that in which he would either die or survive with possible paralysis. He did survive, was returned to the States for recovery therapy, and transferred to March AFB, California, where he eventually returned to flying status. He and the RN told me he had fallen off of the second floor of the compound and landed on his head. They did not go into greater detail, and I did not push it.

I contacted scheduling and told them I would need a copilot for my next flight and the rest of the tour; mine was in the hospital. I also informed our wing representative. Each time I flew from Andersen until I returned home, I had to remind scheduling that they had failed to schedule a copilot with me, and some poor soul who thought he had a day off would be notified at the last minute to go into crew rest for a flight.

We continued to fly. We landed about 0130 in the morning and had been in bed for several hours when there was a knock on the door. I got up to inform the sergeant who had knocked to return later after we had a chance to rest. He told me he had to have my signature on an accident report. He handed it to me and told me I had to sign it. I read it and told him that I would not sign it; it was not correct. After a long discussion, he finally accepted the fact that I was not going to sign the report someone else had written without interviewing me or my crew. I had to remind him that I did not take orders from enlisted people and would not sign any report under the circumstances. He left. When the crew awoke later, I explained what had happened and that they should be prepared to be interviewed.

On the way to dinner that evening, I met our wing representative who asked why I had not signed the report. The way he asked, I knew he had been taking some heat. I asked if he had read the report; he had not. I suggested he read it and then we could discuss it. He did and told me he was very glad I had not signed it.

On our next flight we aborted into UT for several days. When we returned, I received a call from the wing commander for Pease AFB, who was the cadre commander at Andersen (our wing commander was at Kadena). He informed me that he would pick me up for a meeting with the Commander of 3rd Air Division concerning the accident to my copilot. I explained that RN had been present and asked if he should come along as well. He agreed that he should.

He picked us up and asked about the incident. We briefly explained our actions. He informed me that the hospital had thought about bringing charges against me. When I asked what they would have been, it got somewhat muddy. I then asked if I might have some charges myself for the treatment of my crewmember. He assured me not to worry about it. He was a well respected commander, and he confirmed that in my mind by the way he conducted our meeting.

We were ushered into the Commander's office which was full of senior staff. We came to attention, saluted, and reported to the general. He gave us "at ease." We went to parade rest. He then congratulated me on the promotion to major. He went on to say that with that came additional responsibility. He told us that he understood that the crewmembers could be rowdy occasionally and he thought that was okay within reasonable limits. Generally (no pun intended), he politely chewed my ass. He got his point across quite effectively. I respected the way he maintained control of the situation. I have tried to emulate the same approach when I have been required to discuss unpleasant subjects with my subordinates. There is something to being an officer and a gentleman. My part of the conversation consisted of "Yes, sir" and "No, sir." He dismissed us and we returned to our quarters.

An investigation was conducted and a report prepared which I was not required to sign or even asked to sign. A copy of it was on the bulletin board and was confiscated later by my old fellow crew member, Jack. The report went into great detail of how the copilot was with a group and he became dizzy on his way to the room. He sat down on the second of three rails and fell through to the ground which was solid coral, landing on his head. I learned over a year later that the group had been attempting to walk a large electrical cable which ran from the compound to the gym. Everyone had fallen, the copilot was the only one to land on his head.

I learned about flying from that!!!

The copilot was replaced with any copilot available for the rest of the tour. I learned from each one how the crews they flew with operated. While we were standardized, there was still room for individual differences. I think my crew had one of the best operations. I guess the biggest surprise was that our stan-eval chief's copilot could not believe I was giving him a landing. In four months, he had received just enough to stay current. I always felt the copilot might be required to land someday and should damn well know how to do it. I could relate to his lack of activity. If I had gotten more as a copilot, I might have upgraded earlier. He did make a good landing.

The mission was at night and we were in the second cell as usual. The lead aircraft in the first cell had an outrigger gear fail to retract. His fuel flow rate was higher than the rest of the cell. The number two in the cell had a problem I cannot recall. The problems were such that they would abort into UT. The number one and two in my cell would be going to Kadena and we were to return to Andersen alone.

I lost an alternator shortly after takeoff. This was not a big problem at the time. We flew through a lot of weather enroute to the target, and the RN complained about intermittent loss of radar when a second alternator began fluctuating badly. When the copilot began the fuel sequence for the drop tanks, the left tank did not feed. We had no one to follow through the weather if we lost radar. A full drop tank with 19,000 pounds of unusable fuel meant we could not use the other drop tank either because it could create a center of gravity and controllability problem, I elected to abort into UT as well.

We came off of the target and passed our post target information to our cell lead and informed him of my decision to proceed to UT. He concurred and I selected traffic control, in our case GCI. I heard the lead and number two from the first cell ask for clearance to channel 105. They were given a heading of 075. Using my "outstanding knowledge of navigation," I recognized this was not in the direction I wished to take, for the less fuel I used the better control I had of the aircraft. It dawned on me we had made this trip before, so I asked for clearance to channel 105 via the Brass Route. I was told to start climb and was cleared as requested. The lead, not being a dummy, asked for the same and received it. The Brass Route was the normal recovery for the BUFs to U-Tapao. The altitude was above 40,000 feet. Channel 105 was the frequency for the Tacan and an identification for UT, which we used instead of the name of the base proper.

Although we had been separated initially from the other two aircraft and landed ahead of them, we were all picked up by the same bus. After debriefing, we were all sent to billeting and then Crew Control for quarters. I overheard the other two pilots discussing whether we would be able to get air-conditioned quarters. One of them was concerned about date of rank being the deciding factor if quarters were limited; they compared theirs. They were from Columbus, AFB, Mississippi. I was a stranger to them, so was not included in their conversation. I really was not concerned after I overheard them.

We arrived at Crew Control and began to fill out the forms for our stay, which ended up to be several nights. The L/C in charge informed us that he only had one air-conditioned unit in the tanker quarters. The other two crews would be in the BOQ. He would therefore assign them on the basis of rank of the AC's since we were all captains. The pilot who was so concerned initially ran to the counter and gave his date of rank. I had stepped into the corridor and the second pilot asked what he had to beat. My interim copilot asked if he could beat December of 63. He said yes and gave his date, just prior. The copilot replied: "You lose!" The L/C then asked me and I gave mine, which I had known all along was the winner. The first pilot immediately challenged me as to whether I was on the majors' list. I said yes, but since we were all captains, I still outranked them. He then wanted to know my line number to major. I replied that if I outranked him as a captain, I would certainly have a lower line number. He reluctantly agreed and we got the air-conditioned quarters. His RN, a major, was not too happy.

The quarters were not too bad, but not as private or as nice as the trailers. We flew two missions and rotated back to Andersen on the third.

One night at the club while we were at UT, we had enjoyed an hour of free drinks. The whole patio was in an uproar. The DCO was at a table 20 or so feet from ours. The sub copilot began throwing a hard cardboard coaster in the air. He tossed it further each time until it came down on the bridge of the DCO's nose. Bad enough, but then he went over and claimed it. Fortunately, the DCO had a sense of humor. I could see my promotion and career slipping away. I was glad to redeploy to Andersen for once.

I had only one wave lead and several cell leads, but was experienced enough to fly an over-the-shoulder with an incoming crew. We had led well when given the chance and were respected as a solid crew. The RN and I were scheduled with a crew from Dyess AFB, Texas. The rest of the crew had the day and night off.

We met the crew at prebrief. I went over the pilot's paperwork and tried to answer all their questions. I was not an instructor at the time, but performed as if I were.

The crew had bought coffee for the flight. The pilot had a cup during preflight. He did not get out of his seat, but studied the mission while waiting for engine start. He had also flown B-47s and we discussed the differences. The flight was normal and the crew performed as expected. The pilot drank at least another half gallon of coffee through the flight. He never got out of his seat, although I offered to give him a break. The flight was 12 1/2 hours long with an hour and a half of preflight. He did not use the relief facilities. In the B-47 you could not move around, but there was a relief tube handy. He must have had a bladder the size of a drop tank! I got the impression he did not trust the copilot alone in the seat, or me for that matter. I did not care to be the over-the-shoulder person. Although I was listed as the pilot in command, the pilot had to really be bad to try to take over or tell him what to do. We did have a slight disagreement.

We came off of the target with several thousand pounds of fuel short of the required amount to recover with 30,000 pounds at penetration.

The ABC in the wave lead aircraft would call for post-release data after each cell had hit the target. He would then determine if a tanker was required for anyone and evaluate any problems encountered and make a strike report. Our pilot did not want to hit a tanker on the way home, but I was all for following the rules. I was not a very good swimmer.

I did not want to come out and remind him that I was in command of the aircraft since he was a major, and I did not want to make him look bad in front of his crew, for he had six months of decisions to make which would affect them. Fortunately, before I had to, the ABC informed us he had called a tanker. I made sure the pilot and I had a short critique.

The time to return home was rapidly approaching, and to say we were eager is to understate the obvious. Our last scheduled flight was an 0200 takeoff. All went well through takeoff and then my eyes began to tear. I checked with the crew and they had the same reaction. I had the RN go off oxygen and he was immediately back on. The fumes were very prevalent throughout the cabin. It was as if raw fuel was being dumped into the pressurization/air-conditioning system. We went through the procedures and could not get rid of them. It got so bad that tears were flowing over my mask, and my throat was raw. We advised Charlie and went through all the suggestions he and maintenance came up with, to no avail. I advised him we could not continue. He launched the spare.

We burnt off fuel until we could land at 300,000 pounds. By the time we shut down the engines and climbed out, I had a number one Excedrin headache. I had asked the command post to have a flight surgeon meet the aircraft but no one appeared. At debriefing I was told if I wanted a doctor I could go to the hospital, even though someone should have been at the briefing which was just finishing when we arrived. I loaded the crew in the bus and we went to the hospital. I asked for a flight surgeon and was asked my serial number. I gave it and told the airman to get the doctor. He refused and asked for everyone's serial number. After a long discussion, he admitted the doctor was asleep and he would not wake him. I told him I would wake him since we should have had someone at the aircraft, or at least at debriefing to take blood samples. I again had to threaten to call the DCO. I finally won my point and went in to see the doctor. He was not a flight surgeon and was not in the least interested in the fact we had been breathing raw fumes for almost four hours. He gave us some aspirin and sent us away. I have had many flight surgeons in twenty-eight years and never had one who had such a cavalier attitude as this doctor. In fact, most of them are very restrictive in the care and feeding of the crew force. My experiences with the hospital on Guam were not the most pleasant.

I was glad to leave Andersen two days later and return to the garden spot of Western Oklahoma. The return trip was on a tanker. Things had changed. A tanker had left Guam enroute to the States several weeks prior. An engine was shut down and the crew elected to land at Wake Island. There was a full load of passengers and baggage. The aircraft crashed upon landing and there were fatalities. The new rules reduced the number of passengers allowed on board when an engine was carried. We had slightly more room.

When we arrived home we were greeted by the staff and our families. The alert schedule was posted and we were back to the old routine in short order.

BREAK! BREAK!

I felt pretty good. We were a solid crew, with the exception of the co-pilot position. We had been tested in many ways and had confidence in ourselves and each other. That was all very evident when all of us except the EW were taken into a room after our stan-eval ride and learned the unit was trying to take action against him for nodding off during a cruise portion of the ride. As a group, we informed the investigating officer that we had spent six months with him in a wartime environment and had complete confidence in him. We felt the whole thing was unfair. I was never prouder of the crew as when they stood with me in his defense. It was dropped quickly.

The biggest problem facing me was the need for a copilot. I hoped to get some say in the selection, but rapidly found I would not. I was given a copilot who had been flying with an instructor for at least three years. I was told they felt he was ready to fly with a regular crew. This should tell you something about the unit's confidence in him. He had been with us on ARC LIGHT. I talked to his previous pilot, a good friend, and he assured me Rod could handle it. He turned out to be reliable as long as everything went normally.

It seldom did. Change confused him; rapid change was worse. We did persevere, however. I became a much better pilot!

We were scheduled for a day flight. When we reached the aircraft for preflight it seemed to be spread all over the ramp. Hal, my first BUF AC, was now in maintenance. I went over to his car to check the forms which were in a mess. The aircraft had one alternator out, an engine oil pressure problem, and sundry other items which had not either been signed off to fly as is or repaired. We discussed the problems and I agreed to take the aircraft. I also agreed to run the engine when it was ready for checkout if there was not enough time for a maintenance crew to do it and still get an on time takeoff.

The repair did not progress as desired, and I was asked to run the engine while it was checked by the ground crew. I started it and waited for them to check it. The technician yelled up the hatch for me to do something and the RN relayed it. I told the crew chief to put the engine man on interphone so I could receive his requests and talk to him. The man did not want to talk on the interphone. He insisted on yelling up the hatch. I finally told the crew chief that if they wanted me to follow directions to get on the interphone or I would shut down the engine and return it to them to repair. Reluctantly, someone did and we got the engine run completed. I then asked for someone to come on board and collect the tools and trash that had been left. They were not too happy when I finally taxied away. We flew the mission and thought nothing more of it.

The next day we went on alert and Friday morning I found a RBI (reply by endorsement) from the squadron commander in my crew box. It stated that after our flight the maintenance crew had found chicken bones around the throttle quadrant and the autopilot console. The aircraft was also reported as being left dirty.

I said nothing to the crew about the RBI, but asked each one to tell me what his inflight lunch had contained. The gunner, who had ordered them, confirmed it with the inflight kitchen. It was as I suspected. No one had ordered or eaten chicken. I knew Rod and I had not, and I always make a cursory check for forgotten items as I leave the aircraft. I then wrote my reply and delivered it in person to the squadron commander.

I had outlined the condition of the aircraft when we arrived and the fact that I had to ask for assistance on the interphone while I performed maintenance's duties, as well as make them clean their own mess before they shut the hatch. I then ran a listing of each crew member's flight lunch and why it was impossible for chicken bones to have been left by me or my crew. The final sentence reiterated that I would continue to inspect the aircraft after each flight. The commander read it and then tapped the last sentence and told me that was what he wanted to see. I could not believe it. He had no interest in the fact that one of his crews had been falsely accused. The event was not a big deal, but it set the tone of the following months and our next ARC LIGHT tour.

I had shown the RBI to the crew before I took it to the commander. When I told them the results, they took it pretty well. Why not? I was the one who had to answer it. It was thereafter referred to as the Great Chicken Bone Incident. However, in typical SAC crew fashion, they did institute a few rules for future flights. It was the two chicken man policy. We had to have two qualified crew members present when anyone was near a nuclear weapon, controlling device or component. It was also required to have two qualified people when anyone was around the go to war tickets. Therefore, in the future, when anyone on the crew except the gunner, as he had his own compartment, ordered chicken for his inflight meal, he could eat it only when directly observed by another equally qualified crew member.

I did get a chance to respond to the maintenance people. We were still on alert and had an aircraft changeover. We went out to the aircraft for preflight and the bird was full of trash. I called the crew together and went back into the alert shack and told maintenance when the bird was ready for preflight to contact me. When I told them the problem, they suggested I clean it up. I reminded them we were not garbage men and would not do

their work for them. The changeover was delayed for quite a while because no one wanted to admit the aircraft was not ready for the crew. I
had made my point.

The time passed quickly and we were scheduled to return as a unit
to Southeast Asia after the first of the year. The squadron had gained
some new members to replace departing ones. I pinned on my gold leaves
on 1 January. They sure looked better than the railroad tracks of a captain.

The RN and I compared statistics, and while I had onloaded
3,012,000 pounds of fuel, he had dropped 3,548,283 pounds of bombs.
Since we did not refuel out of UT, he had a definite advantage. I bet
him I would catch him and pass him the next tour. I lost.

I went through a period where each Saturday morning I would get a
phone call from the operations officer about a mission we had flown that
week. I would answer his questions while he chewed me out. The following Monday, we would show him the crew had been right, but I never got
an apology or acknowledgment.

For example, we had flown a low level mission and had two bad bomb
releases. At the time, we did not know what caused them. I got my Saturday morning call and was chewed out and informed we needed additional
training. I called the RN to discuss it with him; he told me not to worry
because the bad bombs were not our fault. Sure enough, Monday he took
the bomb folder into the bomb nav office and we compared the data for the
offset aiming points with the other folders for the same targets. He was
right, someone had not changed the offsets and we had used the data as
presented. When I showed this to the ops officer, he just shrugged. The
Saturday morning calls stopped.

There is a low level VFR (visual flight rules) route in Southwest Texas which is open most of the time. It could only be flown in visual flight conditions. The entry is near Fort Stockton, where the terrain is generally flat and rolling. It then swings south, then west, through the mountains just north of the Big Bend country. The route turns north with a bomb run near the town of Marfa. This is where the movie *Giant* was filmed and the set was still there. The big house, which is only a facade, was still standing and made a good visual reference point. The route then followed a long valley and exited to the west.

Pilots loved the route, for there were legs we could descend and fly very close to the ground. The main hazard was buzzards which caused many birdstrikes. There is something satisfying about flying a BUF at 325 knots just above the ground. The nav team was always glad when we reached a leg with a higher enroute altitude, mainly because their ejection seats went down, not up like the rest of the crew.

One leg has a peak which is several thousand feet above the approach altitude. It sticks up above the surrounding terrain like a tower and can be seen 30 miles or more. The RN calls distance to high terrain and advises the pilots to climb in order to clear the obstacle. I never flew this route when the pilots started the climb when the RN suggested. Instead we would fly directly toward the peak at the approach altitude. As the distance shortened, the RN's voice rose in pitch. He would become more insistent the closer we got and I would remind him I had it visual. I would fly directly toward it and then at the last minute, fly to the side and below the peak. One flight we had the nav upstairs. He got so nervous he went back down to the darkness of his station where he could not see out.

Naturally, we could not get through the period at home without an inspection. The dreaded ORI (Operational Readiness Inspection). A horde of inspectors descend on the base and the unit must fly a simulation of their EWO mission. The rules have changed over the years, but basically, the wing must generate the aircraft which would fly missions after the alert force has been launched or an increased Defcon level is declared.

Time frames are critical. No work can be done on the alert aircraft except safety of flight items so they are ready to fly at any time. The wing will then fly a predetermined route, exercising the different requirements of the wing's EWO commitments. Of course, all nuclear weapons are downloaded prior to the exercise. The wing's readiness is then evaluated on how well they accomplish the established criteria. Generally speaking, if they pass the flying phase, the wing passes the ORI.

Once the flying phase is complete, the inspectors then begin to look at everything else. They dig through paperwork, inspect facilities, and overall, make nuisances of themselves. It is necessary and supported, but not particularly enjoyed or appreciated by the inspectees.

I came back from leave just in time to go on alert as the inspectors began their digging. The wing had flown satisfactorily. Senior people came into an area; they were always escorted. This was necessary in some cases, depending upon the area inspected, but more often out of survival instinct of the person in charge of the area.

A bird colonel had come into the alert facility and had a group of horse holders in tow. He went about the rounds with the alert facility manager right behind him to answer any questions and divert attention from anything that might raise questions.

I was just leaving the officer's latrine when the entourage came in. It was just a two-staller with a urinal and washbasin. The colonel walked into one of the stalls with the major right behind him. He turned and asked the major . . . "if he didn't mind, he thought he could handle this one alone." I almost did not make it out of the door before I broke up.

The new schedule was out and we were to deploy to Andersen AFB on 31 March 1969.

RACE TRACK

March 31 was upon us before we knew it. This time we would be flying a BUF to Andersen rather than ride the cattlecar. I approached the squadron commander who had given me the RBI and asked if we would be flying more wave and cell leads this tour. He would not give me a straight answer. He told me he did not know if he would recommend us or not. He did not, but the senior staff at Andersen did. We knew where we stood with him, the artful dodger. The Division thought more of our ability than our own squadron commander.

The flight to Andersen was from Clinton-Sherman to an A/R over the rockies, onloading 67,000 pounds, and coasting out near San Francisco. We met another set of tankers well off the coast onloading another 80,000 pounds; with full tanks, we set out across the Pacific Ocean. We were in cell with another aircraft which was scheduled to lead halfway and then switch the lead to us to finish the route into Guam. I felt I should have been in the lead, but the other pilot outranked me.

This irritated the nav team something fierce. They felt, and I agreed, they were a more competent team. Instead of transferring the lead to us at Midway as planned, the lead waited and gave us a five degree heading change into Wake Island where they turned the lead over to us. This was the last leg into Guam. As we came into radar range of Guam, the navigator said he would like to give a half degree heading change, but did not think the other crew would understand the irony, so he made it a full degree. I made the correction and advised the cell. We then prepared for approach and landing.

Our approach was over the cliff. This approach in VFR conditions can be intimidating. Even when on the glide path and everything in the green, there is a tendency to fly higher than normal to avoid the massive rock which makes up the face of the cliff. Everything tells you that you are clear, but the seat of the pants says, "stay high." This compounds the landing, for the runway is a downhill slope almost all the way. If you are high across the threshold, the aircraft will float . . . and float. If the pilot forces it down, it results in a bounce. I had landed this direction before, and after five months of absence, gracefully put the bird down with a small but solid bounce.

The drill had not changed. We were taken to maintenance debriefing and then to Crew Control for quarters assignment. We found we were on the ground training schedule for three days of Scat School prior to flying. Our first mission this time was an early get up with a takeoff just prior to dawn. Little had changed and nothing of note except this was my first heavyweight refueling since the previous October. The auto pilot did not work in the A/R mode, but with a little effort I got it in one gulp.

I had gotten to the point that the nav would time me and count down to the disconnect. He did this by dividing the amount of fuel by the maximum transfer per minute. He was pretty accurate, except when I fouled him up by losing contact. A stan-eval pilot and radar from our own base were on board giving us our over-the-shoulder checkout. It was as if we had not left. Roddy even performed well.

The routine was the same. We stayed at Andersen for about three weeks and flew the long missions. We were leading this year, thanks to the staff at Andersen. The only thing out of the ordinary was that I had to shut down an engine on seven out of ten flights. The rumor was that I could not fly without an engine out! It sure seemed like it. Then we deployed to U-Tapao.

Things had changed. A new O Club had been built. A new dining facility, and a snack bar which was open twenty four hours a day. A new and separate bar, joined by a covered patio area. All air-conditioned. The covered patio lost the charm of the old one. There also was a move to sod the whole base. What had been bare ground before, now featured green grass, even the trailer area. A new exchange had been erected and the whole base had a new look.

I was with more Clinton-Sherman crews. We initially went into the night schedule. Improvements had been made to the schedule as well. The wave still consisted of six aircraft in two cells. The crew would fly six days on one time frame and then have a day off and rotate to the next time frame. Each day one crew left the group and moved on and another joined. We flew our way around the schedule. Everyone got a reasonably good chance of the same number of day and night flights.

This worked well until a pilot from Griffiss AFB did not make the flight one night. He was grounded and sent home. His excuse was that he was taking medicine for a cold and overslept. Most of us thought the medicine came from a Jim Beam bottle or similar container. Now, instead of a day off with the crew, each pilot was rotated through to cover his flights until a replacement was sent from Griffiss and checked out. Naturally, my turn was on the Ivory/Walnut schedule with an 0317 takeoff.

Each crew EW was issued a tape recorder for each flight. It was his responsibility to hook it up to the interphone system and record all critical phases of flight to include takeoff, air refueling, in-country bomb runs, approach and landing, as well as emergencies when possible. Initially the crews hated the idea; it was viewed as just another way for the staff to intrude in the crew's lives. We came to appreciate it as an unbiased witness to events which the majority of the time substantiated the crew's actions. On long missions when it was not recording, the EW would play music on private interphone for anyone who wished to listen. This was our second year with the recorder.

One of our first flights at UT was a night mission and we were number three. The target was the area surrounding Muy Gia Pass out of North Vietnam, an important point on the Ho Chi Minh Trail. The location of the target required that we attack it at a higher altitude than we normally flew. I had to shut down an engine shortly after takeoff. It was all we could do to reach 39,000 feet and move somewhere near position by the time we reached the pre-IP.

We had a captain from the bomb-nav shop in the IP seat. Roddy was having a bad night. He screwed up the radios and did not get the right frequencies set until after we left the IP. The RN did not hesitate bringing it to his attention. As we neared three minutes to bomb release I began to see large orange fireballs ahead and to the side. Although I had never seen it before, it was obvious it was anti-aircraft fire. I mentioned it to the crew, and the gunner said he had some behind us as well. Although he said it was level according to his system radar, intelligence data indicated it was not capable of that height. It did not pose a threat in any case. Since we were the second cell, the bad guys just waited about fifteen minutes and sent up some fire, hoping to get lucky.

The copilot screwed up the radios again and we were well within 60 seconds to go before we were back on frequency. The RN had a few short things to say to him. We heard the countdown from ground and the bombs were released. As we reached our start climb point, Roddy was catching up to level off 45 minutes earlier. The RN was vocal . . . again.

After debriefing, the captain from bomb-nav observed we had crew coordination problems and asked that we meet with him to discuss them. His critique centered around the RN and copilot. I explained that the crew, with the exception of Roddy, had been together for over a year and were in sync. He then decided we would review the tape to prove his point.

The procedure for the countdown between the nav and RN was to use private interphone. This year a change had been made and they had a choice. Gary and Frank elected to stay on private.

The tape was full of static and difficult to understand until we got on the bomb run. He began to make his points. During the time from the hack to the release, a strange voice came on the interphone asking who was making the countdown. I knew who had spoken. I asked if the captain wanted to press the issue of coordination after interfering with the bomb run countdown. He declined and mumbled something about procedure. We left. The tape had done its job.

The crews in our group were pretty good for the most part. We took turns as lead and everyone got their share. We had a crew from March AFB in our group, and except for one thing, I liked flying in cell with them. It seems every time we were in the same cell, I had an emergency, which ranged from minor to serious pucker time. It only happened when John's crew was in our cell, not the wave. We worked our way through the red bordered pages (emergency procedures) together that tour.

I was lead one night when my gear did not all retract. I immediately passed the word on Charlie channel that I would hold my flaps while I recycled the gear. It was a little late; number two informed me he was pass-ing me on the right and number three on the left. The gear came up and we caught up and took the lead again.

The next night with John in the lead, I was number two. We had just set climb power when the fuselage fire warning light illuminated. The light is located above the copilot's directional indicator on his instrument panel. I had often wondered whether it could be seen well from the pilot's seat.

It can.

I saw it before Roddy. I passed the word to Charlie and John. The nav had the checklist out and we began to work the problem. A fire in the fu-selage can be serious, especially with a full load of fuel and bombs. The light can indicate either an overheat condition or an actual fire. Unless it can be seen, the data on the overheat panel on the copilot's side panel is all that is available to evaluate and make decisions.

The problem was isolated to the air-conditioning/pressurization system. The light went out when the pressurization switch was moved from normal to combat, but illuminated when it was returned to normal. Roddy put it back into combat for the remainder of the flight. This meant that on recov-ery our cabin pressure would be much higher than normal, but not too much higher for the bombing portion of the mission.

I called Charlie and John and informed them that I would continue. If the light came on again, I would abort into the nearest base that could take a BUF. My choices were limited; the last thing a base commander in South Vietnam wanted was a mortar magnet like a BUF on his ramp. I also con-sidered a Jimmy K maneuver, dropping the bombs in the gulf and landing, but then he had a real fire. I just had a light as far as I knew.

The rest of the mission went normally. When we climbed to our recov-ery altitude, the cabin pressure went to 20,500 feet. Everyone was on oxy-gen for awhile, and Roddy thought he would die because he could not smoke. When I think of the WWII B-17 crews with no pressurization, it was not too bad, just inconvenient. It was more tiring.

I learned about flying from that!!!

The following night we were assigned a different aircraft. I knew some-thing was up when the bus pulled up to the aircraft. It is not unusual to see a line truck with maintenance people in it and the crew chief and his assistant doing the primary work, unless specialists are required. It is unusual to see a second lieutenant and a chief master sergeant awaiting the crew. It is more unusual for the chief and the lieutenant to bring the forms on the bus for the pilot. It is a very strong clue that the chief is going to show the lieutenant how to sell a pilot an aircraft he might have reservations about flying. This was no exception,

The chief handed me the 781 and said there was a small, but not serious, problem with the pressurization system. I asked what. He said the aircraft could only be pressurized to combat pressurization and again assured me that the pressurization altitude would be about 16,000 feet at 40,000 feet of altitude. I read the write-up and told him to get me another airplane. He replied that I did not understand, and went through the altitude differential again. I informed him he was the one who did not understand. I wanted another airplane.

He continued the conversation, intent on selling me the bird. I told him I had flown the night before in another aircraft with combat pressurization because it failed in flight; since our mission did not require it, I would not start out that way. If it failed in flight, that's the way the ball bounced. I then asked if he would find me another airplane or if I should get on the radio and call Charlie and inform the world what I was being offered. He found another airplane. The lieutenant got a lesson in how crews don't always accept what is offered because someone with many stripes makes the offer.

We all learned about flying from that!!!

Radar makes the job easier. The aircraft initially flew in close formation when ARC LIGHT started. A midair collision helped change the tactics. By the time we got there, the normal cell flew in trail at separate altitudes with mile separation. We were not dependent upon visual conditions. As long as the weather was penetrable, we would continue. This was the way we had learned SAC's primary mission. A night low-level in mountainous terrain without the ground visible is a wonderful confidence builder.

The formation, if it can be called that since there is separation, can penetrate weather much more safely with radar. If a trailing aircraft has radar problems, the gunner in the lead aircraft can monitor and guide it on his radar.

The thunderstorms in Southeast Asia can build quickly and many times do not have the intensity at the upper reaches that is present in the ones over the central U.S. At least that is my experience. That does not mean there is no turbulence.

I was leading a wave one night toward a target northeast of Saigon. We had been in and out of the weather all of the way, but it was mainly cirrus and light cumulus. The RN did not have any severe weather on his scope as we left the IP on the bomb run. As the site counted down the last few seconds, we hit the top of a thunderstorm and the autopilot kicked off. It was all I could do to maintain a heading and semblance of altitude as the release sequence began. I believe, but am not sure, some of the bombs went up rather than down. Number two and three were higher and did not get any turbulence.

We had a pilot transfer into the wing just after we returned from the first tour. He was assigned a crew and deployed to ARC LIGHT with us. His experience had been in C-130 aircraft. He was in our group at UT. He had a habit which drove the rest of us mad. According to his RN, who I worked with years later, once they were airborne he would turn off all radio switches on his console and monitor only interphone, leaving all radio work to the copilot. He never acknowledged anything the first time; this required extra transmissions until someone on the crew answered.

One day we were leading and John was in number two slot with this guy in number three. Since John was in the cell, I had my scheduled emergency with alternators which turned out to be minor. My RN was guiding us through the weather with an abnormal number of thunderstorms. Each time we changed heading we would advise the cell. John would answer: "Grape two." Number three had to be called several times before someone would acknowledge. Finally, as we neared the pre-IP for the bomb run and I gave another heading, number three pilot piped up: "My radar thinks we should go right rather than left for the weather."

Before I could reply and ask why he waited until now to get in the ballgame, John said: "Shut up. . . .! You had your chance to lead yesterday!"

He actually answered the radio the rest of the flight.

There was a navigator who must have listened to or heard of the disc jockey in SEA who always began his program by yelling: "Good morning! Vietnam!" We flew in the same cell occasionally. If it was any-time after midnight or before noon as we coasted in, Lenny would yell over the radio: "Goooood morning, Vietnam!" I never thought much about it until the movie came out. To my knowledge no one ever told him not to do it.

It was during this period at UT that we flew our 100th mission. The whole staff and flight line always knew, and as the aircraft stopped for park-ing, it was surrounded by staff people and many buckets of water. When available, the commanding general would be present to hand out the hun-dred-mission patches after the wet down. I was always the last one out of the aircraft and took the time this day to empty my pockets of everything I did not want to get soaked. I then left the aircraft. The participants had been patiently waiting. When I stepped off of the ladder, I was herded to-gether with the others who had completed the magic number. We were then doused with water over and over until we were soaking wet. The com-mander then presented us with our patches and a chit for a bottle of cham-pagne each. Our picture was taken. It did not take too long for the sun to dry out our flying suits, but the underwear stayed wet.

The next morning we flew number one hundred and one and the war went on.

The tanker troops had achieved a lot of respect in Southeast Asia. The tankers out of UT primarily ran anchors for the fighters. In other words, they provided A/R for the fighters prior to their strikes and after as well. The anchors were assigned orbits. The tankers helped save numerous planes and crews. Many went beyond the point authorized to assist a damaged aircraft. That effort built a bond between them. It was almost as strong as that for the troops who flew rescue, especially the Jolly Greens. When you know that they will make all efforts they can to get you back if you go down, the willingness to press it increases.

In 1969 at U-Tapao, to acknowledge the tankers' efforts, the base held a YOUNG TIGER DAY. YOUNG TIGER being the code word for KC-135 operations in SEA. It was an all-day party with a big blowout in the evening.

The war effort did not stop, however. We were scheduled for a late evening showtime for a takeoff after midnight, hitting the target just at dawn. This meant we went into crew rest early and did not get to partake in the festivities. War is hell! A schedule was always posted in the O Club. It indicated I was leading the wave with a member of the planning staff along as the ABC.

The ABC did not show up at the briefing. This was allowed since he had helped plan the mission. The IP for the bomb run was on the coast and the target was in the tri-border area. The rules at the time stated that unless we were specifically briefed, we could not overfly any part of Cambodia. Immediately after bomb release, we were to make a combat break to the right, and one minute later, a turn to the left to avoid overflight of the tip of Cambodia. A few miles later we were to start climb and pick up the Brass Route for recovery. We were not briefed to overfly. Pretty straight forward. The ABC met us at the aircraft prior to engine start; he was also a major.

Engine start and taxi was normal. I had put my chapkit under the IP seat so that I could don it after we got to altitude. I noticed the ABC was asleep before we began our takeoff roll. I did not mind; the less interference with the crew the better. The guys at UT had a pretty good reputation.

We leveled off and ran through the systems checks. All looked good. I asked the IP to hand me my chapkit from under his seat. When I got no response after a second request, I turned to see if he had heard me. He was still sound asleep. I put in my seat pins, unstrapped and reached back and got the chapkit and put it on. We continued around the south end of Vietnam and up the coast. The sky was rapidly turning light; the sun was soon to rise. We were the Viet Cong's alarm clock. Our contacts were made with the release agency. All was well with the world, we thought. Without any warning, the ABC woke up.

We had left the IP and were halfway down the bomb run when the ABC made his first request. We had assumed our radio procedure in which the pilot worked with the release agency on the cell frequency and did not monitor GCI. The copilot worked with GCI and monitored both frequencies. We were within three minutes to release, the most critical point of the run coming fast. The ABC told the copilot to get clearance direct from the release point to the climb point and disregard the two 90 degree turns. The nav came up immediately, said we had not been briefed and could not change the route. The ABC began to argue and I missed the 60 second call. When it was repeated by ground with a "Do you copy?", I told everyone to shut up and pay attention to the business at hand and that we would fly it as briefed. They did and we did.

After release, when the copilot was collecting data for the post- release message, the ABC told him to get clearance to start climb early. I replied that we would fly it as briefed. Nothing else was said. We recovered without incident.

I was the last off of the aircraft, and after a quick exterior postflight, got on the bus in time to hear the ABC telling my crew that we would never fly wave lead again. I asked what the hell he was talking about. Apparently, he had been chewing them out while they waited for me. He went on to say that he had never been so ignored as an ABC. He repeated the threat. At least, I took it as a threat. I informed him I had never had an ABC who slept until the critical part of the flight and then decided to have the crew disregard established procedures for no reason. I went on to mention it was his group that had planned the mission and if he wanted it to be changed he should have done so during the planning stage.

We continued to argue as we picked up the number two crew and the threat changed to: "I'll never fly as ABC with this crew again." I agreed and asked if he wished to review the tape. The pilot of the second crew, a good friend from Clinton-Sherman, asked why I had missed the 60 second call; I had never done it before. I told him we had an internal problem. The ABC got off the bus at HQ and we went to debriefing where I explained to the number two pilot what had happened. He advised me to talk to someone immediately. I agreed and we returned to quarters. I cleaned up and returned to HQ.

I asked to speak to the DCO and was told he was not available, but the ADO was and I asked to see him. I started out by saying that if I was out of line to tell me and I would leave, but I wanted my side of the story to come out if the incident was brought up.

He told me to go ahead. I explained what had happened and told him the only thing I was asking was this particular individual never be scheduled to fly with my crew again, as he upset my crew and I could not permit that. I felt in the bomb dropping business the fewer distractions the better. I also mentioned he could review the tape if he wished to substantiate my story.

He leaned to his left and opened a drawer and handed me a letter signed by the 3rd Air Division Commander. The letter, in essence, said to tell the staff and ABCs to leave the crews alone; the crews knew what they were doing and doing it well. I gave it back and said as far as I was concerned that was the end of it, except that I could not permit the individual to fly on my airplane again. He told me not to worry and press on. I went back to my trailer and went to bed feeling much better.

That evening at the club, the nav was complaining about a rule at Andersen that did not allow one to wear a turtleneck shirt at the O Club. In my inimitable way, I was trying to explain that if that was what the commander wanted that was the way it was and we could do little about it. I was waxing eloquently on the subject when the EW came up and asked if I had seen the night's flying schedule. I replied I had not. He informed me that our friendly ABC was scheduled on our bird.

I went ballistic. The nav reminded me of my recent discussion and I told him to get bent; that SOB was not going to fly on my airplane.

As soon as the bus stopped that night, I was into the scheduling office and told them that the scheduled ABC was not going to fly with me. I was told the commander had already been briefed and they could not change it. I informed them that I would not fly on the same airplane with the SOB. I gave them the option of moving either me or him back in the cell. Let him play ABC with another crew, but he was not going to fly with me. I referenced my discussion with the ADO and offered to call him.

I then left for the briefing. They did move him to number two. I lead the gaggle and was the ABC. I heard that he wanted a hundred missions as an ABC. I don't know if he made it or not.

I believed that was that until I checked the flight orders the next night. Guess who was scheduled with whom?

I arrived at scheduling that night, and as I walked in they raised their hands and told me it was a mistake. It had been taken care of. He flew on another bird and I was ABC again. I do think I did a better job as ABC than he did, but then most of the pilot ABCs did.

I learned about flying from that!!!

The DCO at UT had been the commander of CEVG (Combat Evaluation Group), SAC's super standardization unit. He was scheduled to fly with my crew and was the scheduled ABC. I could see no real problem as we were leading again. If we did not screw up too badly, it could be good for all of us. We had already started engines when he showed up. I knew I was in trouble. He had on a white scarf around his neck. Now, most of us did not like to wear the scarf at home and no one wore it during ARC LIGHT, especially at UT at 1400 in the afternoon.

He climbed on board and began to get comfortable in the IP seat. The crew chief closed the entrance hatch. The hatch light on my instrument panel did not go out, indicating a hatch somewhere on the aircraft was not closed or the electrical connections were malfunctioning. Regardless, it was a problem that had to be solved. I informed Charlie and we had an electrician on the way. In the interim, the RN had run through his procedures of hot tips, and we had determined the problem was in the switch in the main entrance hatch. The crew chief was told to inform the electrician, and I am sure he did. The electrician began to inspect all of the other hatches. I told the crew chief to send him back to the main entrance hatch.

Meanwhile the time was passing swiftly; our taxi time passed. The electrician kept checking the hatches in the rear of the aircraft. The IP was getting restless. He was getting upset. We reached a point where we could no longer make the launch as scheduled, so he elected to move to the new lead aircraft.

I advised Charlie. Just before the DCO left interphone, the electrician came on the interphone and informed me that the problem was in the entrance hatch and it would take about 30 minutes to repair. The IP left in a bad mood. I would like to have been in standup that day when the DCM tried to explain to the commander why we were delayed, while the DCO was present. We launched in the second cell.

We had done so well that we got a free trip back to Andersen. I don't recall why, but several crews were flown back on a tanker. The wing was getting in more RTU crews all the time to supplement the cadre units. They came from G and H units and had volunteered or been selected by their units to share the load. They spent several weeks at Castle training in the procedures and the D model equipment. They would then get an over-the-shoulder ride with instructors at Andersen. Once cleared, they were turned loose with the rest of us.

The instructors were taken from the cadre force. When the pilot and RN team was used, the rest of the crew was available as spares. This took many of the lead crews out. The rest of us lead qualified crews did a lot of flying with the new crews in the cell to check out. This resulted in many days with 18 hours between flights. The days and nights ran together, but then time flies when you are having fun!

Our fifth mission in this cycle was an 1120 A.M. takeoff. I was leading as Tan 1. Number two was another crew from Clinton-Sherman. As I approached level off, the pilot of number two called and asked if we had any problem with our number one engine. At the same time the gunner reported a large cloud of black smoke from number one nacelle. I checked the engine instruments and was about to reply in the negative when the EGT pegged, the RPM went to zero and the fire warning light for number two engine illuminated. I pulled the firewall shutoff switch and cut the throttle, calling for the checklist which was quickly completed. My concern was then whether number one had sustained any damage. It continued to run smoothly and the instruments were steady.

I called Charlie with the information. He asked if I was going to continue and if number one engine was OK. I replied that it looked good and I would continue. He had less than five minutes in which he could launch a spare; since we looked good, he did not. We continued on seven engines.

An hour later the number one oil pressure began to drop. I let the engine run until it reached 35 PSI and shut it down. Now we had a problem. We could not continue with two engines shutdown. We advised number two to move to the side and take the lead while we continued along until we received our clearance to return to Andersen. The copilot got a lower altitude for the return and we advised the command post over the HF radio of our situation.

As we returned, I started to add drag devices when we got within UHF range of Andersen. We were told to go to a holding area off the coast of Rota Island, north of Guam. We got clearance to 8,000 to increase the fuel flow. I had the air brakes up, the landing gear down, and the power set to keep the fuel flow rate high. I had lowered the flaps, but the control problem that presented at our weight (we still had a full complement of internal and external bombs) took too much effort, so I raised them.

We had run the checklists and had everything positioned to ensure the operation of all equipment necessary for safe flight. Then I lost a hydraulic pack unaffected by the engines I had shut down.

No big deal. Then I lost an alternator. We rechecked our bleed air system; no indication of leaks was apparent. The engines were adjusted for the best thrust without overtemping or putting too much strain on the airframe. We had seven and eight pulled back as much as possible. Then the fire warning light on number five illuminated. I retarded the throttle until the light went out. I did not shut it down. I advised the command post and told them my weight was at 330,000 pounds and would be below 320,000 if I left holding to land now. I suggested I put it on the ground before something serious developed. I was told to standby.

They came back several minutes later, approving my suggestion, and advising that we had clearance to proceed to Naftan Rock and jettison the bombs. This made sense as it would lower the aircraft weight greatly and quickly, and in turn, give me more flight control. The nav set up a bomb run and the RN set the bombs to go safe. We were at 8,000 feet and the resulting explosion from the "safe" bombs knocked off the aircraft autopilot. I could not believe the intensity of the blast which hit the aircraft. I was glad not to ever be on the receiving end. All of the bombs went. I think they all exploded as well.

After the release, we got clearance and were vectored to the final approach for landing. We declared an emergency and the field was filled with vehicles with flashing lights. It was not as dramatic in the daytime. We landed without incident and taxied to parking, escorted by what seemed to be every blue vehicle on the island. I guess between launches there was little to do.

We parked and were immediately surrounded by people. Someone was dragging up an engine stand to look at the damage before we deplaned. As usual, I was the last one off of the aircraft and had to work my way through the crowd to get to the number one nacelle. When I got there, an L/C maintenance type on the stand was expounding to the audience, made up of senior enlisted men and 0-6's, one of which was my wing commander. He said loud enough for everyone to hear: "These goddam pilots don't know what they are doing. There is nothing wrong with this engine!"

A chief master sergeant standing beside him looking into the engine replied very calmly: "Sir, there is no turbine wheel in this engine. I think the pilot shut down the engine when it departed."

My wing commander tapped me on the shoulder and asked which engine I had shut down first. I explained number two and why. I also added number one was shut down when the oil pressure dropped below limits. He patted me on the shoulder and said: "Good job, Jim."

The flying schedule continued and we were on it the next day. We racked up the flying time.

I learned about flying from that!!!

The year before I had bought each of the kids a small stuffed toy koala bear. When I left the second time and asked what they wanted, my youngest daughter said she wanted a big "koalie bear." Wendy had returned to Illinois in August and the older kids planned a birthday party for Jill's third birthday. However, she was not too happy. She had received nothing from her father. The party was in progress when the mailman arrived with a package for Jill. She opened it and found her "koalie bear." It was almost as big as she was.

My favorite picture of her was taken that day. Her face had remnants of chocolate cake and ice cream and she was obviously tired. But she was hugging her "koalie bear." I could not have asked for better timing.

There was a big push which resulted in a continuous stream with almost no breaks. The targets were in the Cambodian border area, north of the Iron Triangle. Continuous waves of aircraft flew over. It lasted over twelve hours. The birds came from UT, Kadena, and Andersen. We were in the middle of the Andersen group.

Our preflight had gone well. We started engines. The copilot ran his check on the electrical system. There was no indication of power on number four TR (transformer rectifier) unit on the DC power panel. We advised the crew chief to tell the maintenance truck, and I notified Charlie. Since so many aircraft were involved, the taxi plan was complicated and required close adherence to preclude a goat rope.

The electrician arrived. We told him what the problem was and that time was of the essence. We had identified the TR unit and one was on hand for replacement. We proceeded to finish up as many checklists as possible so that when we were repaired we could press on with the least amount of delay.

Then things began to fall apart.

The crew chief told us the electrician was entering the aft bay. I told him to tell the guy the problem was with number four TR unit in the forward wheel well. He said the guy would not listen to him nor get on interphone as I requested. They proceeded to change the unit in the aft bay. I could not get anyone to listen to me or the crew chief. In retrospect, I should have unstrapped, gotten out of my seat, opened the hatch, chewed some ass, and straightened them out. Charlie kept moving us back in the launch.

The interesting thing was that we had all sorts of blue maintenance vehicles around us. The personnel surrounding us were heavy with stripes and leaves.

The electrician came on the interphone and told me he had changed the number seven TR unit. I thanked him and told him to get his ass in gear and change the one that was broken in the forward wheel well. He gave the interphone to the crew chief and proceeded to correct his error. By now we had reverted to spare status. I noticed as the launch wound down the blue vehicles began to slowly depart. I asked the crew chief to tell the maintenance truck that the pilot wanted to talk to someone in authority when we shut down since we had lost our chance to fly because of their screwup. He did, but the blue vehicles continued to depart.

I shut down engines when we were released and left the aircraft heading straight for the last blue truck. One young captain and several mainte-nance NCOs were in it. They denied any knowledge and I vented my anger. I continued at maintenance debriefing, asking why no one listened to the crew when a problem arose. I got no satisfaction but made sure it went into my written critique.

The nav had developed a ringing in his ears and was getting dizzy in flight. He had to tell us once he felt he had to do something about it, for his performance was always top notch and was not affected as far as I could tell. The flight surgeon grounded him. This was a big loss. Frank was one of the best. His replacement arrived, right out of nav school and upgrade at Castle. The RN took him under his wing and brought him up right. He turned out to be very good, even though he had little experience.

The flying hours continued to add up and we were fast approaching a point where we would not be able to fly without a waiver. We were sent to Kadena where the missions were shorter. The RN had arranged for his wife to meet him in Okinawa while we were there. It was a common practice for the tanker troops who were stationed there for longer periods.

Arlene and another wife from Clinton-Sherman were waiting when the bus pulled up to the quarters. Gary and Arlene were like two teenagers. They were both hesitant to run to each other and suddenly became very shy with the crew standing around like idiots. The new nav loved it. The RN was staying downtown with his wife and the nav had a room all to himself. I wish we all could have had our wives there, for the RN's attitude improved drastically.

Two of the Charlies were pilots I flew with during my upgrade. I felt they were looking over my shoulder all of the time. It seemed as if they wanted me to fly and would hold the launch when I was leading and having problems which could be solved in a short time.

We were spare one evening when number three in the first cell blew an air-conditioning duct shortly after takeoff and had to abort. The lead in the second cell was told to move forward and join the first cell as number three. That left two birds in the second cell. We were at the expiration time, but Charlie called and said: "You've got it, Jim!"

I added power and we started our roll. The S1 speed was good. We continued, and continued, and continued. I began to think we would not reach unstick speed before we passed the overrun. We were lighter than the previous aircraft had been, so our takeoff should have been shorter. I could swear we flew between the tanks at the end of runway 24. They are on the beach, well off the end of the runway.

Once airborne our next problem was catching up to the cell. We were to take the lead, for number two had a bad gunnery radar and number three had a bad radar beacon. Since we had launched late we would not receive a tanker, so fuel could be a problem. The new nav asked for 490 knots true airspeed. The RN corrected it to 450. The nav asked why and the RN told him— rather than go faster and catch up, we would go slower and catch up at the entry point for Vietnam-bound bombers. We would save fuel and not have to divert to UT.

He would also be able to get back to his wife. I concurred, but when he asked if I would fudge the figures if our fuel reserve over the target was below the required amount, I told him if we had the minimum we would return, and if we did not we would divert. He got busy and showed the nav some serious navigation.

We arrived at the entry point and I rolled into position behind number three and asked for a gunnery system check. With that out of the way quickly, I moved out and forward to take the lead. The RN kept reminding us to check the fuel closely. At release we had 100 pounds more than the minimum—not bad for a late takeoff and catchup.

We returned to Kadena and I wrote up the aircraft, 5104, for a long takeoff roll. At debriefing I had a long discussion with a maintenance chief. I was informed that there was nothing wrong with the aircraft. It had been written up on the previous mission for the same thing. They had jacked it and greased everything and I was obviously wrong. I asked if he was on board and he said no. I then got the takeoff data and compared it to our actual distance and asked if he could see the difference.

He still insisted I was wrong. I offered to have him write up in the forms that the pilot knew not of what he spoke, but he declined. I can understand his frustration, but it was our butts on the line, not his.

Pilots can be very egotistical. Two things which BUF drivers like to show they can do well are landing and refueling. Especially refueling. Not to be able to get the gas is looked upon as a shameful thing. Having spent some years as an instructor and having flown with many different pilots during this phase of flight, I have seen many different methods. I finally learned to move the ailerons less and use the throttles more for small lateral movements. This took a lot of disconnects and patience. Some pilots can sit behind a tanker and the control and throttle movement is barely discernible. Others thrash about as if they are killing snakes. Many of us fall in the middle to a greater or lesser degree. The idea is to stay in the envelope and onload the gas without a disconnect. When you are proficient enough and have trained yourself to accept only perfect position, then you upgrade to instructor where the exercise is to demonstrate the limits of the envelope without falling off of the boom. One must force oneself to move to the inner and upper limits for they are not at all comfortable. I often have said I could demonstrate the limits without even attempting to do so.

The position most pilots strive for is to stay in the "green." This is the position directly behind and below the tanker, centered on the orange stripe on the tanker belly, and with the center lights of the director light panel, also on the tanker belly, illuminated. Keeping them illuminated means the receptacle is moving, or stationary in a two-foot cubic area. Moving outside that cube causes another light to illuminate. These direct the pilot to move back to center. If one is really good, he can keep the center lights and the next row, up or down, illuminated . . . a one-foot cube. Complicate this with weather, night, turbulence, or all three combined, and it can take some concentration. I have actually been in contact and lost sight of the tanker for what seemed like several minutes, but was actually only seconds. If I had initiated a disconnect, I would have had no idea where the tanker was. By maintaining contact, I at least knew he was at the other end of the boom and I would eventually break out of the weather enough to see him again.

We were leading a gaggle of my compatriots out of Kadena one day. We had an A/R taking on a nominal fuel load for each receiver from one tanker. I hooked up and everything was smooth as glass. Some might say that is unusual. I had been hooked up for about five minutes when I noticed I was adding power to keep up and the tanker was climbing. Then I heard: "Breakaway! Breakaway! Breakaway!" Since I was the only one hooked up, I broke away. The boomer then cleared number two into the precontact position. I was livid. A breakaway had been called and my refueling ability was in doubt with the other pilots. At least that is the way I viewed it. I waited until number three had his fuel and called the tanker pilot and asked for the reason for the breakaway since every indication I had was in the green.

He replied that I had received my fuel and the boomer told me. I kept hanging on and continued to pursue them when they tried to accelerate. The only problem was that the boomer was on tanker interphone; obviously I could not hear him. He assured me that the internal problem had been resolved. I was satisfied. The rest of the cell now knew I was not at fault and could get the gas. My ego was back in place.

I woke up one morning in Kadena and turned on the television. We had been busy and I had not paid too much attention to events back in the real world. The astronauts were just about to land on the moon. I sat down and spent the morning watching their arrival. I was still there when the Okinawan maids came into the room. I tried to explain what was happening on the television, but they had no interest at all.

It was difficult to believe. A monumental event in history was occurring right before our eyes and all they were interested in was making my bed and collecting my dirty underwear. That was dedication.

We redeployed to Andersen and landed at 2300. Twenty-seven hours later we were lifting off returning to Kadena with a small detour through South Vietnam. A typhoon alert had been called and we had to evacuate the aircraft from Andersen.

We returned to Kadena on a dark, stormy night. We were number two and had dodged thunderstorms all the way from Vietnam. Lead landed as we started our final approach. The lead pilot called out that he had no brake chute, and his gunner thought it had fallen onto the runway. I asked the final controller what he wished me to do. I was still high enough to transition and land on the left runway if necessary. I got no reply. He began to give directions to number three. I continued my approach and continued to query him as to what I was cleared to do. I was ignored.

I eventually reached the point where I had to go around as I had no landing clearance. I also did not know if the chute was on the runway. I called the tower on the go and asked for a visual pattern as my fuel state was rapidly going to hell. They refused due to C-141 traffic and weather, and then passed me to approach control. I requested a short pattern due to fuel reserves and was given a vector away from the runway environment and behind the C-141s. I then advised them that if I was not put back in the landing approach immediately I would have to declare minimum fuel and really screw up the pattern. They reluctantly did as I asked. We landed without incident, but the fuel was so low when we shut down we could not read it on the gauges.

I wrote up the traffic control agency unmercifully on a safety of flight report. A month after returning to Clinton-Sherman, I received a letter from the communications squadron commander. He had reviewed the tapes and agreed with my assessment and apologized for the incident.

I learned a lot about flying from that!!!

We spent a week flying out of Kadena. The threat of the typhoon had passed and we returned to Andersen in time for a flight and an on call day. We then joined crews from Clinton-Sherman, who were on Guam, at a beach party which the wing commander had arranged. We went back on the flying schedule the next day.

Roddy had decided to get out of the Air Force, and his time to rotate to the land of the big BX was rapidly approaching. I was not too disappointed to see him go. In my opinion, he would never have upgraded. There was also a thread of dissension among the crew and he always was at the center of it. From the first, he was always reluctant to compromise for the good of the crew and insisted upon having his own way, relenting when the crew faced him down or when a ranking member told him to get his shit together. It was always minor things such as the radio.

A local FM station on Guam played what is now referred to as elevator music, varied enough to satisfy everyone. We always had tuned it in when we moved into the room and did not turn it off until we left. The first night Roddy went over and turned it off. The nav turned it back on. Roddy told him to turn it off and the nav told him to get stuffed. Roddy insisted he had to have absolute quiet to sleep. The nav asked how he could sleep on the airplane. Finally, they asked me what to do and I said I liked it on. That was the first night we spent together. He gradually accepted he could not win them all.

He would never leave the base with us when we were in Kadena or UT. His excuse was that he was saving his money since he was getting out. We learned differently from the crew he had been with the previous year. It seems he was writing home about what everyone else was doing on their off time, and in turn, they were getting heat from home. What they were doing, I do not know, but whatever it was, it was reported. When his crew finally found out who was telling the stories, they solved the problem. The A/C told me they took him with them one night, got him drunk and introduced him to a young Thai prostitute and paid for his dalliance. He never left the base again and the stories stopped. I guess it was just a carryover when he became my copilot.

We landed at 0400 on a Monday morning in the middle of a typhoon evacuation. Since we could not get the proper crew rest, we were not scheduled to fly, but were to stay at Andersen and ride out the typhoon.

It was a good break. We filled the refrigerator and bought some food in case we could not get out of quarters. The RN, who was the experimenter, had discovered the previous year that by modifying the connection of an appliance cord, an aircraft hot cup could be used in the room. He would fill the hot cup with water and drop in a small can of chili. When the paper label came off, he would remove it, and it would be just right for eating.

Our schedule for the next four days was non-existent since there was no flying. We spent the time playing board games and penny poker while consuming the contents of the refrigerator. It occasionally got loud and rowdy. The copilot would not engage in the poker game, but wanted to dig through the coins looking for those that might be of greater value. He was told if he wanted to do that he had to ante up and join the game. He refused. At 2200 the first evening, he informed us we would have to quit playing because he wanted to go to sleep and we disturbed him.

He was politely told to sexually assault himself in a manner which is physically impossible. He gathered his bed clothes and left in the middle of a rainstorm and spent the next three nights sleeping somewhere else. It had gotten to the point I wanted him to rotate home more than the rest of the crew because of the dissension, even though it meant I would play musical copilots for the rest of the tour. He never seemed to understand that we were a crew and he could not have his way. We had enough distractions without his.

The BUFs came back and we deployed to UT again. The night schedule was awaiting, but the missions were short. We had an RTU crew from Ramey AFB, Puerto Rico, in our group. The pilot was very eager to lead and win the war. At least that was the way it seemed. After being dismissed at the end of the briefing, the lead pilot always held a short meeting. Normally, it was just a reminder to keep the heads up and the eyes open.

Each pilot received a sheet which listed the pilot, crew number, PCS base, and the number of missions for each position. It also listed the parking location, taxi sequence, and time for each aircraft. The taxi and takeoff was done for the most part with little radio talk except when difficulties arose. It was always amazing when things went well and the BUFs were in good shape. At a given time, the crews would start engines, and the aircraft would taxi and take off as scheduled with no radio transmissions.

I was parked on the last row. I was lead and would taxi first. The other BUFs would fill in and taxi in sequence. If someone had not taxied, the following aircraft would taxi up to, but not past, the parking space of the aircraft which preceded him in the stream unless he was declared out of the launch. I had just cleared the crew chief off interphone when I saw number three pass in front of me. I called Charlie and advised him of the situation. He had number three taxi across the runway and hold on the hardstand where the spare usually parked. The takeoff and mission went off as planned.

The next night I was lead again; when the pilots met after the briefing,

I looked directly at the pilot of number three and reminded all of the pilots to ensure they knew where they were parked compared to the rest of the cell and pay attention to the taxi plan.

I had cleared the crew chief off when number three came taxiing by. I called Charlie, identified myself, and told him number three had done it again. Charlie rogered me and then personally directed number three on a tour of the parking area to get him into the proper position. It was then we decided that he must think if he got to the hold line first he would get the lead. It did not work that way.

The next night, same group, same briefing by me, to which I offered to personally explain the taxi sequence to anyone who could not understand or follow it. This time he waited until he got into the air.

I have mentioned the Bonus Deal where the gunner using his gunnery system can give direction to the trailing aircraft in case it has lost its station-keeping capability. After level off, the trailing aircraft would move into position and the lead gunner would run through a system check with the radar nav of the trailing aircraft. The number two gunner would go through the same drill with the third aircraft. The readings would be compared. If they were outside of set parameters, a lead change would be made to put the aircraft with the most reliable system in the lead in case a Bonus Deal was needed.

Everyone likes to fly the lead. The crew kept busy and usually got the better aircraft for that cell. It was also good fodder for OERs if you had a lot of wave and cell leads to your credit.

That night we had just leveled off and number two, our taxi friend, moved into position and called for the systems check. The gunner ran through it and the info came back way out of tolerance. The gunner told me there was no way his system was that bad. We ran it several more times. It gradually got better, but still unreliable. I told the cell to stand by for a lead change when number three called in and asked us to check with him. The gunner swiftly gave a reading and the RN in number three came back with an almost perfect reading.

A light dawned, and I asked number two to run another check. This time it was well within the area of reliability. They would never admit it, but we knew they were willing to get the lead any way possible. I kept my eye on the pilot from then on and found they had done the same in other cells. I passed the word.

The schedule had us returning to Andersen on 30 September and re-deploying to Clinton-Sherman on 3 October. We lucked out. We would fly a BUF back and not ride the cattle car. It would also be direct. I reminded everyone I could think of that I would need a copilot.

We left UT at 0900 and passed over Vietnam long enough to leave all but one 500 bomb. As the RN completed his release check, he notified me we had a light on indicating a hanger in the bomb bay. This caused no concern for we had had these indications before. It did not always mean there was a bomb there, sometimes the light malfunctioned. The RN would visually check it prior to landing and that would be that.

At our descent point, I lowered the landing gear, lowered the nose and pulled the throttles back as we started our penetration. The RN notified us that the light on our hanger had gone out. This was not good. It meant that if there had been a bomb hanging on the rack, it may have fallen and was bouncing around in the bomb bay. We had no way of knowing whether the fuse had been armed or not. If the arming wire pulled out when it dropped, there was a chance that it could be armed and detonate if it received a big enough jolt.

Knowing this could ruin our whole day, I advised the command post of our situation and that we would check the bomb bay as soon as possible. If they had no other directions, we would land as planned. They, of course, told us to stand by. As we passed 12,000 feet, the copilot depressurized the aircraft, I raised the landing gear, and the RN went back to inspect the bomb bay. He made a record trip. When he got back on interphone he informed us that the bomb had indeed dropped and the wire was still in the rack. The bomb was lying on the bomb doors near the forward bulkhead. We had no way of knowing if the fuses had spun down and armed the bomb. The seriousness of the situation had intensified greatly.

I advised the command post of our new situation and that I was continuing my approach for landing. I was again advised to stand by. As I started my final descent for approach, I advised them of my intentions to land. They replied to stand by. I then turned my complete attention to flying the best ILS I could and really concentrated on the landing. The fact that it was nighttime added to the difficulty. I really did not want the bomb to bounce around against the bulkhead.

The first several thousand feet of runway 06R had a slight descending gradient. It then began an uphill grade to the end by the cliff. The last thing I needed, or wanted, was to bounce or float until I hit the uphill grade. I have never worked harder on a landing. I reduced power smoother than I ever had, trimmed in shorter spurts and maintained the proper landing attitude. The touchdown could not be felt, it was that smooth. Much different than normal. I never had a better landing, before or since. It must have been the incentive, for the potential bounce of a 500 pounder loose in the bomb bay increases concentration and effort.

I did get a little upset with the MMS crew that de-armed the bomb. They were supposed to wait until everyone was out of the area. They de-armed the fuse while we were at the tail waiting for the bus.

We flew our last bombing mission the next night, and then prepared to fly home. I reminded everyone that I would need a copilot. I was assured one was scheduled, due in from UT. We did the mission planning and waited.

I learned the night before we were to leave that my copilot would be someone already at Andersen. He was a Clinton-Shermanite so that caused no problems. At our pretakeoff briefing, I asked if the proper name had been forwarded to Clinton-Sherman since my flight orders reflected the original copilot's name. I was assured that it would be. I had made the changes to my paperwork.

We arrived at the aircraft with lots of baggage, albeit quite a bit less than the previous year. You do learn from experience. The crew chief was asleep in the wheel well and we could not awaken him. Everyone on the flight line was engaged in a mission launch and had no time for a mere redeployer. I finally waved down a maintenance truck and told the line chief I needed some assistance, and the crew chief needed medical attention. It took a while, but I finally got a stand-in for the crew chief.

We were running late but managed to preflight quickly enough to start engines on schedule. The other aircraft returning with us checked in with no maintenance problems. I checked with the command post, and they assured me the message had been sent, changing the name of the copilot returning with us. We took off on time and headed back for the real world. We hit a tanker shortly after level off to top off our tanks and would hit another off the coast of California.

Our spirits were pretty high. The copilot and I took turns napping, and before we knew it, it was time to refuel again. We came off the tankers and could see the California coast. As we coasted in, we hit the jet stream and a good tailwind. I pushed the throttles up so the bird was cruising at max Mach which gave us 510KTAS. As we crossed the Sierras, number two called and asked us to slow down for they were in turbulence and his nav thought the aircraft would come apart. I complied. We touched down at Clinton-Sherman just before 1400. It was not the smoothest landing I have ever made, but I recovered from the bounce and made a controlled crash out of it.

We arrived at the hangar set up to get us through customs and debriefing quickly. Our families were waiting on the far side of a roped- off area. I recognized that the wife of the originally scheduled copilot was in the group and asked if the Andersen command post had sent the message. I never got a clear answer, and no one seemed too concerned except the family, the replacement copilot, and me. I apologized for the foul-up and attitude of the squadron ops officer.

The wing had a set up a storage area for vehicles, boats and trailers of people who wanted to store them while on ARC LIGHT. I had stored the TR-3 so that Wendy would not have to worry about it. I disconnected the battery cables and covered it with a plastic tarp. A set of keys was kept in the bomb squadron orderly room in case the Security Police needed to move anything. A procedure had been set up, so they did not have direct access.

I went to the squadron a few days after returning to pick up my keys and was told by a major pilot, who had returned earlier and was running the administration office, that I had to get the 1st Sergeant's permission before I could pick up my car; he was not available. I told him it would be a cold day in Hell before I had to ask an NCO for permission to get my keys, since the major was clearly in charge, had access, and appeared to outrank the sergeant. He said I had to be escorted by the 1st sergeant to the Security Police for identification. I explained that I did not need escorting since I was not entering a restricted area and was sure the Security Police could identify me by my ID card and the car's registration.

They did. It was not a problem. I removed the plastic tarp which was covered with pigeon poop, hooked up the battery, jumpstarted it and drove it home.

BYE BYE BLACKBIRD

It was October and the wing was back in the alert cycle. The base was scheduled to close at the end of the year and everyone was wondering where they would be assigned. Naturally, we had filled out all kinds of dream sheets as to where we wanted to go. Very few had chosen BUF bases which flew the black bellied D models. Thirteen out of 17 months of TDY were enough for a while.

While we were at Andersen, the RN and I had gone to a briefing by personnel to encourage transfer into the FB-111 program. Not many showed up. We volunteered to the colonel running the show that we would like to go as a team. He took our names and all but assured us that when Clinton-Sherman closed we would be chosen.

The day arrived when the crews were assembled in the base theater for their assignments. I had considered what I thought were all the bases and hoped it would not be Loring, Minot, Grand Forks, or many others. I kept my fingers crossed for FB-111's. Almost every instructor was sent to Castle. I heard them call all of what we considered good BUF assignments and then they called my name.

Blytheville AFB, Arkansas. The only BUF base I had not considered. The RN also got Blytheville, as well as enough crew members to make up four crews. We both went to the follow-up meeting for those of us who were not satisfied with our assignments. It was crowded.

I asked about the FB-111 assignment and was told the B-58's were phasing out and their crews were filling the FB-111 slots. Blytheville had been scheduled to phase out the BUFs and become a C-130 base, but when the B-58 phase out was announced, it was decided the C-130's would get Little Rock AFB instead. The wing at Blytheville needed crews, for it was to continue to operate. We were chosen.

While we were trying to get answers, an L/C team member kept popping in the room and telling us he wished he was going to Blytheville. I offered to trade places with him. He declined.

Housing was of immediate concern. We called the housing office at Blytheville (Hooterville) and asked about the availability. We were assured plenty of field-grade housing was open. It was the middle of November. Our orders came in and a special class had been set up at Castle for G and H difference training. Hooterville had white bellied G models. The course was a ten day course and we finished just prior to Christmas.

I signed out of Clinton-Sherman and we took the kids to my parents in Illinois. Wendy and I went to California. We stopped at Hooterville on the way and were told there was no field grade housing and none would be available for six months. We stopped on our way back and got the same answer. Wendy stayed with the grandparents, and I went to sign in at Blytheville. I learned a captain had been assigned a field-grade house. I was told by the housing officer that they assigned it before they were aware it was a field-grade house. I pointed to the chart on the wall which identified them and asked why I could read it and they couldn't. All I got was mumbles.

I went to the squadron and asked to have Gary as my RN when he signed in. I was told they would if they could. I then talked to a captain who also had just been assigned a field-grade house. Since I was number one on the list, I questioned it and was told it was too late to do anything. I brought it up to the squadron commander. He said there was nothing he could do and that was the way it was. The housing officer advised me not to rent or buy downtown. When I asked what I was supposed to do, she said the best deals could be had in Memphis. I tried to explain that I was a crew member and could not commute 100 miles each way to work. She never caught on and I gave up. I did not even think to go to the IG.

We began to look around and could find nothing to rent we would live in. I finally bought a new house. My brother was with me when I agreed to buy it. He swore that I'm the only person he knows who bought a new house for $50 down. We were very glad we lived off of the base during the next two years.

When I first met the squadron commander, he asked me if I was ready to go to ARC LIGHT. I informed him that I would be ready when all of his pilots had two tours. He did not appreciate that. We had been told he had been at Blytheville since he was a 1st lieutenant. He was now a senior LtCol. He did not understand. Of course, as far as I know he never volunteered to join the war either. When he asked an A/C, who had spent most of his career in F-4s and the last few years in green underwear, if he was ready to go to ARC LIGHT, the pilot replied that he did not see any green ribbons on the commander's chest. He and I became good friends.

Gary and I were assigned to the same crew, and for the first time I had a strong copilot. The nav, I found out shortly, was weak. He needed help to find the aircraft. The EW was experienced. Everyone but the gunner was from Clinton-Sherman and had two tours under their belts.

We flew our wing checkout program in the G model with no difficulty and were signed off. Our first mission without an "evaluator" had the squadron commander on board. I know he was evaluating us also, but not formally. I could not have asked for a better day for flying. It was clear and blue as far as the eye could see.

We hit the tanker about an hour after takeoff. It was a small off-load. When that was complete, I began to wax eloquent to the copilot about the differences in the D and G while continuing to hang on. I went on to bore the hell out of him and the rest of the crew with chatter and demonstrations. Twenty-six minutes later the tanker told us he was disconnecting. We had reached the end of the A/R track. I admit I was showing off. The rest of the flight was just as smooth and the crew did well.

Later, in the squadron, the commander asked if I had ever thought about becoming an instructor. I told him I had been upgrading when the wing closed, and when I felt comfortable in the G model, I planned to come talk to him. Two days later I began upgrade to instructor and completed it shortly after that. I could not convince the staff to upgrade Gary even though he had more experience in the equipment (he had spent years in E models) than the other wing RNs. He was also a better RN. I had the nucleus of a good crew and hoped we would get a chance to prove it.

Once we were settled, Gary and I met the wives at the club for dinner one Friday evening. We were seated and the waitress took the ladies' orders. Gary said he would order for me. He did, and when the waitress left, Wendy asked how he knew what I wanted. He explained that he had lived with me more in the past two years than she had. She agreed. He also got the order right.

The base/town got the name "Hooterville" after the town in the TV series *Petticoat Junction*. It was appropriate, although I believe the one on TV was more up to date!

We were not too welcome, for the base had been scheduled to close. The crew force was stable in the sense most of them had been there a long time. In many cases it was the first assignment out of Castle. Not all of the crews had been to ARC LIGHT when we arrived. That did not endear us to them either.

The current ORI route ran just north of Clinton-Sherman. When we tried to advise bomb-nav shop of some of the things that might help or hinder the wing's plan, we were ignored. Little things, such as identifying a road they had as paved and were using as a visual timing point for the pilots as "an unpaved red dust mess," or the way the selected radar offsets really looked on radar. I found the general attitude to be that nothing new was accepted and was to be ignored. I also found that scheduling and bomb-nav took advantage of the crew force.

I really got them going when I informed them that I had never flown an ORI as an aircraft commander or that I had never been on alert when one was initiated . . . in fact, that I had only flown on follow-on sorties twice, once as a copilot. While the flying chances changed, in 13 years of crew duty, I was never on alert when the wing got an ORI or similar exercise. At Hooterville, I flew in every one while I was on station, but never off of alert.

The housing situation had not changed for most of the troops. My EW was living in a trailer with his goods in storage. He was continually told he would get in a house in short time. The supply system was undergoing a change. Instead of taking an old flying suit in and exchanging it for a new one, they had to be ordered. The sizes were new also. He had ordered new flying suits, and when they arrived, turned in the old ones. The new ones did not fit. He could not get the old ones back. I went to the operations officer and explained the problem. He asked if the EW had any in storage and I said I thought he might, but it cost $15 each time he was allowed to get into his stored goods and he was short of money since he had just had a PCS, was living in an overpriced rental unit and the housing office was still playing games. I was then told there was nothing he could do and that the commander could not even get a new flying jacket. I got the picture, so I asked if the EW could fly in civilian clothing. I was told not to be ridiculous. When I asked if he could fly naked, he threw me out of his office. The crews from CSAFB gave him the name Mr. Ed, after one end of the famous TV horse.

I was not making too many friends in the staff. I was continually catching them disregarding regulations as they pertained to crew duty and rest. I was not bashful about bringing it to their attention. Every other unit I had been in held a morning briefing prior to mission planning each day. This brought new changes to the crew's attention and was an opportunity to keep them informed about everything as a unit. When we questioned starting one, Sam, a newly arrived A/C from Pease, and I were told it was not necessary. Although we tried and tried, we could not get anyone to listen to us.

I noticed the nav was having difficulty coping with the flights. It started with the low-level portion of the ORI route. He got sick and threw up. This was not unusual for the guys who flew downstairs. Low level could be turbulent and hot, and with no outside references, it was easy to succumb to motion sickness. Every nav I had flown with before had lost his lunch, cleaned up, and kept navigating. This one did not. He just quit and the RN did both jobs. This happened on every mission when we went low-level, which we almost always did.

A typical mission would be a departure to a point north of Blytheville and was the ARIP for a refueling track which terminated in the vicinity of New Orleans. After departing the tanker, we would perform an extended 270 degree turn and begin a celestial navigation leg which would terminate about twenty minutes short of a low-level entry point in New Mexico. The first flight the nav called for 480 knots true airspeed at the beginning of the nav leg. I was used to excellent navs and gave it to him. Just west of Fort Worth he asked if I could slow to 320 KTAS. His excuse was that the wind had changed. I slowed as much as I could. The leg was reliable. The next flight he asked for 480KTAS, and when I questioned him, he swore he needed it. At Fort Worth, I was again asked to slow down. When he asked for the increased speed on the third flight, I told him he would get 430 as he had planned and he could try to navigate. It worked with no changes. The RN and I had discussed it and were working together to remain reliable and get the nav up to speed.

We were returning from a trip to the East Coast and were on a nav leg which would terminate in Northwest Arkansas where we would enter a VFR low-level route. As we crossed from Ohio into Indiana, I asked for a radial and distance from Tulsa Vortac to preclude setting up a holding pattern and have a direct route into the low-level. He told me to stand by. As we crossed the convergence of the Mississippi and Ohio Rivers, I asked again. He said he would have it shortly. I asked again 10 minutes from termination point and got the same answer. I gave up and pulled a radial and distance out of my ass and got clearance from center. When I asked about it after we landed, he said he was too busy. The RN and I continued to discuss our options.

We had our first tour at Columbus AFB, Mississippi, our satellite base. We had aircraft deployed on alert, and the crews changed over every week—a lot like Reflex. This spread out the force and increased the targeting problem for the Soviets. The base had been a SAC base, but was now an ATC base for pilot training. The alert facility and alert area ramp were retained by SAC. We were not appreciated. We caused the base problems. People were constantly using our reserved parking slots and did not understand that the flashing red lights meant to pull over and wait. It was a break from the grind at Hooterville, however.

It was the first trip to Columbus which caused my first run-in with scheduling. I found out after we returned and were put to work a day early that we should have gotten an extra day off after satellite alert. I took it as my fault for not being up to date on the regs, but gave them a hard time for not asking if we knew since satellite alert was new to us and they were aware of it. I paid more attention to changes and other related areas. Volunteering to work on my time off, or being asked was one thing; taking advantage of me was another.

Prior to the trip I was sent to the command post to review a classified manual and ensure that I knew all the rules pertaining to ferrying of nuclear weapons. The regulations which governed carrying passengers in bombers had to be reviewed. I did as I was told. We took an aircraft with both on our first trip to Columbus to swap out with one already on alert.

It was shortly after the Director of Training told me I had been considered for a TDY, but my name had not been sent forward. It seems a requirement for a highly experienced ARC LIGHT pilot came to each wing and the individual selected would spend a 90 day TDY working on improving the mission. My name was considered, but not forwarded, because I had returned less than six months earlier. The decision makers did not think I would be interested. Needless to say, this was a good opportunity to help improve things, as well as enhancing career potential. I let them know that I was upset for not even being asked if I was interested. I definitely was . . . as it was, Dudley went.

I was asked if the crew would like to take a BUF to McGuire AFB for an open house. I said that we would. The crew, plus an extra EW and two crew chiefs were on the flight orders. We had a training mission enroute and one on the return trip. The day of the flight we were just short of engine start when an engine man appeared and informed me he was to go with us. I tried to have him added to the flight orders. I was told he was not on the list of maintenance flyers. I told the supervisor of flying he could not go, and the DCM appeared and said he wanted an engine man with us. I asked for him to be put on flight orders and was told it would not be done; he would go as a passenger.

I called the command post and was told the same thing. Using the manuals and regulations as my reference, I told the command post to change my flight clearance to go direct at 18,000 feet. Additionally, they could cancel the tanker and low-level route and send a weapon with ammunition for one of my crew members. It got real quiet. I would either be cancelled, fly direct with the changes, have the engine man put on flight orders, or be told to disregard the regulations. They put the guy on flight orders and he was carried as a crew member, not a passenger. I did not make any friends over it. The squadron commander who had made sure I reviewed the regs was the acting DCO that day.

We arrived at McGuire in late afternoon. The runway is not as wide as most BUF runways, and looked even narrower. It is just what you are used to. We landed, and due to the narrow taxiways and signs along them, I asked for wingwalkers. I did not want my wing tips coming in contact with anything along the way. The "follow me" truck began to get impatient, and no wingwalkers appeared, although repeatedly requested. I deplaned the crew chiefs to perform that duty and taxied to parking. I was parked at the end of a row as requested. I had quite a reception—maintenance officers and chiefs as well as a contingent of Security Police led by a captain.

The open house was being held at the same time as one at Fort Dix, right next door to McGuire AFB. I still do not understand how or why, but a scheduled peace demonstration against the Vietnam War was to be held on Fort Dix on Sunday. I had orders when I left Hooterville that if my security requests could not be honored, I was to leave and return to Hooterville. I also was ordered to leave if the demonstration spilled over onto McGuire. We cocked the aircraft as if it were on alert and climbed out. I had been led to believe everything had been prearranged.

I informed the SPs that I wanted an armed guard on the aircraft at all times. I was told there would be a roving patrol. I told them my directions were to have an armed guard or leave. I was told it was impossible. We went to the command post for the tanker unit to resolve the situation. I insisted I had to know in order to leave and stay within the crew duty day. I finally was at the point to call for directions when a tanker from Griffiss AFB called in, asked for two armed guards, and wanted confirmation prior to landing. The captain turned to me and told me I would have my guard.

I explained if the demonstration spilled over, or any like disturbance occurred, I was on orders to leave ASAP. I told him that meant I would load the crew and make a cartridge start, taxiing as soon as the engines were started. I expected them to clear any obstructions, including people. I would be taking off when I reached the runway. They agreed and we set out a plan of action with them and the tower.

The day of the open house was a gray one. The ceiling was between 2,000-3,000 feet with no sun. The Thunderbirds put on their demonstration, although somewhat limited. We stood by the aircraft and answered questions for the public. It was a great day. The people came to see the airplanes and nothing else. I think we made some friends that day. They were really interested, and the main question was if we had been to Southeast Asia. We told them we had but the airplane had not, for it was a G model and only D models were there at the time.

Once we got a feel for the crowd, we opened the bomb bay doors so they could get a better look at the bird. We did not open the cockpit area. I had noticed the airlines had some aircraft on display as well as Air Force cargo birds. They were set up so the public could enter at the aft part of the fuselage, walk through it, look in the cockpit and then exit at the front entry door. Each aircraft had long lines. I noticed a long line at the end of our bird. It seems they had lined up to enter the bomb bay, thinking it led into the fuselage. The forward bulkhead of the bomb bay stopped the line. We put the nav there to answer questions and tell them why they could not go into the cabin.

I had one gentleman insist that the aircraft was radio controlled. I tried to convince him that it was not. We were the crew. He disagreed. I asked what made him think it was radio controlled. He said that there was no entry door like the other aircraft; therefore, it was sealed and could only be flown by radio control. I took him over, opened the hatch, and let him look inside the cabin, thinking that would convince him. I am not sure it did.

Another gentleman was standing just in front of the nose and muttering to himself. I eased over and he was saying: "Man! That is a big son of a bitch!" I agreed with him, and he asked if I had flown it in. When I said I had, he asked if I was sure. So much for my image as a pilot! We had a pleasant conversation. He seemed surprised that an ordinary looking guy like me had flown that "big son of a bitch." He wanted to know if I was going to fly it out. I told him if he went to the end of the runway the next day at 1000 he would see us depart.

It was a good day. The people were interested and asked many good questions. It was hard to believe the demonstration was going on next door at Fort Dix.

The next day the weather was worse. It was raining with low, fast moving clouds. We taxied carefully down the narrow taxiway and lined up on the runway. The RN was picking up radar returns off of the south end of the runway and suggested we delay until it had passed. The tower had no like returns and told us we would have to depart or clear the runway, since a T-39 was inbound. We heard through the command post the 8th AF commander was on the T-39.

I elected to leave the runway. Rather than taxi down the narrow taxiway I decided to do a 180 and return to the hold line. I had never made a 180 degree turn on a narrow runway before and wished about halfway through that I was not doing it at that time. I could envision the BUF up to its axles off the runway and the 8th AF/CC diverting. Since I was in 8th AF, this had meaning, especially when the cockpit was halfway through the turn and I was sitting over the grass beside the runway. Luckily, we did not depart the runway but completed the turn and returned to the number one slot. The T-39 landed and the RN agreed the returns had diminished and we should leave. We did.

Alert duty had not changed much over the years. The FNGs were always introduced in ways which took advantage of their lack of experience. The favorite targets seemed to be copilots. My copilot, Mel, had decided to get out of the Air Force. His position was filled on flights and on alert mostly by copilots which we had just upgraded to combat- ready status. The one I was assigned permanently had not completed his check-out. I went on alert with a brand new first time ever on alert copilot.

The first night I was sitting in the library when Ron came in. At 1030, he stood up and said he was going to bed. I told him that he could not go until we were relieved at midnight. When he asked why, I told him we were on "red alert" and another crew would take over at midnight, and then we could go to bed. The reason I gave was that it gave us a few minutes head start. I wove a long and confusing tale of the necessity for immediate response. He bought it. I left the room and went to bed. He realized his leg had been pulled when he talked to the RN a few minutes later. He learned quickly. Two days later he was replaced by another new copilot. I was passing the library and heard him briefing the new guy about "red alert" and the need to stay up until midnight.

The replacement copilot took in the morning briefing with great attention to detail. Having been caught once, he cautiously asked me what they meant when they said our aircraft was to get a tire rotation. I explained that the aircraft had been on alert for an extended period at a heavy weight and the tires would tend to get flat spots. To preclude this, maintenance jacked up the aircraft and turned the tires. This was half true.

We began our daily preflight and the tractor pulled up in front of the aircraft. The crew chief asked me to set the parking brake. I did. He made the hookup to the tractor and asked me to release the parking brake. I did, as we continued our preflight. The tractor pulled us forward about three feet very gently. I was asked to set the parking brake. I did. The crew chief disconnected the boom from the front trucks and the tractor left. He replaced the wheel chocks and asked me to release the parking brake. I did.

We completed our radio calls and other items. The copilot then turned to me and asked when we were going to rotate the tires. I asked if he had been paying attention to what we had just done. It slowly dawned on him that he had been had again.

The nav team had a favorite trick with a new crewmember, preferably a copilot. We would complete the daily preflight and get off of the aircraft. The RN would ask if the copilot had made the "echo check" of the AGM-28s. Obviously, he had not. The nav team would then give a lecture on the importance of the check and then brief the copilot on his duties in the check. It consisted of sending him to the rear of the missile, leaning into the tailpipe and making loud noises while the nav team stood at the front of the missile and checked the resonance. The copilot usually caught on when he heard the laughter and looked out to see the rest of the crew, crew chief, and often the security guard, all but rolling on the ground.

The RN had another trick which he and I would use on new copilots. After we completed our preflight, we would recock the aircraft for an alert start. Some items were done with power on, some with power off. The co-pilot had to set the starter switches. As he turned to do this, the RN would reach above his head and grab one of the throttle cables which ran through the throttle quadrant, under the floor of the top deck, and just above his position on the lower deck. He would pull one and the corresponding throttle would move forward to the idle position. I would then ask the co-pilot what he was doing and show him the throttle and move it to cutoff. I would then have him undo what he had done with the switches and re-set them. This would go on until we broke down laughing or he finally caught on.

Another version was to prearrange with the RN to pull the cable mov-ing the throttle to idle or cutoff, depending upon the situation, while the pilot gave the copilot a line of bull on a new way to alert start or cutoff by voice command, or whatever came to mind at the moment.

It was late spring. We were on alert at Hooterville. Just after dark, the alert horn went off and we ran to the aircraft. The copilot and I arrived first, with the nav team close behind. The crew chief was not present yet, so the gunner cleared the engines for start. I fired the cartridges and saw a large flash on the left side of the aircraft. The gunner yelled: "Fire!" and I saw him and the rest of the crew running down the ramp. There was a wall of fire on my left. I advised the command post of the fire and that I was shutting down. By then, the fire trucks had arrived and were extinguish-ing the fire which turned out to be from fuel spilled during the start.

The exercise continued without us and was terminated in a few min-utes. The crew returned and we had a "Come to Jesus" meeting about leaving us in the aircraft without telling us what or where the fire had been. The maintenance team had arrived. I had already entered the engine explosion during start in the 781. The deputy DCM was in charge and smelled as if he had been enjoying adult beverages.

He told the crew chief to load another cartridge and the pilot would fire it to check the system. The pilot told him that he would not fire any cartridges until the system had been checked and the forms signed off by proper authority. The pilot was accused of being afraid to fire the cartridges. The pilot agreed that he was apprehensive since he had fired the first one which resulted in the present problem and that he was not stupid enough to do it without some repair. I also went on to say that when the aircraft was in working order and the forms signed off I would accept the responsibility for it; until then, it belonged to maintenance.

The crowd had grown as the other crews wandered by to see what was going on. The number two nacelle cowling had been removed and an inspection was in progress. The starter was in a million pieces. So much for trying to fire another cartridge. It was obvious that it would have to be replaced. A new one was ordered and was delivered shortly thereafter. The actual work fell to two young maintenance troops, while the chiefs stood around and gave advice.

The new starter was finally in place, and the deputy DCM told the crew chief to load a cartridge and the crew would test it. I asked him to sign the forms and he replied if the system checked out he would do so. I told him if he wanted the cartridge fired he could do it, for I had been bitten too often by performing maintenance's duties. I added when it was repaired and the forms indicated it, I would accept the aircraft and attempt to put it back on alert.

He then told me I had to do it for the aircraft had nuclear weapons and EWO material on board and his people could not get on the aircraft. I suggested that we could remove the EWO material and give him the aircraft or he could find someone qualified and we would escort them. He then said he had no one qualified at the aircraft. I just stood there. The crew chief volunteered to do it if someone would show him what to do. We finally agreed on that procedure. We escorted him and he checked the system by firing a cartridge. It worked as designed and we were back in business.

The wing was hit with an ORI and brought the nav problem to a head. The mission was flown mostly in the daylight. Our A/R track was east to west ending over Southeast Missouri. Our celestial nav leg was from the Little Rock area to the east coast with a small turn about half-way. We were not scheduled for an AGM leg as we did not have them assigned to our sortie. We would fly the route but it would be a long radar nav leg to the low-level entry point in the Midwest.

The weather was clear-severe. We could see forever. We started the nav leg and the copilot and I kept track of our position by radio aids. According to the rules we could not assist the nav with them or advise him of his position. Since it was a clear day we could also map read. As we passed Columbus, Mississippi, we were about ten miles south of course. No problem. I asked the nav how we were doing and his position was similar. We kept drifting slowly to the right. When we reached eighteen miles right, I asked if he knew where we were and what our limits for the nav corridor were. He admitted he did not and to stand by for a course correction. As we hit twenty miles right of course he asked for a twenty degree turn to the right.

I turned thirty left, rolled out, gave the copilot the aircraft and cleared off of oxygen and interphone. I unstrapped and went downstairs. I stepped between the nav team and told the radar where we were. He said he knew. I then asked if he would tell the dumb son of a bitch next to him where we were and went back upstairs. The nav never caught on and continued to do his thing. He was happier than a pig in shit with a ten mile nav leg termination, which in reality, he had little to do with it. He spent the next three hours backing in his nav leg.

The RN and I went to see the bomb-nav people. I explained what had been happening and requested that an instructor-navigator fly with us. I was told that since we were reliable one was not needed. I asked who would have to answer if we were unreliable and they agreed with me it would be the RN and me. I asked for an instructor again. I was told I had no case. I asked to have Gary upgraded. I was told there were too many instructor navs to justify upgrading another. I asked that since there were so many, let one fly with us. I was turned down again. The squadron staff was not interested in our problem either. They all agreed that no help would be forthcoming until he was unreliable or failed a checkride.

They also agreed that would reflect on the rest of the crew as well.

The problem was solved for me a few weeks later. The wing had only two instructor pilots present in stan-eval and I was the only other IP available. I was approached as to whether I would like to go to stan-eval and replace the pilot on S-03, who had just received notification of an assignment to Castle. I replied that sounded good to me. I was then told all I had to do was to volunteer to take that crew to ARC LIGHT as it had been the pilot's turn to go when he got the assignment. I said thanks but no thanks, there were other pilots who should go before I went again. The argument then was that I could not go to stan-eval unless I went ARC LIGHT. I still refused to volunteer. I also knew no other instructors were available to go to stan-eval. I went to stan-eval, but not ARC LIGHT.

The problem stayed with the crew, however.

The upgrade to instructor pilot was normally followed by a short TDY to Castle to attend the Central Instructor Flight Course (CFIC). I was no exception. The course was a two-week program involving classroom and flight instruction. The tankers and bomber pilots were in the same class, as we had an interlaced mission. Each student was required to teach a short class as well as be the recipient of the instructors' knowledge and experience.

One of the tanker IPs told the story of finally being convinced by his bomber friends to take a ride in the BUF. He went into great detail—how he donned the helmet and parachute, made the oxygen and interphone connections, and sat in the IP seat. After each of the pilots had taken a turn at refueling and made it look simple, they convinced him that he should also get into the seat and give a whirl. He admitted that he had not paid much attention to the movement and equipment changes the pilots in the seats had made. The copilot unstrapped and left the seat.

He got into the seat. He connected the shoulder straps and seatbelt with the help of the other pilots, noticing the closeness of the control column to his body. He moved the seat as far aft as he could, extended the rudder pedals, got his bearings, and was ready to take the aircraft. The other pilot relinquished control and let him attempt refueling. He admitted as he tried to control the big bird, with little room to maneuver, that his respect for the tribulations and ability of bomber pilots rose dramatically. It was tough going.

Upon completion and separation from the tanker, a seat change was made. He noticed that the seat had a parachute in it and he had continued to wear the one he had originally strapped on. No wonder the control column was so close. The BUF pilots, of course, did not let him forget it.

The course was a big confidence builder for new instructors. Each flight consisted of a two-ship formation. A tanker took off with a BUF one minute behind. Once we had cleaned the aircraft up and were settled into the departure, the tanker cleared me into the contact position. I moved forward and he hit me with the boom. We began our practice which would continue to the A/R track and through it. All A/R was done with the autopilot function off. The autopilot function is like power steering and requires less effort from the pilot. However, if the bank exceeds 10 to 15 degrees of bank, it takes a greater amount of effort to overcome it. With it off, the pressure is not present. The maneuvers we proceeded to complete made it easier if the autopilot was off. I noticed the shadows move around the cockpit, but was so intent upon not falling off of the boom, I paid little attention to anything else. It was just like back in flight school, in trail formation, with one exception, we were actually connected. We continued in this manner while providing the IP with a limit demonstration. I have always contended I could do it without trying. Finally, my turn was up and another pilot got into the seat. I watched as he went through the same sequence I had and began to appreciate the fact that I had held on through it all. The tanker climbed, descended, made turns exceeding the normal, and of course, the airspeed varied throughout it all. Later, when the IP told me I flew a good aircraft, it meant a lot to me. I guess you could say I went to play with the big boys and was asked to stay.

The next six months went quickly. I spent most of my time either in the air or on alert. While stan-eval crews were supposed to pull less alert than the other crews due to the heavier flying schedule, it did not happen that way with us. We pulled 113% of the average crew alert duty.

Mr. Ed was still the operations officer and our relations had not improved very much. I had a night mission with my new crew and learned something which had not been discussed. I should have known it.

The standard departure to the south at Blytheville involved a turn to the west following flaps up, followed by an immediate turn north. It was not unusual to get a temporary holddown if there was traffic on the civilian airways just west of the base. The flight had a water takeoff due to our weight. We received our takeoff clearance with a 2,000 foot holddown until passing a radial after our turns. I took the runway, applied power, and hit the water switch. We reached S1 speed and the copilot took the throttles. Then it dawned on me.

The holddown meant that if I continued and raised the flaps with the water on I would exceed my altitude and possibly exceed the flap retraction speed schedule. If the copilot reduced the power to maintain the speed schedule, the water would stop and reinitiate when the throttles were advanced. This could cause one or more of the engines to flood and flame out. I recognized this would not be good. I took the throttles, cut the water switch, and hit the drain switch. I flew to the holddown altitude, started my turn and then began to slowly advance the throttles. Our holddown was terminated and we raised the flaps when we rolled out to the north. The copilot and I had a long discussion as to what had occurred. I made sure he understood why I did what I did.

We both learned about flying from that!!!

I approached Mr. Ed with this information and recommended we make sure everyone knew about the potential problem. I was informed everyone knew. I insisted that there were pilots new to the G model who might not know and it never hurt to remind people of what could happen. I was dismissed. I then made sure I contacted every pilot who had come into the unit after I had and we discussed it. Most were like me, and had not even considered it. I felt better, but continued to wonder about Hooterville's approach to safety.

The flying was good. The instructor shortage kept me busy; I spent most of my time upgrading new instructors, pilots, and copilots. The other stan-eval pilot was giving about 75% of the flight checks. My new crew was very good and very well balanced. The nav team was solid. The copilot had come with us from Clinton-Sherman and was ready to upgrade. I was determined to upgrade him, for he was good and he deserved it. In that six month period, I did not get in the left seat except for an ORI mission when I flew with my crew and very seldom when I flew with others.

Race Track Two

As time passed, I recognized that I would have to return to ARC LIGHT in either January or February 1971. I had not received any leave for the fiscal year. When I changed crews, my previous crew was just going on leave and the new crew was just returning. If it had not been for an old friend from Clinton-Sherman working in scheduling, and a considerate chief of stan-eval, I would not have gotten any before I left again. As it was, I returned with 17 days of leave left which was to start several days after I returned from ARC LIGHT. More about that later.

It was a coin flip between Sam and me as to who would go first. His crew agreed to go as a crew and they left in January. While the pilots were scheduled to go, the massive crew changes which seemed to be a way of life for some crews did not always mean the whole crew was due to go.

My crew also volunteered to go as a crew. Part of the decision hinged on retaining the positions in stan-eval when we returned. The only exception was the copilot. Hal had completed his upgrade, and I convinced the squadron he should get a crew rather than go to ARC LIGHT a third time as a copilot. I went to the new operations officer when we had decided to go and told him the crew would volunteer if I could have my choice of the new copilots. His response was that I did not want the one I had selected. I reminded him that I had trained most of them, spent two tours myself, and I thought I could select a copilot who would fit in and do a good job. The squadron relented with warnings that I would have all kinds of trouble. Chuck caught on quickly to the mission and it was a relief to have a strong copilot while on ARC LIGHT. He caused me no difficulty.

When it was known that I was going to ARC LIGHT, I had people come to me and ask me to bring them back a particular item. I was a horse's ass about it. I said if they wanted something they could make the trip themselves. The ones who asked either had not been or were working hard not to go again.

We went to Castle to transition into the D model and become acquainted with ARC LIGHT procedures before deploying to Andersen, and then to U-Tapao. We arrived at Castle and were in class with a crew from

Ramey AFB and one from Grand Forks AFB. The pilot from Ramey, an L/C, and I became good friends in the next few days.

The ARC LIGHT procedures came back quickly. The D model was like an old girl friend. It was just a matter of getting the feel of things again. The academic classes were very informal and I found myself joining in and leading much of the discussion. I felt comfortable discussing things which had changed and surprised myself with how much I had retained about the mission and the D. Most of the RTU instructors had been ARC LIGHT during the periods that I had. The atmosphere was good for learning.

The crew had all had one tour, except the copilot, and he was up to speed quickly. The training missions were primarily emphasizing cell procedures. Each crew had the opportunity to lead. I was quite comfortable with the crew. They were very professional and we went through the training with high marks. Crew coordination can be one of the hardest things to accomplish. As a stan-eval crew we had not flown together that often, especially with the new copilot.

Our last flight was a night mission which involved the normal heavy-weight refueling, and then out over the Pacific where we descended and flew a low-level route coasting in with a camera bomb run. I was quickly in and got the gas. The instructor and I then alternated contacts with the tanker. We would hook up and then see who could maintain the longest contact while slowly working the rudder pedals to maintain position. Then alternating and using the throttles. When the tankers finally departed, the gunner called me and thanked me for the beer. I asked what he meant. He said he had bet the gunners on the other crews that I would have my fuel before either of their pilots. Talk about a confidence builder.

The time at Castle had passed all too quickly. We were scheduled to deploy on a tanker from Westover AFB. Three BUF crews from the bomb wing at Westover were on board as well. Since they were a D unit they did not have to go through RTU. We gathered at the terminal at the designated time and were told the aircraft required some maintenance and would be delayed several hours. A young captain AC from Westover had been designated as the troop commander when they left Westover. He was, therefore, responsible for the passengers. That was all right with Bill and me until he began to give orders. He did not confer with either of the senior officers, out of courtesy, but began to tell everyone that they could not leave the area and laid down some rules which did not apply to the situation.

Bill turned to me and asked if I would like to go to the club. I answered in the affirmative. We gathered our crews and left. We returned in plenty of time. I guess the captain was so caught up in his authority he did not think we could be responsible; however, he did not broach the subject with us. I doubt he even missed us. We let him run around and be important. The aircraft had been delayed long enough that when we arrived at Hickam AFB, we had to stay overnight due to crew rest for the tanker crews. It was my third time through Hickam and the first time I got to see it in daylight.

We spent the night in the BOQ and had a leisurely breakfast in the O Club the next morning. Everyone was ready and on the bus except our "leader." While we waited for him, his navigator decided to tell us all about ARC LIGHT. I do not want to say he was dense, but he was not too observant. I was, and had been wearing my ARC LIGHT baseball cap. It was adorned with personal and unit items embroidered on it. I occasionally removed it and replaced it, but he never caught on. He even got some of the story straight. The "leader" finally arrived and we went to the flightline.

The flight into Andersen was typical. The relief cans filled up several hours out and some people were sitting with crossed legs. I had forewarned my crew and we rode it out.

The schedule at Andersen was easy. It called for an ARC LIGHT indoctrination and EWO study. The squadron commander at Hooterville when I arrived there had been promoted and was now an ADO at Andersen. I did not make an effort to see him, recalling all the help he had been to those of us coming into his squadron the previous year. The indoctrination was a rehash of the RTU and the new way things were operating. The only real changes were that now the waves were made up of one cell and there was an area for delays, giving more flexibility in changing targets after the wave was airborne.

The second night we were at the club. I met a pilot I had not seen since Little Rock. He was working in EWO plans and informed me that an ADO would be taking the EWO certification the next day. The name he gave me was a colonel who had been the deputy and then DO at Clinton-Sherman when we closed down. He had also been my neighbor.

Andersen had an EWO commitment. Each crew passing through had to study and brief the mission to a senior member of the staff who would certify the crew knew the data. The six new crews were ready the next morning. Our "leader" acted as if he were still in control. He was always in front wanting to be noticed, trying to lead the group.

As we prepared for the certification, my friend told me one crew would have to give the briefing portion of the certification. He asked if I would volunteer. I replied that the "leader" would be a good choice. He needed and wanted the exposure. I was told they did not like to use the cadre unit crews as they were continually going back and forth. I disagreed. It was decided the crew numbers would be put in a hat and one selected. The winner/loser would give the briefing. I drew my own number and have always wondered if all of the slips had S-03 on them. I did not check.

The time for the briefing had come. We were all in our seats in the briefing room. My crew was up front with the maps and materials spread out ready for quick reference. The other crews were aligned by crew in the audience. The colonel walked to the front, shook my hand, and asked how everything was going at home. We had a short personal conversation. The only one who seemed to miss this was the "leader." I went through the briefing as I always have, covering the material, leaving out several obvious things which I could be questioned on. The rest of the crew gave their presentations. We waited to be interrogated. The colonel thanked us for the good job and asked the questions of the other crews. It was a pleasure to watch the "leader" dance. They even got most of the answers right.

It had not sunk in yet to the "leader" that some of us had been there before. Our last day we had a "gee whiz" dog and pony show. Prior to the briefing the "leader" had ensured that he had a seat up front, although the L/C should have been there. He and I ended up in the back row. We were told our flying assignments would be given to us at the end of the briefing. The briefing consisted of how many sorties had been flown and how many bombs, numerically and by poundage, had been dropped since the first BUF mission.

The 3rd AD vice commander gave us a pep talk and answered a few questions. The staff officer came in with the flying assignments. The flight schedule was on a twenty-four hour rotation. Each crew would start at a given point and work their way around the schedule. The briefer started with the Westover crews. Each was starting with the morning flights, as was the crew from Grand Forks. Bill was put in the afternoon schedule. I will never forget the briefer saying: "Major Hooppaw, because of your experience, you will be in the Ivory schedule." That was the middle of the night. Our "leader" stood up and looked around to find out who I was. I guess it finally dawned on him that someone else had been there before. I found later this was his first tour as an A/C. The next morning we deployed for U-Tapao to join the war.

We flew our first mission as number three and everything came back quickly. The only real change was the addition of the timing box. We would take off with a planned target. The lead would contact a ground agency on a secure radio. They would confirm the original target or give coordinates for an updated target. The nav team would then determine when we had to leave a specified point, exiting the box to strike the target on the scheduled TOT (time on target). Timing was a critical element and even seconds off of the TOT was frowned upon. Depending upon TOT and target location, we might go direct or enter the timing box for a delay. It generally worked out fine.

We had practiced defensive procedures at Castle and the crew responded well. The typical procedure was that the EW monitored all electronic emissions from the ground and air sources and notified the crew when the aircraft became an item of interest. He also identified any threats to the crew as to type, location and intensity.

For example, on the practice bomb runs after the cell left the IP, the EW would notify the crew of tracking radar in particular. This call would generally be the type of radar and location from the nose of the aircraft, such as, "TTR (target tracking radar) 12 o'clock." If the radar locked on, the EW would notify the crew of the lockon and advise the pilot to start a defensive maneuver. If in cell, which we inevitably were, the pilot would then advise the rest of the cell on the UHF radio by means of a code word and the direction to start maneuver. We became very proficient at Castle in this activity.

Most of the targets we hit during this period were in an arc to the south and west of North Vietnam. We would occasionally hit the passes on the Ho Chi Minh Trail leading out of the North. The closer we got to the border the greater the chance of artillery or missile launches against us. We did not get within a reasonable range for fighter activity. We flew above the ceiling for most artillery and did not consider it a problem, although it could easily be seen below us firing at other targets.

This was especially true at night. The sky was really lit up at times. The missile threat had also been small up to this point. When we went in certain areas we were escorted by Iron Hand aircraft. They would fly the same route as we did, at a lower altitude and in a position to intercept any signals we received. In theory, if a missile radar locked on us, they would receive the signal and send a missile down the radar signal to the missile site.

The procedure the missile people on the ground appeared to use, as we understood it, was to locate the inbound aircraft, and then make a short lockon of the intended target, fire a salvo of missiles, and then take down the radar to preclude being hit from the Iron Hand birds. This meant the missiles would be launched without an extended guidance signal, rise to a predetermined altitude and detonate—a lot like the firing of rifles at low flying aircraft . . . one might hit something.

Once the bombs were released, the RN normally turned to his optics and looked for detonations in the target area. He looked for confirmation of any secondary explosions indicating we hit something in addition to the ground.

Our first mission target was slightly north of Khe Sanh. Our Iron Hand was in position. The interphone sounded like the missions we had flown at Castle. "TTR, twelve o'clock" and shortly after that: "TTR, twelve o'clock." This occurred all the way down the bomb run. The Iron Hand reported a SAM launch and we were diverted 90 seconds to release. We saw nothing. We hit the secondary target. We reported the electronic signals and the reported launch to the intelligence officer at debriefing but little was made of it.

The second night we had moved up to number two and the target was in the same area as the previous night. The flight went pretty much the same, with the same results, except we hit the primary target. The EWs in the cell had stronger signals. There were some indications of a missile launch after release, but could not be substantiated by the Iron Hand escorts.

It looked as if it would be a way of life as long as we bombed in that particular area. It did not seem to pose a serious threat. We again reported it to intelligence and were not listened to, by all indications. The EWs were convinced there was a missile site in the vicinity of Tchepone, Laos. We were told that TAC had not confirmed any sites; therefore there were none.

I had bought a radio which could pick up Radio Hanoi. I started listening to their version of the news as I prepared to fly each night. They reported shooting down B-52s about three or four times a week. Since we would have known instantly if any were lost, I gave little value to the rest of their version of the news, but it was interesting. They seemed to be strengthened by the demonstrations back in the States. We all worried about our friends we knew to be POWs. When a BUF goes down it is impossible to cover it up. We had lost several in earlier years, none by enemy action, and the crews knew immediately. One was lost off the cliff at Andersen one afternoon in 1969. An airliner full of military people waiting for takeoff watched it. We were at UT at the time and knew about it within hours. I found the BUF crews were not as accustomed to losing an aircraft as those of us who had flown B-47s

The third night we were scheduled to be number two again. The number one aircraft developed maintenance problems and we moved up to the lead. The target was in the area of Ben Karai Pass in the southern part of North Vietnam, although not inside the border. We went through the timing box and ensured we had our Iron Hand support. We departed the box and started the arc to the IP.

We left the IP and the EW began to call: "TTR, twelve o'clock" every 30 seconds or so. Just like the previous two nights. This continued through the bomb release, following which I broke to the left in a 55 degree bank as normal. Number two released and three was in the process when the EW called: "Lockon! Lockon! Start Maneuver!"

I called the codeword to the cell and told them to start maneuvering. I switched off the autopilot, pushed the throttles to the firewall and started to break back to the right. My first concern was to get away from the other aircraft and have more maneuver room. Then the RN called that he had the missile launch in his optics. The gunner called that he had the missile visual, passing between number two and us. I had begun to turn back left when I saw the trail of the missile pass over us on the right. It started to arc back toward us and exploded. It was close enough to hear and feel the shock wave, but it did no damage. A second one had been launched and exploded above and to our rear.

I could not have been prouder of the crew. Everything went just like we had trained. This was the acme of crew coordination. No one got excited . . . there was really no time. The tape of the attack and our responses were later used as a training aid, as an example of how to do it. When we were away from the area and the EW reported no more signals, I called the cell to stop the maneuver and advise of any damage. The reports were negative.

In addition to the normal after release report, we now had to report the missile attack. The copilot handled the reports after I checked them. When he passed the message form to me, I could not read it. It was just a lot of squiggles in grease pencil lines that had no resemblance to numbers or letters. Apparently, the shock had begun to set in. We filled it out together and he sent it. I agree with Winston Churchill: there is nothing as exhilarating as being shot at and missed.

The debriefing was the most intense I have ever had. The intelligence officer kept telling us that there were no missile sites in the area. We told him there were now. I suggested they take our position at the time and figure out the size of the area the optics cover at that altitude and transpose that on a map; they would have a general area of the site. We were told that TAC had not confirmed it so it was not there. The rest of the cell got the same line we did. The escort had also reported the firings. We were interrogated as to exactly what our actions were, as if it were our fault. I guess in a way it was, since we were dropping bombs. The word was out immediately and we were referred to as the Blytheville Missile Magnets.

Two days later we were told that TAC had confirmed the site. They finally believed us. I don't know what they thought we had seen. The rest of the tour we were very attentive.

Fourteen years later I was working in the 57th Air Division. The commander had just returned from a Red Flag exercise at Nellis AFB. He called me in and told me he had sat through a BUF crew debriefing and the debriefer was critiquing the crew on defensive procedure coordination. He then gave them the above example of a missile attack on a BUF cell and how well the crew had worked together and that he had been a member of that crew. The general then said that the L/C debriefer knew me. I acknowledged that he was probably referring to my old radar; we had indeed had excellent coordination. The general then told me the rest of the story.

He was flying F-4s in Southeast Asia at the time and was called upon to go to the area we had identified, to see if it could be confirmed if a missile site was present. He and his wingman flew down a ridge line and could not identify anything either electronically or visually. They did a 180 and came back over the same area. They confirmed the missile site by dodging several missiles. We had never met before he became the commander. It was eerie talking about events which were interlaced but separate. It is a small Air Force.

The copilot was on his first tour and we thought he should benefit from all the experiences available to us. We broke him in gently by taking him to the local community, Sattahip. The town was located several miles to the west of the base and transportation was needed to get there. A baht bus, small pickup truck with bench seats in the rear, or a cab was it. The cabs were safer. We made sure he understood that if he felt the driver was going too fast or dangerously, to tell him firmly: "lao lao." We did not tell him that meant go faster, but he learned quickly.

We had told him we would show him around and then take him to lunch at a restaurant overlooking the Gulf of Siam. The first stop was at a jewelry shop, then a souvenir shop, a leather goods shop, and then a tour of the open market. The open market consisted of all types of local food items. Some were unrecognizable, some were, and we wished they weren't. The odors were enough to turn a strong stomach. This was, of course, the point of the whole exercise.

The copilot had a strong stomach and kept asking for lunch. After we ate we continued to visit shops and found an Indian tailor who informed us all he needed was a picture of a garment and he could replicate it.

We did take him some pictures and he did make clothing which was well worth the cost. I still have and wear a tweed Newport jacket he made for me.

The custom in the shops was to offer liquid refreshment to potential customers. This took two forms, Pepsi or Sing Ha (Thai beer). John the tailor quickly learned that my crew preferred the local product. We stopped often to check on the status of our clothing, especially if we were thirsty.

John seemed to like to measure fittings. Especially the pants. It could almost get personal.

Mission number three had made an impression on me, especially the interrogation I went through before the confirmation of the missile site. I made sure that everything was done by the book as much as possible. The book was SAC Manual 55-2. The guidelines were laid out and easily understood. One of these rules spelled out when Iron Hand was required. It was determined by the location of the target. If it was north of a specific latitude, Iron Hand was required; if it was not available, the cell was directed to abort the bomb run and proceed to the secondary target.

We had our target and had left the timing box. The copilot had gone to GCI frequency and was working the Iron Hand support. He told me we would not have the support for the bomb run. I thought the target was above the cutoff latitude. I asked the nav to recheck, which he did with the same result. I then called GCI, after confirming the tape was on, and asked them to confirm negative Iron Hand. I was told Iron Hand was not available.

I had referred to the manual to confirm my position and then informed them that we would proceed to the secondary target. When asked why, I told them those were my instructions. They came back that Blue Chip said go and I replied again I could not. Blue Chip was 7th AF HQ in Saigon.

They repeated that Blue Chip said go; again, I refused. I was then asked for a reference. I gave them chapter, verse and page number of SACM 55-2. We proceeded to the secondary and dropped along with number two. Number three withheld and we had to take him to the tertiary target. We made the full circle.

I could have gone ahead and hit the primary target, but if anything had gone wrong at all, I would have been in deep doodoo for disregarding the manual. After the third mission I was taking no chances and played by the rules. No free style.

Nothing was said at debriefing about the action I had taken, and I was not called to task for it. The following night the mission briefer gave us an emergency change to SACM 55-2. The change said if Blue Chip said go, that overrode the instructions in the manual. I had no problem with that. The rules had changed and I would play by them. A similar incident never arose again.

Shortly before our arrival at UT, the South Vietnamese invaded southern Laos under the mission name Lam Son 719. It was a major incursion and many of our flights supported it. We were particularly busy during the pullback and return of the forces to South Vietnam.

We had progressed to the day schedule and were all set for a quick return when we got a target change. We left the box and the copilot asked me to come up on the other radio. I selected it and heard an F-4 talking to someone on the ground, but could not hear the replies. The F-4 pilot was directing the group, which was in a bomb crater, to lay their tee shirts on the rim of the crater for identification and he would lay down some 20 mike mike (20MM gunfire) to keep the bad guys away. He also relayed that while he did that, a cell of BUFs was laying down a strike as close as possible to delay a larger group of bad guys. In addition, some choppers would come in low from the other direction and pick them up as the BUF strike went down. I realized we were the BUF strike.

We led the cell in and listened to the pickup after we laid down the strike. The guys on the ground got out. It was the most satisfying mission I ever flew. The results were immediate and we knew we had helped some guys in deep trouble.

On our 15th mission we had the lead of Grape cell and the commander of the wing at UT as the ABC. When we called for our enroute target update, we were told it would be sent encoded. The ground unit's secure radio was inoperative. This was a lengthy process and we were still working on it as we entered the timing box. The nav took the TOT; he and the RN had to navigate in order to lose eight minutes so we could hit the target on time. They chose to lose it by making small turns and reducing the airspeed only slightly. The target was all the way on the eastern side of the arc, which required even more turns and leaving the box earlier. This made losing the time more difficult, for we had to leave the box as soon as we decoded the message. We hit the target seven seconds off TOT. We thought that was pretty good.

We recovered over Cambodia (the rules had changed) and let down from the east. Approach control vectored us through a small cumulus buildup and the ABC got upset. He called and asked why we were sent through the only thunderstorm in SEA. He was not in a good mood.

The senior staff all came out to meet the aircraft. The general was the first off and away. This was normal, but the DO stayed until we deplaned. He came up to me and told me to come to his office as soon as I finished debriefing. This did not give me great comfort. I went through debriefing with great anxiety, but with no real clue as to what I had either done or not done.

I went to the DO's office. It was full of staff weenies. I was asked to explain the comment the general made when he got off of the airplane. Since I had not heard it, I was at a loss, and wanted to ask why they did not ask the general to explain. I kept my mouth shut for once. The general had said that he had never been on a flight which had so many turns in it. If he had paid attention he would have known what we were doing. I asked if I could bring my nav team into help explain. This was granted.

The nav team laid out the map and indicated where we got the coded message and where we were when we finally decoded it. The need to lose time for an ontime TOT was evident. They had elected to lose it by maintaining a close proximity to the original course in case the winds changed as we progressed around the arc. They also pointed out the numerous turns in the arc. I also reminded them that our TOT was within seven seconds.

They assured us that this would be easy to explain and released us.

All in a day's work. It was not unusual, we learned, for the general to say something without someone asking him for further clarification. I have since learned this is common in dealings with staff, senior officers and commanders.

One of the entertainments of the day was at the maintenance debriefing area. There was a large screened cage which held a large boa constrictor. The snake just lay there most of the time. A rat had been put into the cage at some time and was still alive, scrunched up between the wire screen and the wooden wall. He did not move and looked extremely frightened. It was the first time I felt a little sorry for a rat.

The big event only occurred about once a week. The airman in charge of the snake would put a live chicken in the cage. The crowd was always immense. Sometimes the chicken became lunch quickly; more often it would be ignored until the pangs of hunger struck the snake. I have never seen a chicken stand so still. We were hurting for good entertainment.

The staff began to pump us up about the impending visit of the vice commander of SAC. It was a big deal to them, but for the crew dogs it was just someone to watch out for and keep away from unless directed to appear. We learned that he would be flying a mission during his stay. I was approached and asked if I was an instructor, and I admitted I was but in the G model. It should have been evident by the S in the crew number. However, I told them I had a lot more time in the D than the G.

A few days later I was told the vice CINC would be flying with us. I again reminded them that I was not an instructor in the D model and asked what to do if the general wanted in the seat. I had no doubt about my ability to manage the situation and fly the right seat, but I did not want to be put in the position to embarrass myself or the vice CINC. I was told not to worry, and we were moved up several time frames to accommodate the ride.

The day of the flight came and the briefers made comments throughout the mission briefing about the vice CINC being a good guy and not to worry. They also mentioned we were a good crew and even had a few slides about the ensuing event. In our mission package, there was a briefing book with a short history of each crew member for the general to read. At the end of the briefing the DO came up to me and asked if I was an instructor. I again replied that I was in the G model. He nodded and left. We went to the aircraft with the knowledge the general would appear at engine start.

The aircraft was in exceptional shape. I had just called for the start engine checklist when I saw a vehicle pull up to the nose of the aircraft. A minute later a Fairchild pilot, whom I had flown in cell with many times before, came up the ladder. I asked him what he wanted and he said he was taking my place. I asked why and he asked if I was an instructor in the D. I said no. He told me that was why. I was very pissed. I could have been replaced prior to the briefing and I would have accepted it gracefully, but at engine start? Someone screwed up and I was determined to let everyone I could know it. I called Charlie and advised him to change the name of the pilot. When asked why, I told him I had been replaced. It was a surprise to him as well.

I was taking my time. I wanted to be there when the general appeared. However, everyone was rushing to get me out of the area. There was no doubt in anyone's mind that they had one very irritated pilot. I finally got into the truck. The general drove up as we left. I was taken back to the HQ building where I was met by the DO and other senior staff members. They apologized profusely for any embarrassment. I asked why they had waited so late. I was told the general's aide had flown the night before and made a landing. The general decided that he wanted one as well. He happened to mention it to the staff after we left for preflight. They told me I was to fly later that day replacing Dudley who had replaced me. That really made my day!

I went back to the trailer and got some rest before the next briefing. I noticed most of the staff left me alone and no jokes were made during the briefing. I was lead and was not worried. I knew the Fairchild crew was a good one.

Our target was just short of the DMZ. We approached from the south with a combat break of almost 180 degrees after release. We got the normal radar signals inbound and the EW called them to the crew. We had released and were ready to roll out of the break when number three aircraft called out the SAM lockon code word. I called for the cell to maneuver and simultaneously went into my own maneuver. I asked the EW what he had. He said no signals. I checked with number two and he said the same. I asked three and he said he had nothing. I called for the cell to stop maneuvering. The crew rode me all the way home . . . so much for being a missile magnet.

After landing I asked number three crew what had happened. They were a newly arrived crew on their first mission and the EW had an over-the-shoulder EW with him. The over-the-shoulder EW had recognized a signal and tried to bring it to the EW's attention without interfering with the bomb run. The new EW interpreted it to mean a threat lockon was present and reacted accordingly. At least he did something.

I caught up to my crew at the club. They had been there for a while. I asked how the mission had gone. They said the first thing the general did was to get hooked up and ask the pilot: "How is it going, Jim?" Dudley replied that he was not Jim and gave a short explanation. They flew the mission as briefed until the return, when the general got into the left seat and Dudley in the right. The copilot was in the IP seat. I was told the copilot had to ensure the switches were set when required; the general was intent on flying the bird. The landing was not the most graceful, but they did not crash . . . badly. This is not abnormal for someone who may have flown the aircraft at one time, but whose job was now not directly involved in flying. I do not fault the general, but am now glad that Dudley was in the right seat.

There were more crews who had not been to ARC LIGHT previously. Those of us with experience were flying the lead most of the time. Gradually, others began to check out as leaders of the pack. It was about this time that a new controversy arose.

The radio transmissions had always been held to a minimum, especially once on the bomb run. The normal work with the MSQ sites involved them giving directions and the lead responding with the heading given and his call sign. Two and three were silent. As the aircraft came within the sixty seconds to release time frame, replies were shortened to just the cell call sign for acknowledgment of receipt. A new theory had developed among the newer crews that the lead should read back all the information to ensure the following aircraft got the headings. The old heads did not feel it necessary. The trailing aircraft were station-keeping, and if in position the heading should be the same as well as the fact that the countdown could be missed. Since a difference of opinion had surfaced, the decision was made to poll the crews. It appeared the staff was leaning toward change. Then we flew a mission as number two behind a newly checked out lead.

The target was just short of the North Vietnamese border and we attacked it from the southwest with a large turn on the break. Everything was looking good and the lead was reading back everything and then adding his call sign. As the countdown continued, the readbacks seemed to get longer. At 20 seconds, the site began with: "Heading 047. Standby for countdown, five, four, three, two, one, hack!" Lead had begun to repeat the heading and was still talking when the countdown occurred. My RN said he had the hack and good timing. I told him to drop. Fifteen seconds after the last bomb, I began my break and informed lead I had dropped and was in the break. Three echoed the same. Lead was still heading northeast and was past the border. The site acknowledged our drop and lead started to turn.

He was now in number three position with a full load of bombs. We had to go to the secondary for his release. Since he had not heard the hack, they determined they had a radio problem. I agreed, but it was the operator, not the equipment. The original lead moved to number two position and they released while positioned off of us.

At debriefing I wrote up and explained the events as they had occurred. I reiterated why I thought the radio procedures should not be changed. Number three did the same. I probably overdid it when I said the chatter sounded like a clatterbone in a goose's ass rather than a professional. I had an excellent example. Who knows how far across the border he would have led us, if we had not been on the ball. The subject was closed soon after.

We took our R and R in Okinawa. It was a shopping spree and we had a good time. It had been difficult to get new flying suits, and I had heard that the open market in Naha had almost anything for sale. We went down and began to look around. Hundreds of stalls filled the area with all kinds of goods. The further back we went the more interesting the wares. I finally found a stall filled with new military equipment. Sure enough, there were plenty of flying suits. I bought several for a mere pittance and wondered how much some supply type had made when they sold them to the Okinawans.

We returned to UT refreshed and ready to complete the tour. It was an interesting return. The tanker providing the transportation had a few airline seats and a VIP package—four airline seats, two facing each direction, with a table between them. The troop commander for the return trip was an L/C member of the staff at UT. In addition to the BUF crews, there were some other staff, some enlisted men and two attractive young lady sergeants. It is easy to guess who got the airline seats. The ladies were with the troop commander and another L/C.

The aircraft had a maintenance delay. The troop commander warned everyone about the delay and the rescheduled takeoff time. He warned that anyone who missed it would not only miss the flight but would also face dire consequences upon returning to UT. He and his entourage then adjourned to the club for refreshments of a liquid nature.

Everyone showed up and the aircraft departed. The troop commander and his assistant had been very attentive to the ladies, to the disgust of the rest of the passengers. Then we hit a little turbulence and the ladies produced the previously consumed refreshment all over the table and their two admirers. It was a pleasant experience for the rest of us.

The flight schedule continued and we slowly worked our way around it.

We were having lunch at the club one day when the nav came up and asked if we knew our previous squadron commander was on station from Andersen. I was not interested. The staff often came to fly a mission. This gave them an opportunity to see what the crews were doing, and as a bonus, get combat pay and a $500 a month tax break. The sharper ones came at the end of the month and flew on a late night mission which passed through midnight to the next month and got credit for two months on one flight.

I checked the bulletin board for the flying schedule and saw the ex-commander was flying with another crew in our wave. This was fine with me.

When we arrived at the briefing, he was waiting for us. He told me, when he saw we were in the cell, he had the scheduling change him to our flight since we had been one of his crews at Hooterville and were in the lead. The staff were not stupid. They checked the crews before they scheduled themselves to fly. They looked for two things: ARC LIGHT experience and an experienced crew, preferably a select one. These were usually in the lead aircraft and the birds were better as well.

The ex-commander was a good passenger and did not interfere with the crew. He had flown several times before and was familiar with the mission. As he departed our company after the flight, he commented to us how well he thought we had done. I could not keep from reminding him that we should do well; I had done it more than 200 times and the crew, except for the copilot, who had performed extremely well, had over 100 missions.

The flight was a night flight and we began our preflight about an hour before dark. As I finished my walk around, the copilot called me over to his side of the aircraft and pointed out something that concerned him. The wing flaps were down as they always were at this point. The left flap had a large right angled tear on the leading edge of the flap where it fit into the wing structure when retracted. There are all sorts of metal lines in this area, including fuel lines. It looked as if the flap had been torn during movement of the flaps and possibly weakened the lines as well as tearing the metal.

I called the crew chief and asked about it. He was unaware of it. This sounded odd. The ground crew is required to inspect the aircraft after flight and before we arrive. If it had not been there when inspected, how did it occur? No one knew. I asked for another airplane and wrote it up in the 781.

A truck appeared and an L/C maintenance type got out and asked what the problem was. I showed him the tear and told him I was concerned because it had not been in the forms, and no one knew how it happened. He told me it was metal fatigue. No problem. I would take the aircraft. I said it was written up now and I would not take the aircraft until it was repaired. He then said there was not time to repair it. I asked for another aircraft. I was then informed he had 20 years of experience and knew what metal fatigue looked like. I told him I had 13 years of flying experience and did not fly aircraft with metal fatigue that was not inspected or repaired. I also asked if he was so sure it was metal fatigue would he guarantee the rest of the flap skin would not begin to fail as well. When I asked if he was willing to sign it off "fly as is," he paused and seemed to change his mind.

I noticed the crew and the maintenance people had walked away from us. The discussion had become heated when I was told I had to take the aircraft. He finally realized I was not going to take the aircraft as it was. He had no authority to force me to do so. I had offered to pass it up the chain for resolution. We both began to cool off and he agreed that it should be repaired prior to flight. I offered to complete the preflight if they would begin repair and it could make the next wave. He got me another bird while we finished the preflight.

Just prior to our return to the States we were scheduled for the shortest ARC LIGHT mission to date—one hour and fifty-five minutes. This was short even for flights out of UT. I planned to make it even shorter if I had the chance. Then we took off.

As we left the IP for the target, number two called and said he had an engine seize up. He would finish the bomb run and return to UT direct. He was scheduled for an RBS run on a site in the northern part of South Vietnam. Our aircraft was the alternate for the run. He returned to UT. We went to the RBS site and logged four hours. So much for record time.

Our redeployment to the States turned out to be a goat rope. The tanker was returning to home station at Lockbourne AFB, Ohio. The route was to leave UT, proceed to Kadena, then Andersen and on to Hickam. At Hickam the tanker crew would change over and the bird would depart for Beale AFB, California. After dropping off some passengers, we would then proceed to Lockbourne, change tanker crews, and fly to Loring AFB, Maine. We would then fly to Blytheville and the Lockbourne crew would return to Lockbourne. The whole goat rope revolved around crew rest for the tanker people. This precluded them from stopping at Hooterville on the first pass across the continent.

We had several BUF crews and passengers from other services as well. Andersen was the last base prior to the States. All the passengers were gathered together for a customs and safety briefing at the terminal. They were given customs forms and told by the briefer they would be responsible for filling them out and giving them to me prior to landing at Hickam.

I had been selected as the troop commander. My joy knew no bounds. I told them I would have them collected no later than one hour out of Hickam. The boomer agreed to tell me when we were one and one half hours out.

At the appointed time the boomer came back and told me. I then turned to the gunner and copilot and sent them up the aisles to collect the forms. Most of the passengers had not even started to fill out the forms; others acted as if they did not know what they were. Almost everyone, aside from the crews, had to have help. They were finally gathered and passed to the boomer who put them away so well we almost never found them when we got to Beale.

We landed at Hickam and the customs people advised us that they would only check the tanker crew and those not continuing to the Mainland. The rest of us were told to take nothing off of the aircraft. We were bused to the terminal to wait for the aircraft to be serviced. Three hours later we left for Beale.

We landed at Beale and customs told us that because the aircraft was continuing only those deplaning at Beale would be checked. We were on the ground less than two hours. We had jokingly tried to get the tanker crew to stop at Hooterville so we could get home earlier. We even suggested they could declare an emergency and land. They declined.

At 12,000 feet in the departure they blew an engine. We suggested they go on to Blytheville, knowing they would do what we would have done and return to Beale.

Customs had to be called back out as we were now going to spend the night. The civilian agent was assisted by some Air Police. One of the APs was checking a young sailor's luggage and found a magazine of doubtful redeeming value. He then began to dig deeper and came up with a stack of film of the same nature. This was turned over to the civilian agent. The sailor, after conferring with some of his friends, went to the agent and asked if he could declare it as art. The agent told him no.

We finished, put the baggage on a bus and went by base operations to drop off the customs agent. The sailor, within the agent's hearing, said he doubted that his "art" would be destroyed. The agent turned and asked if the sailor had a match. He said yes. The agent told him to come with him. He took him to a 50 gallon drum where he had the sailor burn his own materials.

The crew rest problem now solved, we went direct to Blytheville the next day. We had a resounding welcome. The new operations officer was the only person to meet us. This was no surprise. We had not heard from the wing at all while we were gone.

When we left, we had been set up for leave two days after returning. In our absence, this had been changed to two weeks later. We had a few days off and then were back in the normal routine. Our leave was moved back another week. I was due seventeen days and would lose it if not taken by the end of June, the end of the fiscal year. I reminded the squadron, scheduling, and the new DOT that I did not intend to lose leave again this year. They all assured me I would not. It was then moved back to the last seventeen days of June.

I had been to Europe and Asia. Wendy had been to Arkansas and Oklahoma. I had written from UT and told her to pick a place within reason; we would go there on leave if our parents would watch the kids. When I returned, I asked her where she wanted to go and she had not made a decision. I do not think she believed we would actually go somewhere.

When the leave was finally solid, we went to Memphis to see a travel agent and asked her to make up her mind. After much deliberation she chose Jamaica. We made the arrangements for the last of June.

Several days prior to my leave, I had to go to Columbus to fly with a crew coming off of alert and returning a BUF to Blytheville. I was to give a check to the copilot on my old crew. The crew came off of alert and went into crew rest. The next day the aircraft broke during preflight. We called Blytheville to replan the flight. It would be a FSAGA (first sortie after ground alert). It would fly a mission similar to the EWO. All of the systems would be used and evaluated as to whether it would have been reliable if launched to strike its EWO target. The DOT was considering delaying us as much as two days.

I reminded him I was to go on leave and any delay would cause me to lose it and I had reservations for a trip I had planned on his word that the leave was solid. He was not too concerned. I reminded him that I had gotten the runaround since I had returned from ARC LIGHT. He said that was too bad and I suggested he could explain that to the IG. Somehow we launched later that day and completed the flight. I went on leave as scheduled. I did not make any friends, however.

Wendy and I were in Montego Bay, Jamaica, when a cruiseship landed and the tourists poured into the duty-free shops. I went in, looked around, and then left. I had spent the last four months looking at the same items for a lot lower prices.

The choice of where we stayed was made by looking at brochures. Wendy picked out one that looked nice. It was Half Moon Bay Inn and it was nice. We went on a tour and were the last ones picked up by the bus. The tour guide was explaining all about Half Moon Bay Inn when we got aboard. We learned that it was very exclusive and was where the Vice President of the United States, and many other prominent people who visited Montego Bay, stayed.

I sat next to an older man who was from Arkansas. When he found we were living in Arkansas, he became a fast friend. He and his wife were staying at the Holiday Inn. He kept telling me he would rather have gone to Hot Springs for his vacation. He told me what he was paying for his room, which did not include meals, and kept trying to get me to tell him what I was paying at the exclusive resort. I never told him that he was paying more at the Holiday Inn than I was at the Half Moon and I had meals included.

The trip was well worth it. It did not make up for all the times I had been gone, but it was something we had been able to do together for a change.

The copilot had found a place for lunch. It was unique. A turn north from the main gate at Hooterville and into Missouri brought us to a small gas station, general store, liquor store, and fast food restaurant, all in an area about 30 square feet. They served some great sandwiches. It was not legal to buy a can of beer and drink it on the premises. The purchaser received it in a small sack which just fit around the can. It could not be identified as beer. We took a lot of new guys out for lunch and beer in a sack.

CHANGES

It was a new period. The wing was sweating out the ORI. Everyone was sure we would be hit as soon as the eligibility period started. We were not far off. Each crew had certified, by briefing to the staff, that they were capable of flying the mission as planned. The low-level route was in Canada. We wanted to fly it before the ground was covered with snow. I doubt there was a crew more confident than mine that we would do well. We knew that if we were not on alert when it was called, we would get a sortie that had AGM-28s, because the nav team had phenomenal luck with them.

The first week passed and no ORI. We were on duty in the stan-eval office when the team landed the next week. We were not notified until 55 minutes after the exercise kicked off. Two of us lived in town and had to go home for our gear. When we checked into the squadron, the chief of stan-eval was having his equipment checked by the inspection team, and was frantically trying to find a pair of long underwear.

I learned our position in the launch and that we would have an observer from the inspection team on board. I would have preferred to have had no extra men, but was not really concerned. The flight was going smoothly though A/R and the AGM leg. Then we entered low-level.

It was still daylight. The check points were falling on time and in place. We left the IP at dusk for the first set of targets.

Then everything went to hell in a handbasket. The RN selected the final offset and told me to center the FCI. I could not get it centered. As we approached the target, I rolled level for the tone. At its termination we started timing to the second target and turned toward it. We had just avoided going out of the corridor. The data was called to the RBS site and the nav gave a new heading. I turned to it automatically and did not check the map. The copilot did not refer to the map either. The RN was having real trouble with the bombing system.

The nav team recognized shortly that we had missed a leg, turned short, and were out of the corridor. The presence of the observer kept them from mentioning it on the interphone. They tried to ease us back into the route before the second set of targets. The copilot and I finally recognized we were off course. We were rapidly closing on the second set of targets and the RN was not at one with his bombing system. We missed the targets completely and did not get back on course until departure. The rest of the flight was very quiet. We knew that we had blown it badly. Some days you get the bear and some days the bear gets you.

We got back and learned that other crews had experienced difficulties as well. It did not make us feel any better. The wing had busted and busted badly. As in all ORIs, if the flying goes badly, the inspectors really started to dig. They found a stack of awards and decorations including at least one silver star in the squadron commander's office. None had been presented. Many things which related to the items some of us had questioned for up to a year previously were written up.

I knew that any action would fall on us harder than anyone else, and rightfully so. We were a stan-eval crew. We prepared for the worst when we went to bomb-nav for a critique. The individual briefed us as to what went wrong and somehow forgot to mention something I had found out. The tracking handle and 13 other components had been changed on the aircraft after we landed. This only meant to me that the first bomb run was questionable; after that it was pure crew error. The first release was the only reliable one. He told us that we would be removed from stan-eval, which we expected. We would lose our instructor status and combat-ready status and fly at least one practice mission to be requalified. Then we went to the ORI debrief at the squadron.

The same individual gave the debriefing. There were other crews, ready and lead, who had done as badly or worse. They kept their combat-ready status and we lost ours. The briefing had no resemblance to what we had just been told by the same person. I broached the DCO after the briefing and questioned the difference in the two briefings. I think I said the briefer had lied. I was told to be quiet and not to worry. I could see that some kind of deal was struck. By hammering a select crew, who deserved it, the wing could keep its combat-ready status. I was even willing to accept this, but when I questioned the briefer, he denied that he had told us otherwise. As far as I was concerned, he had lied and made sure his shop got by as cleanly as possible. I knew I would eventually get a chance to pay him back.

The worst thing about the whole mess was that no one wanted to have anything to do with us. We were lepers. It seemed as if associating with us would somehow put them in the same position we were in and so we were avoided. We drew into ourselves as a crew and continued to operate as we had before.

Once the inspection team left, the corrective action changed somewhat. We had lost our instructor status and were downgraded to a ready crew. We remained out of stan-eval. I learned the chief of stan-eval was one of my main detractors when punishment was meted out. I was not disappointed about not returning. The instructor status would require some additional corrective action. The gunner and EW had not lost their instructor status as they were not involved in the unreliable activity.

The runway was shut down for repairs and we went to Loring AFB as a unit. We maintained satellite alert at Columbus. We were pretty well ignored at Loring. I had a good friend in the staff who kept me apprised as to what was being discussed in staff meetings as it pertained to our status and who was supporting whom. The wing commander, for example, asked if I had been told what my status was and what I could expect. The answer was no. He then was reported to have told the DO to let me know where I stood in the wing. I'm still waiting. A new squadron commander was inbound.

We flew a pilot proficiency mission at Loring. The operations officer was to fly as the IP. I had checked him out as an instructor the year before. I suggested the copilot should get some left seat time. He agreed. The next day when we were ready to start engines I got out of the seat. He told me to stay in it. I told him I was not an instructor and could not perform those duties. He tried to talk me out of it but I was adamant. He reluctantly took the seat and the copilot had a good workout.

The wing had begun to replan and recertify the makeup ORI as we finished the tour at Loring. I was told the wing commander had told the staff that he would take my certification briefing. I had no problem with that. The crew studied and prepared our song and dance for the wing king.

The certification involved each member covering his responsibilities as they pertained to the mission. We briefed it straight up and then covered the "what if's?". The wing commander, squadron operations officer and our "friend" from bomb-nav were present. We covered everything, and the wing commander complimented us on our knowledge of the mission and asked for questions. We were thrown some softballs which we answered quickly and then the commander said we did well.

He then told us that the staff knew the first target was obviously difficult with the offset aiming points that were used. Therefore, the wing plan was that if we had any difficulty with it, to forget it, and concentrate on the second target to ensure that release was reliable.

I thought for a few seconds and then said that we would have to decide quickly, get the tone on and off before we concentrated on the second target. He asked why. I then explained if we did not, the bomb plot would score the first tone they heard against the first target, regardless of what we were aiming at.

He turned to the bomb-nav representative and asked if that was true. The new L/C swallowed hard and answered in the affirmative. The commander then told him to personally contact each of the 10 crews that had already certified and modify the wing plan to reflect the information the bomb-nav shop should have known. I could not help smiling at the bomb-nav man. I had just been able to innocently show the wing commander that the bomb-nav people had not paid a hell of a lot of attention to the wing plan or the certifications. My crew and I had done a better job than his staff experts. Revenge can be sweet, especially when it presents itself unannounced.

The wing commander then turned to me and said he thought we could do a good job. If we did not, wherever he was sent he would take me along. I knew a threat when I heard one.

The make-up ORI was flown and the wing did well. We were very reliable. I tried to get the money for the best bomb since my nav team had an unbelievable 100 foot score on an AGM-28, much better than the best bomb. I lost.

We flew a mission which, if passed, would reinstate us as instructors. It was a typical mission—two releases at Matagorda Bomb Plot in Texas, with a VFR backup route. The chief of stan-eval and his RN were along to complete the recheck. We arrived at the entry point and could not enter on the first scheduled time due to thunderstorms. I elected to delay and see if the weather would pass and enable us to make the second entry time. The IRN, I learned later, had washed out of pilot training and did not like pilots. He tried to get my RN to tell me to abort and go to the VFR route. The RN told him I was in command and would make that decision. He knew I would not enter the route if the weather did not change. It did not, and we pressed on to the VFR route when the second entry time expired.

I got my clearance from center and let down to the point where I could declare VFR as we prepared to enter the VFR route. We had two entry times. We were at the max airspeed for below 10,000 feet. It looked close as to whether we would make the time. The nav called entry as the five-minute pad expired. The radar told me we were not at the entry point. I notified traffic control that we would be delaying under VFR conditions in the area and meet our second entry time. They rogered it.

I then heard the IRN tell the IP to go to private interphone. I switched to monitor private as did everyone else on the aircraft. I heard the IRN tell the IP to take command of the aircraft and get me out of the seat for I had violated safety of flight.

I went back to normal interphone and waited. I knew I had done nothing wrong and in a way hoped the issue would be brought up. The crew told me later the IP said I had done nothing out of the ordinary and all was well. We completed the flight and were instructors again. However, I was not a flight examiner and could not give instrument checks. I stayed well clear of the IRN. I did not know what his problem was.

The chief of stan-eval gave me my critique and asked if I would like to come back to stan-eval. I said no. I had a good crew and would continue to instruct and leave the evaluating to others. He then told me that most of my crew would return to stan-eval and that I should reconsider for I would get a different crew. I still declined. He then told me I could not consider an assignment which had just come in for an instructor position at Castle. I asked why I could not consider it and was told it might not be filled at all. I told him I still did not wish to return to stan-eval.

We had been on alert at Columbus. The return trip was to be on an ANG C-130. Weather precluded flying into Blytheville, and we landed at the naval air station at Memphis where two buses met us for the rest of the trip home. The C-130 crew tried to drop us off on the ramp in a horrendous downpour, but I was able to have them wait until our transportation arrived. The first bus filled up and left. Our bus driver had left Hooterville with less than a full tank of gas, planning to fill up at the naval station. We started back alone and it was after 2000.

The bus started to sputter as we started up I-55. The driver kept it going for about 20 miles when he had to pull over. He stopped at an all night filling station and they had no assistance nor a phone we could use. We forgot we were in rural Arkansas. We piled back on the bus and continued up the interstate. The bus was making slow but steady progress. At the intersection of US Route 63 and I-55 it all but died. The driver was able to get across the overpass and coast into a service station.

The station had no mechanic and nothing but a pay phone. They only accepted correct change and credit cards after 2100. I had no change and the troops had spent theirs in vending machines. I finally convinced the attendant to make change for $1.00 and tried to call the command post collect. They would not accept the call.

We had always been told to contact the command post if we had difficulty. It was manned around the clock and could contact anyone on the base. I was somewhat upset that they would not accept the call. The knew me and knew we were enroute from Memphis. The supervisor of flying was standing in the command post when the call came in but could not convince the controllers that I would not be calling unless there was a problem.

I then called home and asked Wendy to call the ops officer who lived across the street. Apparently, she got through. Another bus arrived two hours later. We did not get home until 0230 in the morning.

I went into the squadron commander's office the next morning with a chip on my shoulder, ready to demand that someone tell me what the hell I was supposed to do and why the command post was not responsive. Before I could utter a word, the squadron commander who had turned out to be a good one, informed me that he had taken care of the problem. He and the DCO agreed with my position. They apologized that no one was minding the store.

I was scheduled to fly a mission on Wednesday with my crew and then on Friday with another crew while my crew was to fly with another IP and give a pilot just back from Squadron Officer School a requalification ride. On Wednesday we were at the end of the runway waiting for takeoff when a C-54 landed. It was obvious that CEVG had just arrived. I was glad to get in the air and not be subject to them the first day of their visit.

We walked into maintenance debriefing after the flight and I was told to call the scheduling branch. I did and was informed that Friday's schedule had changed and that I was now flying with my crew and giving a requal check to the returning pilot. I reminded them that I was no longer a flight examiner. I was informed that as of 1500 that day I was back on flight examiner orders. Since the scheduling officer had been originally scheduled to give the check, I knew I had no chance at rebuttal.

It was 0500 Friday morning when we got to base ops. There were four CEVG evaluators in the flight planning room. I asked why they were there and was told by the IP they were going to evaluate my instructor skills. I pointed out that I was not instructing, but evaluating. I offered to let him take my place and give the requal ride. He declined and said he would just evaluate my evaluation. This seemed odd, but I had no choice but to go along with it.

The flight went well until A/R. The initial contact was made followed by an immediate disconnect. I reset the system and the pilot went in again. It was impossible to get the tanker system to mate with ours and we eventually aborted the refueling. The tanker cleared the track and I began to clean up the checklist. The refueling doors would not close.

I went to private interphone to discuss our options with the RN as to whether we could go low-level due to airspeed limits on the open A/R doors. I referred to my map, suggesting a route back to Blytheville. The pilot was flying the aircraft and we were proceeding to the end of the track. I knew if we could not close the doors we could not go low-level. In the interim, the nav asked for an increase in true airspeed. The pilot acknowledged and advanced the power. I turned to look at the airspeed; before I could reach the throttles, the IP was retarding them, for we had passed 305 KIAS, the A/R door limit.

The pilot and I had just busted the ride. He should have known the limits and adhered to them, but he did not. I was evaluating, but also in the seat, so I bought it as well.

At the low-level entry point we aborted and returned to Blytheville where we spent two hours in the traffic pattern. Our critique was pretty good, except for the A/R doors. The evaluator said he recognized the position I was in, but could not ignore it since everyone on the aircraft was aware of it. However, he put it in the cruise portion of flight and I received a conditionally-qualified with no corrective action, instead of a failure. Every other wing had done poorly. No one was too upset and rather seemed relieved it was only a CQ. The new DCO was very understanding. Naturally, I had a different opinion. I also knew who my friends in the wing were.

It was about this time I was approached as to how I felt about an assignment to Castle. I was very cautious how I answered. I had been through this before. I initially said no. I knew the odds were with me going. Other than the stan-eval IPs, there were three in the squadron other than the ops officer. One had just been identified to get a maintenance squadron and the other was the fair-haired boy. I was the third. I was also selected.

The procedure in those days was for the nominated instructor to go to Castle for an interview with the wing commander. If the results were positive, he would be hired. I left in December for my interview. I arrived at Castle without my baggage, which had been sent to Monterey. I did have a uniform, all the necessities except for low quarter shoes and black socks. I wore gray socks and dress boots to my interview with the DOT and made sure he knew what had happened. I also assured him that as soon as the BX opened I would buy some socks. My boots were black. I felt they would suffice.

The interview consisted of my presenting my flying records and some personnel records to the DOT. He then called the bomb squadron, RTU, stan-eval, and CFIC. They each sent representatives who went over the records, and then gave a thumbs up. Once I had their approval, I was then taken in to see the DCO. When he approved, I was then set up to meet the commander. At that time he was a brigadier general.

The interview was reasonably short. I spent the time trying to cover my boots with my pantlegs. I was asked questions about my experience and views. The general then mentioned that being an instructor meant that the students would try to kill me with their lack of knowledge. When I replied I had already learned that, he told me I was hired.

I spent the next day looking at housing. We had put our house in Blytheville up for sale, expecting a long wait. It sold in two days with two back-up buyers. So much for not living downtown in Hooterville.

I flew commercial airlines to and from Blytheville. Actually, it was from Memphis. On the return flight we stopped in Dallas and two young soldiers fresh out of boot camp took the seats next to me. I was in civilian clothing. Their carry-on baggage was stacked knee high in front of them. They were both three sheets to the wind and their conversation was how they were ready for anything now that they had completed training. Once we were airborne, the one in the center seat asked where I was going and I told him Blytheville. He asked what I did for a living and I said I was in the Air Force. He asked if I was a sergeant. I replied I was a major. He moaned: "Oh shit!" He passed that bit to his buddy, and after losing their lunch a little later, they both went to sleep.

I began to prepare for transfer. I was still in the alert and flying schedules. I wanted to leave the first of February and was told I could as long as an upgrading copilot passed his pilot checkride. Otherwise, I would have to wait until he did pass and would pick up his alert line until he did pass, which could be for an undetermined amount of time. He passed on the last day of my alert tour. I took my crew rest time to finish last-minute items and signed out before anyone could change his mind. I was very glad to leave Hooterville.

My Favorite War Stories

Baked Ham

You had to be there.

It was the spring of '68 and we had been on Guam forever. At least it seemed like forever. The routine had become almost routine, not quite, but almost. Just when we thought we had it down, something came along to change it. I don't recall which number mission it was. It was unusual in two ways. First, it was a daytime takeoff. It seemed we only flew at night. Those were the ones you remember. Secondly, it became memorable after the first thirty minutes, which normally were spent in the slow climb to 30,000 feet trying to get comfortable for the next 10 to 12 hours of flight.

We went through the normal briefing. I noticed we had an extra man on board. The flight orders identified him as a pilot, colonel, and DCM. This was a little odd as few high ranking staff flew with a captain with only a few missions and in number three position. Senior people usually flew with the most experienced crews. We got maintenance men or low-ranking staff who could not make it onto one of the lead birds. Maybe he had no choice. Anyway, I was not about to ask. He did not show up for the briefing, or if he did, he did not identify himself to me or the crew.

The preflight was normal and the bird was in good shape. I wonder if the fact that the DCM was flying with us had anything to do with it. He showed up just prior to engine start and took his position in the IP seat. I gave my normal briefing, modified for an 0-6, and he had no questions. This was before Irving. In fact he said little at all.

Engine start, taxi, and takeoff went smoothly, and I paid little attention to the IP, for I assumed he knew what he was doing, and he replied correctly when required to do so.

We went through our checklists as we settled into our departure climb-out. It looked as if it would be an uneventful mission as we passed 12,000 feet, ran our station checks, and I cleared everyone off oxygen.

We passed 18,000 feet and settled in for a long ride.

Then all hell broke loose.

There was an explosion behind my seat, and I saw what I thought were sparks flying past my helmet. At the same time I felt something hit the back of my seat. I calmly pressed the interphone button and asked in an unusually high voice: "What the hell was that? Everyone on oxygen and report in!"

My first thought was that some piece of equipment behind my seat had blown up. Everyone checked in quickly, the copilot with the cabin pressure, which was normal. I loosened my oxygen mask and was met with an odor reminiscent of holiday meals back home. The autopilot had remained engaged and the engine instruments all were steady, so there seemed to be nothing wrong. At the same time I noticed the items I mistook for sparks had hit the windscreen and were sliding slowly to the bottom of the cold glass, leaving a trail of grease. It was fat.

The copilot had turned to check the bunk area and informed us that the oven had exploded. I instructed the IP to disconnect it and he did. He said nothing other than to acknowledge my request.

The oven was unusable now that the latch had been broken in the explosion. The jolt I had felt in my back had been the latch which had hit the back of my ejection seat. We are fortunate that it did not hit the side of the aircraft, for it might have gone through the skin. Naturally, the crew had frozen flight dinners to be heated in the oven.

The copilot could see the oven from his seat and explained to the crew that it had exploded when a can of C rations had been placed in it to heat up and apparently had not been opened. When it got hot, it blew. Everything was quiet until a voice from 150 feet behind me (gunner) asked: "Who was the dumb son of a bitch who did that?"

No one answered.

The rest of the flight was uneventful. The radar-nav, using his ingenuity, had rigged up a temporary latch, and we were able to heat our frozen dinners.

Ten hours later when I was taking write-ups, a quiet voice from the IP seat reminded be that the latch to the oven was broken. I made the appropriate entry. I checked after landing and there was about a half inch dent in the back of my seat.

The colonel was met by a staff car when we landed. I don't recall ever seeing him again to recognize. I do know he never flew with us again. That was one of the best smelling flights I have ever had. It certainly beat stale sweat and flatulence. I have often wondered how long it lasted.

TAKE THAT FOR RAYMOND SHERMAN!!!

We landed at UT about 0200. It was 0330 to 0400 by the time post-flight and debriefing were completed. It was too early to go to bed on this schedule, and we had no food or refreshment in the trailers. The O Club would not open until 0600, so food was out of the question for a while. We discussed this on the bus returning us to the trailers with a crew from Fairchild. At this point, Louis, my new gunner, spoke up and suggested we accompany them to the NCO Club as the bar was open twenty four hours a day. I expressed my concern as to whether we might not be out of place since all but the gunner were officers. However, Louis and the Fairchild gunner insisted if we were their guests it would cause no problems, and besides, at this time of the morning who would object, especially if we conducted ourselves as the officers and gentlemen he knew us all to be? The logic of his argument convinced us.

The bus dropped us off at our trailers to stow our gear, and we walked to the NCO Club about four blocks away. It turned out to be a pleasant stroll as the night was somewhat cool and not as oppressingly humid as the daytime.

We entered the club and proceeded to the bar in the rear where we ordered some snacks and a round of beer, followed shortly by another round. We proceeded to discuss and solve the problems of the world as the time passed and the beer flowed.

After a while, a man in civilian attire approached our table, and while he was not inebriated, he had obviously been drinking. He stopped and asked if we happened to be a B-52 crew. We assured him we were and introduced ourselves by position. He did the same.

"My name is Raymond Sherman, and I'm in the Merchant Marine. I have been hauling bombs over here for four years, and I've never met anyone who flew the aircraft that dropped them. I want to shake your hands."

We invited him to join us and pulled up a chair. He shook hands with each of us solemnly and expressed his support and hoped our efforts would help end the war. He then asked who actually dropped the bombs. We explained each person's duties briefly and identified the RN as the one who actually released the weapons. He shook the RN's hand again and asked that the next time he dropped a load to say: "Take that for Raymond

Sherman!!!" The RN assured him he would do it.

Mr. Sherman then stood and remarked that he must return to his friends and would like to buy a B-52 crew a drink. We told him that was not necessary, but he insisted so we agreed and thanked him for his generosity. He asked what we were drinking and we told him beer. He went to the bar and returned, not with one each, but a whole case of Oly which he sat on the table. We invited him to help us with it but he declined and reminded the RN to "drop them for Raymond Sherman."

Such hospitality could not be overlooked, so we stayed until the gift was no more than an empty box. Someone noticed it was close to 0600 and the O Club dining room would be open for breakfast. We thanked the NCO Club and waved farewell to Raymond Sherman, Merchant Mariner and friend to B-52 crews.

The thought of a good breakfast and then to bed was overpowering, so we set a course for the O Club. The copilot said he was very hungry and a large breakfast was in order as we followed him into the dining room. Since the gunners had taken us to their club, we waived tradition and asked Louis to join us. We ordered, and the copilot, true to his word, ordered a large stack of pancakes and sausage. While we waited, we drank coffee and discussed how we would fulfill Raymond Sherman's request.

The food arrived and conversation ebbed as we turned to the task at hand. The copilot took a few bites and began to nod, his head gradually dropping lower and lower over his plate. Before we could prevent it, his head was resting on the stack of syrupy pancakes. He began to snore softly.

Louis, who had only ordered coffee, gently raised the head, removed the plate and lowered the head to the table. He then remarked that we should not waste food and finished the plate. Hoping not to attract too much attention, we quickly finished, gathered the CP and returned to the trailers and bed.

The crew was not on the schedule to fly for a few days and our commitment to Raymond Sherman was delayed and almost forgotten. When we returned to the flying schedule we discussed it, but in the preparation and accomplishment of the mission, it was overlooked. Several weeks passed and we were scheduled to fly with an ADO on board. The flight was uneventful, the checklists run without error, the RN was cleared for bomb release, and the interphone fell silent.

At the hack, the bomb release light on the pilot's instrument panel began to flicker as the bombs left the aircraft. As the last bomb left, the RN announced: "Bomb's away, pilot. Take that for Raymond Sherman!!"

The checklists were completed. We cleared the target area and began our recovery. When all was quiet, an unfamiliar voice came over the interphone: "Who the hell is Raymond Sherman?"

I suggested if he would buy the beer we would explain. He did and we did.

JACK

He would have been easy to caricature. He stood about five foot ten with medium build and was in his early forties. His hair was black with a touch of gray beginning to show. His nose was large but not overly so, and below it he wore a full mustache, bushy, but within the limits for an Air Force officer. The plastic nose, mustache and glasses which can be purchased as a costume fit his description.

I first met Jack in 1963 when our B-47 unit was replacing his at Benguerir Air Base in Morocco. Our crew changed over with his, and he kept us in stitches the whole time. He had it all in the right perspective, serious when necessary, but irreverent. His unit was breaking up and he was going to B-52s.

I was later assigned to Clinton-Sherman and met him again. I was assigned to the crew with Jack as the radar-navigator. As I got to know him better, little bits of history came out.

He had been a bombardier on a B-26 in the big one (WWII). His bird had been shot down in 1944 and he became a prisoner of war. His personality would have fit right in with *Hogan's Heroes*, but I am sure his experiences were much more grim. It was something he did not talk about much.

An alert tour with Jack was an experience not easily forgotten, but certainly enjoyed. He would take over the intercom and relate a full episode from *Boston Blackie* or a James Cagney movie, playing all the parts himself with the sound effects to go with it. He always seemed to catch something in a movie everyone else missed.

The chief of stan-eval was an older gentleman and wore glasses at all times. He also had a hearing aid built into the earpiece of the glasses. Jack would meet him in the hallway and move his lips to say: "Good morning, colonel." The colonel would then be seen adjusting the volume of his hearing aid. Jack would then turn and go back down the hall and say something to the colonel in a loud voice. We would then see the colonel readjusting the volume. Jack did this every morning the colonel was on alert.

Each morning briefing was started with a time hack which the briefer would give to the crews. Jack spent an entire alert tour taping the sounds of Big Ben, chimes, train whistles, and other noises, ending it with a countdown for a missile launch. He added a time delay and left it in the rear projection booth, locking the door as he left for changeover. The briefing started. As the briefer called for the time hack, the tape kicked in and for about five minutes that was all that was heard.

Each Sunday on alert there was an argument as to which football game to watch in the Officer's Lounge, AFL or NFL. It would finally come to a vote, and many times Jack would cast the deciding vote. The game would start and five minutes later he would leave. He also did this for other controversial programs. I think I am the only one who ever noticed that he left.

The EW on his crew was a good guy, but could sometimes try one's patience. There were few experiences or conversations in which he did not voice an opinion. He was knowledgeable on many things, or at least had an opinion, which he made sure was heard. Jack loved baiting him as much as everyone else. Sometimes it was easy. Travis especially liked to enter discussions of flying, and to hear him talk, one could guess that he was a pilot.

The BUF used water injection on all models except the H. We were flying the C, D, and E models at Clinton-Sherman. All alert aircraft were loaded with water to augment their takeoff. However, when the temperature reached 40 degrees and was forecast to stay below that for any period of time, the water was drained. Conversely, when the temperature was increasing and was forecast to stay above 40 degrees, the water would be loaded. At certain times of the year, this was a daily occurrence, dumping at night and loading the next morning at preflight. I have seen them loading when the order to dump came over the radio.

In most cases, when the word to dump was passed, the pilot and copilot would go out with the crew chief to dump the water. Sometimes another crew member would replace one of the pilots. The two-man policy had to be observed at all times someone was in the aircraft. All it involved was putting power on the aircraft, throwing a few switches, removing power and recocking.

I was on alert with Jack's crew. The pilot, Wiles Loveable, was a piece of work himself. He loved to bait people and could do it with a straight face.

He loved to watch the reactions. He and I had been at the aircraft for some scheduled maintenance when the word came to dump the water. We did so. The day was a blustery one with a few showers, but the ramp was mostly dry, except under the wings where the water drained onto the pavement.

The pilot turned to me and asked if I would help him get the EW. Naturally, I said yes. We recocked the aircraft and went back into the alert shack. He told me to disappear.

When Jack and Travis came in, he asked if they had seen me and they replied they had not. He said we had to dump water and he did not want to go out again, and he could not find the copilot. He then asked Travis if he knew how to dump the water. Travis immediately assured him that he did. The pilot then had him go through the procedure several times, with the warning that he had better not screw up his airplane. Travis assured him he knew all about the procedure. Jack, on the other hand, had reservations and voiced them. They finally left and I heard them going down the hall with Jack still voicing his doubts about Travis' ability. Once they had left the building, I returned to the library and sat down with Wiles.

Fifteen minutes later we heard them come in. Jack was giving Travis the devil and Travis was mumbling to himself. When they came into the library, Travis began with: "I've got a question." The pilot then began to accuse him of breaking his airplane. Travis denied it. They went round and round with Travis admitting that the water did not drain. The pilot then asked him to explain what he had done. Jack kept saying he had told him he did not know what he was doing.

Travis went into a description of his actions as long as the Michigan Hog Law. Wiles kept saying that he had broken his airplane. Finally, when we could no longer keep a straight face, the pilot asked what they had seen on the ground as they approached the airplane. Travis thought and thought, and then it dawned on him why the water had not drained. He did not speak to us for a while which was a blessing in itself. Jack would not go out again to drain the water unless a pilot was present.

Eligibility for promotion varied. In the spring of '67 it looked as if there might be a small chance that I would be in the primary zone for major. I decided to go to Randolph AFB at San Antonio, Texas, to check my personnel records. I figured if there were any errors, I had time to correct them. If I did not fall in the primary zone, then I would have over a year until the next board to make any adjustments. It was also recommended that one check his records, for it showed an interest by the individual. I needed all the help I could get. I planned to fill all the squares and cover everything that might be a tie breaker. I do not know if any one thing made any difference, but I made the effort.

I mentioned that I was going to make the trip on my CCRR after the alert tour. Jack asked if he could go along and check his records since he might be considered for promotion to L/C, and had never checked his records at Randolph. The company sounded like a good idea, and we agreed to leave as soon as we got off of alert the following Thursday. He asked which car I was driving. I said the TR-3. He asked if I thought it would make the trip. I told him that if I did not think so I would not own it.

We set off and the trip went quickly as we each took turns driving. We arrived at Randolph and checked into the BOQ. We went to the O Club and had a good leisurely meal before turning in for the night.

The next day we went to the records section and requested our records for review. It took a few minutes before they returned with them. We were ushered into a room half full of glum looking L/Cs who were poring over their records as if they were searching for something that could tell them what they were seeking. It was like a library.

I sat down with my folder which was about three quarters of an inch thick. Jack sat down a little behind me. He had a stack of records, most of them in German, about four inches thick. It did not take me long to review what few items were in my folder. I did find a copy of orders for an air medal which had someone else's name on it. I turned it in to the monitor to be filed correctly. I found nothing out of the ordinary and was about to leave.

Jack's whisper came to me: "Hoop! Hoop! Look at this! Look at this!"

The other people looked up as if we had committed some social faux pas such as loudly passing gas. He had a stack of records in front of him. The ones in German were from his period as a POW. He was holding a thin piece of paper and passed it to me.

It was a citation for the Distinguished Flying Cross. It went on to say that "although grievously wounded, Lt E . . . continued to maintain his station and ensure the release of his bombs on the target before bailing out of the fatally damaged aircraft." I told him that sounded pretty good and he told me he knew nothing about it. It had never been awarded although it was in his records. The event had occurred in 1944; this was 1967.

When he had completed his review, he asked what he should do to ensure that his records at Clinton-Sherman reflected the medal. He was told they would make copies of the citation and prepare a letter for him to take with him. The rest of the trip he was walking on air, and rightfully so.

Several weeks later, the base had an open house and a special ceremony during which Jack was officially awarded his DFC he had earned twenty-two years earlier.

The following year we were in Southeast Asia. I had my own crew and Jack was still with his. The aircraft were maintained to keep the bomb-nav system continually reliable. To ensure that this was possible, the aircraft were required to have an electronically scored release during a set period of time. Most of the releases we were making were not radar synchronous using the bombing system, but directed from the ground. Therefore, on many missions one of the aircraft would be scheduled to make an RBS practice run on a radar site in South Vietnam. Safety measures were used to ensure nothing was dropped except a tone. If there was any indication of a hanger in the bomb bay or external racks, then that aircraft would not make an RBS run. One of the other BUFs in the cell would be the alternate. No one liked to make the run. Often the aircraft had to break cell and go off on its own, extending the length of the flight. It also seemed a little ludicrous after dropping more than a hundred live bombs to go and make a simulated release. However, we did it when asked.

One evening we were in the same wave with Jack's crew. We were flying out of Andersen. All the counts and no accounts were at the briefing. The briefers covered the material and then it was announced that the aircraft Jack was flying in was scheduled to make an RBS run. Jack stood up and said that he would not make an RBS run. The room got extremely quiet.

The full colonel taking the briefing asked him to repeat himself; Jack did. The colonel then asked Jack to explain.

Jack quietly said that in 1944 he had been shot down and spent the rest of the war in a POW camp. If he was going to go to war again, he was going to be serious about it and not play games he could play at home. There was a long pause and then the announcement that the alternate aircraft would make the run. No one to my knowledge had the gall to make an issue of the situation. Respect for an old flyer was never higher among the troops.

I have always felt I was fortunate to serve with Jack. He had seen the elephant and rode it home. I lost track of him when the wing broke up later and he retired. I will never forget him.

IRVING
(The best kept secret in ARC LIGHT)

I always spent a lot of time shopping at each of the bases and in the surrounding communities. I did not buy that much, but it helped pass the time and I met some very interesting people at the different shops. Each base had some concessions at or near the exchange, but the more interesting ones were off the base. I normally was not looking for anything in particular but waiting for the inspiration to hit me. I found some neat and unusual items. It kept me busy and out of the bars, and with walking several miles, reasonably fit.

The best shopping was outside the gate at Kadena. The Army, Navy and Marine bases also provided good shopping. I would leave the base at the BC street gate and methodically enter each shop, inspecting the display cases. If something struck my fancy, I'd make a deal with the shopkeeper. There were camera shops, watch shops, jewelry shops, stereo shops, and shops with a combination of all these items. The most interesting were those which did not seem to receive many military visitors, such as the stationary shop I found that had an excellent selection of drawing and graphics equipment.

One of the best deals was a Koza Coffin. This is a box 3 feet long and 18 inches deep and wide. They cost five dollars and were great for storing things in. I still use them.

There always seems to be some obligatory purchases, in addition to gifts for family and friends back home. These items may or may not have any useful purpose, but are reminders of the visit. Generally, a casual look at one's household goods can indicate the countries visited by the family or military member. For example, camel saddles from Morocco, steins and cuckoo clocks from Germany, silver goblets from Spain, monkey pod from the Philippines, geisha dolls from Japan, and brass candlesticks from Thailand. When the same items are priced in the States, their purchase is justified.

The East-West Gift Shop is one of the larger buildings in downtown Koza. The shop contains seven floors of goods from all over the Orient. The items vary from cheaply made toys to expensive and exquisitely carved wood and ivory items. It was easy to spend several hours there and still not make a purchase.

I normally made my trips alone, more for the privacy than for any other reason. In our environment, which was not that different from alert, it was still good to get off by oneself for a short period. One particular day, the copilot joined me for a tour of the East-West Gift Shop. We went to each floor and inspected the goods with care. I'm not sure how the idea began, or even whose it was, but the copilot took the ball and ran with it. Or, as we say on the OER: "He showed great initiative." We bought a small wicker basket about four inches wide, ten inches high and twelve inches long. We also bought two small locks as well as a few other items.

We also bought Irving that day.

Irving was a habu. A habu is a deadly snake indigenous to Okinawa, whose main purpose in life seems to be to engage in a fight to the death with a mongoose. It is reported to be a two- stepper. In other words, it bites you, you take two steps, and you're dead. The copilot somehow came into possession of a plastic nametag in Japanese. He filled the basket halfway with grass, the non-smoking kind, introduced Irving to his new surroundings and added the locks. He added the nametag and swore to everyone it was Irving in Japanese. He then put the basket in the refrigerator to keep Irving sluggish, as he explained, and prepared for the debut of crew E-13's newest member.

We were due to rotate back to Andersen in a few days and decided that would be the proper time to introduce Irving to this fellow aviators. Tom was a few steps ahead of me. The day of the flight he let the rest of the crew, with the exception of the gunner, in on the game we were about to begin. We established how everyone would play it, and how to deter any potential unbelievers by suggesting they open the basket and look. The gunners lived in another area of the base, so we figured he could take his chances. We would monitor his reactions for future reference. He was informed after the first flight.

The copilot was a stereo-typical Texan, with a tremendous flair for the gaudy and flamboyant. Understated action was alien to his thinking process. He appeared at the bus clad in a new flying suit. He had taken it to a local embroidery shop for modification. The decorations must have taxed their skills with a sewing machine. It could not have been done in less than two days of hard work, and they may have added a few items on their own. On his head he wore a bright blue baseball cap, which did reflect the squadron color. His rank (1st LT) was in the center front, but not overly obvious with the other decorations. The bill of the hat had a series of small white bombs arrayed around it, giving the immediate impression of the field grade insignia of farts and darts (clouds and lightning) which festoon the bill of a wheel hat of a L/C or higher. A snake adorned the back.

The rank on his flying suit was subdued (black), which at the time was not approved by SAC. His left sleeve, at the shoulder, held a Confederate flag; on his right the Stars and Stripes. His name tag was a thing of beauty: black with white lettering and what must have been a history of his short . . . and soon to be shorter, if this was any indication of his state of mind, career. His right breast bore a subdued SAC patch with a cobra bearing bloody dripping fangs superimposed in the center. The *piece de resistance* was not readily apparent. He turned around and it appeared in all its glory. He couldn't find a habu in his rush, so instead, he had a large cobra which stretched from his waist to the center of his shoulders. It was coiled and in the strike position, red-eyed and spitting venom. Since we only flew with name tag and rank on our flying suits, he stood out like a bastard at a family reunion.

When I regained my composure, I suggested he change into proper attire before his and my careers were summarily terminated. He replied that everything was packed. Enroute to briefing I discussed his future with the crew, squadron, and the Air Force. We discussed the proper dress and decorum of the SAC flying officer, and I believe I threatened an article 15, court-martial, and bodily harm, not necessarily in that order, if anyone from the staff should see his sartorial splendor and question my sanity in permitting it. Throwing caution to the wind, I directed him to keep his seat when the senior staff entered the briefing room and in general be invisible. Fortunately, we were flying in number two position and were sitting in the second row. Oh yes, in his right hand he had the basket with Irving.

We arrived at operations just in time to gather what we needed and take our seats. The copilot, carrying Irving, was stopped by the weapons officer and asked what he had in the basket. He replied: "A habu. His name is Irving."

"A what?"

"A habu."

"I don't believe you," the major said.

"Well, open it and look!"

"Well, the briefing is about to start. Why don't you leave it out here in the hall?"

"Okay, but he might get loose, or someone might open it by mistake."

"On second thought, take him with you, but don't open the basket!"

"Yessir!!" the copilot replied.

The comments from then on were basically the same.

"What's in the basket?"

"A habu."

"Bullshit!"

"OK. Open it and look."

"Noooo. You're crazy enough to have one!"

It was discovered that by holding the basket up to the light, the weave was open enough that the outline of Irving was visible in the grass. The conversation was then more like the following:

"There's no snake in there!"

"Look and see."

"Well, I don't want to take a chance, you crazy bastard, you might have a snake in there."

"OK. Hold it up to the light."

This was done with great caution by the unbeliever.

"I'll be damned! You're not kidding! There is a snake in there!"

The basket would then be passed back to the copilot very quickly and gently.

The more difficult questions were answered with more thought.

"How do you feed it?"

"We keep it in the refrigerator to keep it lethargic and lower its metabolism rate. The house girls catch mice for us and we put them in when it is cold. He can eat when he warms up."

"What if he gets loose in the airplane?"

"We just depressurize until he's either too cold to move or dead and then put him back in the basket."

Thus began the illustrious career of Irving the habu, seventh member of crew E-13, and only snake (of the reptilian persuasion) in the USAF that flew on a BUF. There were those I must admit that thought the crew was a little squirrelly to begin with. We played the game for several missions and began to notice the word had gotten out about the Clinton-Sherman snake crew. We also noticed a dramatic drop-off on any staff members scheduled to fly with us. That in itself was worth the whole game. Since there are only five ejection seats in the D model BUF, the gunner jettisons his tail turret and steps out. Extra people became a liability if the aircraft had to be abandoned in a hurry.

The guys we didn't mind were the maintenance troops who busted their butts keeping the birds flyable. They also caused the least interference and it was worth it for them to get flight pay, combat pay, and a tax break. When you had problems with a BUF over the middle of the Pacific Ocean, it was nice to have someone on board who might be able to help fix it.

Everyone scheduled to fly was required to attend the briefing, and each pilot was required to ensure the extra people were briefed on safety, mission procedures, and what he expected of them during the flight. I usually held this briefing at the end of the preflight and just prior to engine start. In most cases, the extra person would fly in the instructor pilot seat, between and slightly aft of the pilot and copilot. Example of briefing: "I want you on interphone at all times. Keep your oxygen on or immediately available at all times or when I direct it. I expect you to be in your parachute for takeoff, departure, air refueling, in-country, landing and any other time I direct it. You can use the bunk unless one of the crew wants it. If I tell you to go downstairs and prepare for bailout, I expect you to do it and do it rapidly. The RN will advise me when you leave and will then eject. Do not delay, for if we must get out immediately, and you do not take advantage of the opportunity, you will be in command of the aircraft. I will order the RN to go and follow him. Keep communication to a minimum, unless it is an emergency. Do not talk on the bomb run, and DON'T TOUCH THE BASKET!! Any questions?"

Naturally, the copilot had placed the basket in the center of the bunk.

I was seldom asked any questions, never the obvious if the guy was enlisted. However, he would corner the gunner before we got on board for engine start. We all knew what he was asking.

The gunner would later confirm. The question concerned what was in the basket. He would tell them and add any embellishments he thought were halfway plausible. No one ever moved the basket. Some never got out of the IP seat the whole mission. No one flew with us twice.

I became known as "Habu."

When a new crew arrived at Andersen, they were given an over-the-shoulder ride. In other words, an experienced pilot and RN would fly with them and sign them off. A reverse over-the-shoulder was also used. Two crew members of the new crew would fly with an experienced crew, observe, and thus learn the operation. This was done prior to their regular over-the-shoulder ride. Since it was not possible to send a whole crew on one aircraft, they would break up in teams. The teams were P and RN, CP and nav, EW and gunner.

One evening at pre-brief, while the copilot was working the weight and balance, I noticed on the flight orders we had a CP and nav flying with us. They arrived shortly thereafter, and I sent the nav to the bomb-nav briefing with my nav team. We spent a few minutes explaining the paperwork and generally reviewing the mission with the CP. He listened attentively, and when I asked if he had any question, he asked: "I see you are from Clinton-Sherman. What do you know about the snake crew?"

Tom got a great big shit-eating grin on his face, reached under the table, sat the basket up on it and said: "Meet Irving!"

Our new friend's only comment was: "OOOOOh shit!"

The game continued for about two weeks. We were scheduled as the manned spare at Andersen. As we came out of the briefing, the DO stopped the copilot and asked what he had in the basket. When he was told, he became somewhat disturbed; there were no poisonous snakes on Guam.

The copilot steered him to the side and explained the game to him convincingly . . . almost. We thought we were home free. We ran our pre-flight, started engines, and taxied into position, cautioning the nav to keep his mouth shut. We sat there in the middle of the day with the sweat pouring off of us through the launch of both cells and until they were out of catchup range. The time had dragged by, and finally the radio came to life. It was Charlie.

"Habu, you're released. After debriefing report to the DO's office... and take the basket!"

Apparently the DO had second thoughts about our story and wanted, living or otherwise, proof. Needless to say, we were not overjoyed or in any hurry to comply. It is seldom, so crew members thought at the time, that an invitation to visit the DO was for anything of a positive nature.

Six sweaty crewmembers and a basket eventually arrived at his office. We were met by our wing representative, an L/C, who explained the DO had to attend a meeting and he would investigate the situation. In fact, there was an absence of people in general. The only ones present were the L/C and two clerks. I pleaded for secrecy from everyone present for our game and the reasons for it. They all agreed . . . if.

The copilot set the basket on the table and everyone gathered around. The three staff members were somewhat tentative. As if on cue, Tom got a case of the shakes, like a dog passing peach seeds, and developed a slight stutter as well. The observers edged back a little. In order to keep from bursting out with laughter, I started a conversation about the mongoose and habu fights and the deadliness of the habu. The locks were opened and removed. Time slowed to a crawl as Tom's shaking hands reached for the lid of the basket. He quickly threw the lid open and the three inspectors jumped about three feet up and back. I am not so sure some of us did not jump back with them. No snake appeared, they cautiously approached the table and peered into the basket.

Sure enough, there was Irving lying quietly on his bed of grass. He did not move. He could not move. He just lay there in all of his rubber glory.

I reminded the inspectors of their promise of secrecy and explained that while most people were not really believers, they were not willing to open the basket and look. I reminded them of their own reactions. They agreed and the L/C informed the DO as well as our own wing commander at Kadena, who liked the story so well he said to keep it a secret and if anyone gave the crew a hard time, just let him know.

We had clear sailing from then on. Or should I say clear flying? The secret held throughout the tour. Irving became an integral member of the crew and amassed 33 combat missions. It only ended when the copilot broke his neck. The fun went out of the game. Irving languished in the refrigerator. We returned from a mission one day to find he was gone. I have been told by impeachable sources that Gross Grogan and Dirty Denny had snakenapped him, but could never substantiate it as a fact.

The game was a success and a good diversion. However, it has not been forgotten. For years afterward, as a CCTS instructor, squadron commander, and even DO, I've had people ask me: "Weren't you the AC of the Clinton-Sherman snake crew on ARC LIGHT?"

There are probably some out there who are still not sure about Irving.

CRUISE

The bomb runs were completed and we had been reliable. Our departure from low-level left us in a good mood. We now had about an hour of deadhead time back to Fairchild. The forms would be filled out and last-minute items reviewed. We would review the activity we would be accomplishing in the pattern as we covered the initial penetration and approach. It had been a good mission so far. I looked forward to some time in the traffic pattern before we finally landed.

Life was good. I had plenty of time to recall.

CASTLE
"You've got to be tough to fly the heavies."
Unofficial motto of the 328th Bombardment Squadron (Heavy)

We left for Castle the first week in February. I decided to beat the weather. We would take the southern route through Dallas to El Paso, Tucson, San Bernardino, and up the valley to Castle. We spent the night in Little Rock and visited my sister and her family, on leave from Liberia.

The weather held until we entered Dallas. It began to rain. I was driving the TR-3 with Bret, and Wendy had Jami, Jill and the critters. As we left Fort Worth the rain turned to sleet.

The cloth top of the TR-3 is not airtight in the best of weather. In fact, it only slows down the elements. We had prepared. We were wearing heavy clothes. The heater/defroster was at the max and kept us warm to the shoulders.

The speed limit was 70. We had maintained that most of the trip. As we left Fort Worth, the windshield began to ice up and the defroster had little effect. The windshield wipers had frozen up. I had to slow to 55 mph and allow the heat to thaw the wipers and the defroster to keep the windshield clear. Each time I tried to speed up it iced up. The ice did not build up on the highway. It lasted for about an hour. I could see Wendy in the rearview mirror and she was not happy. She had no idea why I kept slowing down and it was irritating her. We finally drove out of the sleet and arrived at Abilene where we spent the night.

I had to explain why I had been driving so erratically. The rest of the trip was easy, just long.

I signed in at Castle and began what would be one of the best assignments I had while in the Air Force. All new IPs were assigned to the 4017th CCTS initially. We spent our time teaching simulator and checking out in the F model. As slots opened in the flying squadron, the pilots would be reassigned. I had many friends from Clinton-Sherman, as well as other bases, who had come to Castle. It was good to work with them again.

I was visiting the required base agencies as I was in-processing and stopped at flight scheduling. Sitting across the room at a table was an old friend I had gone to high school with. We greeted each other. We were doing the old: "Where have you been and what have you done?" thing. Another officer leaned over to RK and said something. He turned to him and replied: "Dummy, of course you know him. He was your flight commander in ROTC!" It is a small world.

The 4017th also ran the simulator train which visited each base on a set schedule. The train consisted of several railroad cars which held the simulator in one and the power equipment in another. It also had a car in which the NCOs, who rode from base to base, lived. They would set it up when they arrived and perform the maintenance.

We IPs would then meet them at a particular base and provide simulator instructional rides for the local crews. We usually ran two three-hour periods in the morning and the same in the afternoon six days a week, sometimes seven. Each IP team had two IPs and we would alternate the morning and evening schedule. We were responsible for the required periods. The local instructors and evaluators gave stan-eval checks and upgrade rides. It got old real quick.

The emphasis was on emergency procedures. We had a basic curriculum to follow. However, we had some leeway in how we introduced the emergencies.

My first trip was to Wurtsmith AFB, Michigan. It was an H model base at the time. I had never been in an H and we had no H model simulators at Castle.

The H is basically a B-52G with improved engines and systems. The biggest difference was the engines. They are fan engines and do not use water injection. They provide much more power. On normal training missions full power was not used for takeoff. A thrust gate setting was calculated and the pilot set the power to that point. I had never seen one, much less used one. The dash one did not explain how to set it. I was reluctant to ask and show my ignorance, so I observed the first crew determine the setting and position the gate. It was really very simple. It is moveable and precludes advancing the throttles too far. It could be overridden if necessary by just pushing the throttles against it to move it forward.

I needed a landing for currency and was scheduled to be picked up by a crew at the end of their transition period. Although I was instructing in the simulator, I had never been in the seat of this model airplane. I was picked up and got strapped into the copilot seat as the AC taxied to the end of the runway. We were just going to take off and remain in the visual pattern for a full stop landing. I found it flew just like a BUF with a lot less throttle movement. The pattern was short and I never really found the instruments. In the other BUFs, the flight instruments were in the same position and had the same relationship in the pilot and copilot seat. In the H they were mirrored, or backwards. I'm glad I did not have to fly an instrument approach. I did find the airspeed indicator and lucked out with the rest.

I was glad to have this trip come to an end. The BOQ rooms did not have televisions. The only TV was in the office, which was usually full of young airmen, and our tastes were different. The club bar had one but I did not like staying there all evening. We had radios in the room, but the signals were so weak a station could not stay tuned in. I spent my time planning my patio in my new house, reading, and at the base theater.

I had a lot of friends from Clinton-Sherman in the 4017th and was asked if I was interested in teaching academics. I decided to give it a try. I found I enjoyed it. I found I learned a great deal more about the BUFs because I had to be able to think on my feet and answer all sorts of questions. It made me a better pilot. We not only taught the main F program but G and H difference. We also ran a short program for senior officers who would be division or wing commanders, vice commanders, and DOs.

We had to fly as well.

It was not unusual to fill in for a flight line instructor with students. The first missions kept one on his toes, especially if the student crew contained two new copilots fresh out of flying school. Many were intimidated by the instrument panel itself. It held 40 engine instrument alone. There were 13 fuel gauges and a full complement of flight instruments for each pilot—flap and gear indicators, warning lights of a varied nature with a few other gauges thrown in, plus an overhead panel, side panels, and a throttle quadrant console containing many more.

The war in Southeast Asia was heating up. Not long after I left Blytheville, many of the crew were deployed to Andersen. It was not long before the BUFs were going farther north of the DMZ. Most of us were glad to be out of it, but also missed it a great deal. This became evident a week before Christmas 1972. Linebacker II started.

The bombing of Hanoi brought mixed feelings. I missed the mission greatly, and in a way was with many friends while they participated. Blytheville got hit very hard and lost many people . . . people I'd flown with, pulled alert with, and even trained to some extent. Other bases also had losses. As the names of the missing and captured appeared in print, I found I knew a good portion of them. When I saw the name of Louis, my gunner, and then saw his picture in a national magazine, I felt I should be there as well. The experiences I had been through made it easy to imagine what they were going through, and I could easily put myself in their places.

It was very real to me.

It was more dangerous and intense for them. It was not a pleasant period to live through; I could only imagine what the families were going through. I appreciated my family a great deal more and hoped my absences had not been as rough on them.

I had an annual checkride. In the critique the evaluator went over many minute details . . . not errors, but techniques. This went on and on until he finally presented me with the paperwork to sign. I looked at it and then at him.

I did not sign the forms. When he asked why, I told him that to be so nitpicking and exact he could have at least ensured that my name was spelled correctly on the forms. The room was full of pilots, who had overheard most of the critique. They broke out in hoots and hollers.

The work was satisfying and the hours were more reliable than I had ever had before. The best thing was no more alert. The wing was soon going to change from flying the F model to flying the G and H models. This required a whole new curriculum. The training program was undergoing a new approach. The new term was ISD (Instructional Systems Development) and we were all involved.

The bomber pilot academic section rearranged the schedule for us to work with several civilian contractors who wanted to sell a new training program to the Air Force. We spent days reviewing each academic class we taught. We provided them with the data, what each pilot needed to know to operate the systems. We recommended what we felt they should know to complete the mission. It was an in-depth study and took several weeks of meetings. This was all to be applied to the new G and H program. The idea was to economize and save time as well as money.

We had emphasized that six hours of academics was close to the saturation point, especially when trainers were added at the end of the day. They took copious notes, nodded their heads and agreed with us. The program they returned to us was nothing more than what we had given them, rounded out to an eight-hour day of academics with trainers on top of that. It was not used in the presented form.

The 4017th was conducting training in old WWII buildings that used swamp coolers in the summer. They didn't help much. Afternoon classes were often sleep inducing gatherings. The worst I recall was a class I was teaching in August at 1430. The subject was SAC Tactical Doctrine, classified secret. This required the windows to be closed and the room secure. A lawnmower was droning outside. Twenty minutes into the class I had lost at least one third of the class to the sandman, and was about to succumb myself. I asked if anyone was retaining anything. The response was negative. I dismissed the class and advised them to check out the manuals and read them when they got the chance.

I had been asked when I upgraded at Hooterville if I was interested in attending IPIS (Instructor Pilot Instrument School) and had replied that I was. However, like most things at Hooterville, nothing came of it.

At Castle I was teaching the base instrument school as well as the students. It was recommended that I attend IPIS. This time it came to pass.

I had broken a bone in my right hand 10 days prior to my departure for IPIS. I convinced the flight surgeon to remove the cast the day before I left with the understanding I would have it reevaluated at Randolph and hopefully be back on flying status. I bought a hand splint and it helped. I drove in a car with a stick shift all the way.

I got to Randolph and was immediately asked how I expected to fly with a broken hand. I said I would fly the simulator which we had to do anyway prior to flight. If I had no problem, I would ask the flight surgeon to take me off DNIF status. I flew the simulator with no difficulty with my hand. (I can't say the same about the procedures and performance.) I was put back on flying status. My instructor was still not convinced and asked what I would do if it bothered me in flight. I said I would fly with my left hand. I had used that hand more on the flight controls than I had my right hand. All worked out well.

IPIS was a good school, although it was directed more toward initial flight school instructors and single-engine center-line thrust pilots than to multi-engine types like me. We had a going disagreement when it came to recalling formulas for things like rate of descent on final. I insisted my formula for the BUF was to set my throttles for 25,000 pounds of fuel flow, look at my rate of descent instrument and make any necessary adjustments. I also made the comment to my flight instructor that I had never flown a back course ILS except for a demonstration and knew no one who had. I flew plenty of them during the rest of the school and none since.

I had never flown the T-38 and asked many questions about it, both to the instructors and the other students who had flown it. They impressed upon me that on takeoff the pitch of the nose should be 7-10 degrees. Having flown aircraft that unstuck in an almost level attitude, I gave this a lot of thought. The simulator did not have the same feel as the aircraft. The first flight, I added power and we began our takeoff roll. As the take-off speed approached, I pulled back on the stick. I used about the same force I was accustomed to using in the BUF.

The nose rose to about 15 degrees of pitch before I could stop it, and for some reason the instructor's voice raised a few octaves as he assisted me in returning it to the proper pitch attitude. I spent the rest of the flight using very little force on the control inputs. The instructor was very observant as well.

One discussion in academics was concerning point to point navigation. When it got redundant, I mentioned that I had two officers downstairs who got paid quite well to give me a heading, and then I explained how to do it to prove I did understand.

We discussed the evaluation process and how to reduce the stress of an evaluation to the evaluatee and get the best performance. I mentioned that if things looked good, I would clear off the interphone at the 12,000 foot check, go downstairs for relief, and give the pilot a break. When I mentioned downstairs, this really brought out the hoots of derision from the single seat, single engine crowd.

We had a disagreement over SAC's method of evaluation. The instructor told the class that everything was written down and copious notes were taken which to him seemed a waste of time. I tried to explain that we had the luxury of doing it. It gave the evaluatee a break, for if there was a question as to whether an action was correct or not, the evaluator had a record of it. Many times it saved a failure whereas a strictly subjective decision made at the time might be forgotten or not recalled correctly. I did not change any minds, but the discussions were worthwhile and everyone learned about different approaches to evaluation.

It was a good school and the instructors were very good. Their relationship with the students was also good, and the atmosphere was excellent for learning. I know, for I learned a lot.

The promotion list for L/C was released the first part of June 1974, and had some surprises. Those who we thought had a lock, in some cases did not make the cut, and some of us who did not think we had a chance were on the list. It was a large list. I expected a long wait before I would be able to change from gold to silver, and the silver looked so much better on the uniform.

I had changed positions. Although still on the bomber pilot instructor manning list, I was working with the Director of Academic Training. I was making the schedule for the old program and trying to plan it so we would have a smooth transition into the new G and H program. It was good experience. I had been at an early meeting on the 27th of June and returned to hear my secretary tell me I was in trouble. The commander wished to see me immediately.

I finally got her to admit the reason. I was out of uniform. I checked everything. I was in 1505s. I disagreed, for I could find nothing amiss. Shirt and slacks matched, belt was centered, buckle shined, name tag in the correct position with the correct name, wings and rank in the proper position. The gig line was straight. She then gave me a big smile and told me my rank was incorrect. I checked the position of the leaves again and then realized what she was telling me. They were the wrong color.

The orders had arrived for the first group to pin on the new rank. It was a big group and my number, 782, was well inside the pack. The commander just happened to have a set of insignia for me.

As we began to change over to the G and H course, we received directions to take the F models to other bases where they became little more than static displays which were moved around occasionally to confuse the Soviet satellites.

I was to fly one of two to Blytheville. The Castle DO, who had been the tanker squadron commander at Blytheville while I was there, scheduled himself on the flight. Although we knew each other at Hooterville, we became better acquainted at Castle.

I called the bomb-nav shop at Hooterville. The old bunch had been replaced and Gary, my first RN, was in the shop. I identified myself to a captain and was told Gary was not in the office. I asked him to give Gary the message that his A/C would be arriving at 1500 on the date of the flight. When he passed the message, he was very concerned that a colonel had called, was coming to Blytheville, and wanted to see Gary. Gary understood the message and told him it was just an A/C, now an LC, and would not be inspecting anything.

Our aircraft was in pieces when we got to it. The other one was in working order and they launched on time. We finally got off three hours late. Our arrival at Blytheville was spectacular, at least from the right seat where I was sitting. The DO wanted to make the landing. He was a tanker type with very little time in the BUF, only because the DO was required to fly in both bomber and tanker. The approach was normal and everything looked good. He flared and the aircraft started to drift to the right. He then dumped the nose and the front gear made contact with the runway which resulted in a very high bounce, and the aircraft weathervaned to the left at about a 30 degree angle to the runway and was closing on the left edge.

I was on the controls as we bounced and told the pilot that I had it. I pushed in full right rudder, right and then left aileron, took out the aileron and held on. We hit again, near to, but to the left of the centerline and somewhat aligned. I deployed the brake chute and began to relax as it took hold and we stayed on the runway. As we taxied in, the DO told me never to tell anyone about the landing.

I learned about flying from that!!!

We taxied to the parking area and shut down. There were two cars to meet us. The DO left with the wing DO. As each of my crew deplaned, they were handed an ice cold can of beer by Gary. The crew asked if I was treated that way everywhere I went. I said yes, but doubt that they believed me.

The first aircraft had landed much earlier and was met by the same two cars. When the occupants of the second car found it was not my bird, they left without greeting the crew.

The 4017th had moved into a new building . . . a preformed concrete structure which had no windows except in the stairwells. The cooling problem we had suffered with in the old buildings was solved. The new building was air-conditioned and always on the cool side.

We got a new squadron commander just prior to the move to the new building. He was a tanker pilot and had never flown bombers. As we went through each room and office, many things were thrown out. Some had been there since the school opened and no longer had any practical use. Two B-52 instructors went past the dumpster and found the large picture of the YB-52 which had hung in the commander's office. This seemed like a slap in the face, for no one had asked if we wanted it. The size itself made it valuable. The pilots rescued it and it hung in the bomber instructor pilot office in the new building. The commander became aware of it and the feelings of the instructors, but since he was a gentleman, never mentioned it.

I continued to pick up additional responsibilities and found myself filling in for the Director of Academics more and more. He in turn was working closely with the squadron commander. The work was enjoyable. I was also going to night school for a master's degree. The classes were held in the building I worked in all day.

Lunch time at Castle during this period was a time when many problems were solved, and close coordination with the other squadrons and DO staff was accomplished. The DOT usually sat at a large round table at the O Club. He was joined by the flight line squadron commanders, operations officers, and flight commanders. As the acting Director of Academics of the 4017th, I was accepted. It was a free discussion period and a time when we could coordinate and propose actions, which if taken in normal channels would be lengthy. The DOT was a very experienced individual and was our conduit to the senior staff in training matters. He was also very easy to work with.

Castle was a CCTS unit. We trained the BUF and tanker forces as a daily duty, but also had the responsibility of an EWO commitment, which involved everything other units were involved with except alert duty. The squadrons were made up of instructors of all flying specialties; everyone had to maintain the currency of their position and assigned aircraft. The academic instructors filled in when required and made up additional crews when necessary.

At one time, I was current in the B-52 D,F,G, and H. No big deal, everyone was. However, when teaching an academic class, it was easy to use the wrong terminology when discussing hydraulics and electrics. Then it was necessary to tell the students to ignore what had just been covered and start all over.

Once we had successfully changed over to the new course, each instructor on the flight line would be assigned a student crew which would be going to a base together, or at least to the same model. If it was a G base, they trained in the G. If it was an H base, they trained in the H. The instructors were qualified to teach in either and had to keep the manuals and checklists up to date for each one. Occasionally, if a bird could not fly, it would be replaced with the other model. That meant the instructor had to have checklists and manuals available in order to change at the last minute. The students were not required to do so. Since there were differences in the models, a last minute change made things interesting to say the least.

Instructors were upgraded and served at SAC units and then could be assigned to Castle. Overall, the experience level and knowledge were well above that of the field units. At the time I was assigned, pilots were interviewed, selected or rejected; that changed in later years. It showed in some of the instructors we had. For the most part they were the best of the best. Competition for positions and promotion was intense. Most of the pilots would have gone anywhere to have the honor of commanding a bomb squadron. I know I would have.

In 1975 I was the DA (Director of Academics) basically, except for having the title on my records. This was not unusual to work in a position without actually having the position title. The commander often sent me to the daily standup meeting held by the wing commander. I was exposed to many other experiences as well as to the senior staff. Each time we had a senior officer academic class, we provided a coffee meeting which included the wing senior staff, 4017th staff, and the colonel(s) or general attending the class. Therefore, I was no stranger to the senior staff. The squadron commander retired in late summer and we were assigned a brand new colonel.

The new commander's appearance was imposing. He was tall with wide shoulders and wore his hair in a flattop cut. I quickly learned he was an excellent man to work for. He listened and discussed things with his staff. It was under his command that I was finally made the DA. I was now responsible for the academic training of all crew positions of the BUFs and tankers. I could be blamed for things now with no recourse. All of the academic units were under my direction. I had been around a few years and the relationships were solid. The instructors knew and performed their duties well, and kept me out of trouble.

I had been presenting a briefing to each class when all of the specialties were present. Different specialties went through the school on different time lines. They all finished at the same time and went to the flight line together. The briefing was about an hour long and covered SAC in a general sense. It could be said that I was recognized by most of the students.

There was not enough housing on the base for the students, and some were sent to motels in the surrounding area. Wendy decided she would like to have a waterbed. She had used one at her brother's and suggested I might like it as well. I wanted to try one before I was willing to spend the funds for a complete new bedroom outfit. We checked the yellow pages and found a local motel that had rooms with waterbeds. We arranged with a neighbor to watch the kids and reserved a room for the night.

We went to the motel when I got home from work, about 1700, to pay for it and leave a few items. I drove in and noticed a group of young men around the swimming pool. I was still in uniform and thought nothing about it until we left the room and were back in the car. Then it came to me—many of the men were students and had just seen me check into a motel with a very attractive lady, stay a while, and then leave. I am not sure what they thought, but I am sure they recognized me.

I was rapidly getting close to four years at Castle. History indicated that four years was the maximum. I knew an assignment was somewhere out there for me. I had noticed many of my flights also had the wing commander on board. He was a good pilot and knew the mission well. I knew this was a time to do well myself.

One night I was scheduled for an H model qualification ride. I had not flown one since the landing at Wurtsmith in '72. The flight consisted of the DOT as the IP, the wing commander, another pilot, RN and me.

The commander was in the seat from takeoff through the first part of the air refueling. The other pilot got his checkout and they called me. I was in the EW seat and came forward. I strapped in and the IP told me to take it when I was ready. I told him I would take a minute to get oriented. It was pitch black. The only light was the tanker right in front of us. I took control of the aircraft and moved forward slowly into the envelope, stabilized, and the boomer made the contact. I had just settled in the green when the tanker went into a thirty degree banked turn to the left. I surprised myself, stayed in the green, and held on through the turn. I had expected more difficulty, for I had been flying backwards in the EW seat and had never refueled the H before. I knew the throttle movement was much different. We returned to the pattern and did some pilot work. I found I liked the H.

I was flying with one of the flight commanders of the bomb squadron and a British wing commander who was attending the VIP course. He was getting a few rides in the BUF before reporting to SAC HQ as a liaison officer. The flight commander was the assigned instructor, and I was along for the time and to fill a seat. We did the flight planning quickly without the help of the British officer.

Cliff, the flight commander, put me in the right seat and the Brit in the pilot seat. We went out to slip the surly bonds of earth. Once we were leveled off and inbound to the A/R track, I asked the Brit if he'd flown the BUF before. He replied: "Oh yes!" I asked if he had refueled and he replied: "Oh yes!" I then asked if he had encountered any difficulty and he replied: "Oh yes, I was all over the bloody sky!" I thought: "Oh shit!"

I turned to Cliff in the IP seat; he was laughing. I motioned to him to ask if he wanted in the seat. He shook his head and kept laughing. When we were stabilized in the precontact position, the tanker IP advised us that his student pilot was getting his check ride. As an afterthought, he mentioned that they would not have an autopilot for the A/R. This really made my day. We would have to have the autopilot off as well. No real problem. It just requires a little more effort. With an inexperienced BUF pilot, who had just admitted he had difficulty under normal conditions, it should really be a roller coaster ride. I again silently offered the seat to Cliff. He just laughed and shook his head.

The Brit was right. He was all over the bloody sky—not dangerous, but unable to maintain a contact. We did this until the tanker called and said we had only five minutes of track left. I told the pilot to try again, and if he could not get the gas, I would attempt it. He didn't and I did, just as we finished the track. The tanker pilot receiving a checkride was a 1/Lt with just a little experience, but he flew the best autopilot off platform I've ever been behind.

Several weeks later, my squadron commander called me into his office and asked how it felt to be the operation officer of the bomb squadron. It was quite a surprise. I asked if he was telling me something. He told me to get my office in order, for the wing commander wanted me in the new job as soon as possible. This was an unusual move. The normal move was from the flight line to the academic squadron. I am not sure what I did to even be considered, but I have always been grateful to the squadron and wing commanders for giving me the opportunity and supporting me.

The new job was challenging. I had been in the academic squadron for almost four years and did not know how I would be accepted by the flight line instructors, even though we had flown together and knew each other. Additionally, the current squadron commander was the first RN to command a B-52 squadron. The bomb squadron was great. We quickly established a good working relationship. It was good to be back in the middle of a flying unit.

I tried to do all the things which I wished the operations officers I had worked for in the past had done. The mission came first, but not to the detriment of the crew force when there was an option and it did not affect the mission. I knew they would perform to the best of their ability and anything I could do to keep away the minor crap would help and be paid back when I had to ask for them to do something undesirable.

I was at a party at the club one evening about five months later and found myself talking to the wing commander. He eased me over to the side of the room and told me that I would be the next bomb squadron commander, but not to mention it to anyone but Wendy. It is impossible to describe the feelings I had the rest of the evening until I got the chance to tell Wendy. The job almost all pilots wanted was going to be mine. I was also getting the best of the best to work with, and the job could be a step toward further promotion. Since that squadron commander position has become an L/C slot, everyone who had it before me and after, to my knowledge, has been promoted to full colonel. The change of command occurred in July.

I have never enjoyed another job as much as I did the command of the 328th Bombardment Squadron (Heavy). I loved being an A/C and an instructor. I could now be both as well as a commander. One of the things which made it so enjoyable was that the operations officer was a classmate from Greenville AFB who had shared the tribulations of flying school with me. If we had only known. We worked together well, and when my time was up, I was glad to recommend Johnny to replace me, which he did. He could do things with the crews which, if I had attempted, would have gone over like a lead balloon. The difference in position had something to do with it, but it was primarily his personality.

I had flown with my flight commanders while in the 4017th. One was an English exchange officer. Mike became a good friend while he was in the 4017th with me and we still keep in touch. Cliff and I had flown together often. He was one of the best pilots I have known. Bob and I had flown together as well. Dick and I had attended SIU at the same time. I was a class ahead of him. He seemed to follow me around the Air Force to different bases and held many of the positions I had held. The RN and EW were well experienced and provided good assistance. The first sergeant and I shared some experiences which we both could have done without, but his concern for his troops increased the respect I had for him.

While in the 4017th I had learned about noise complaints. For a long time the complaints were taken by the base instrument school. Some were legitimate and others were just from people who did not like the Air Force. One civilian had worked at McClellan AFB at Sacramento. When he retired, he moved to Merced, bought a house right under the final approach to Castle and began to write complaints to the base and local paper. Then there was the individual who lived off of the runway, near, but to the side of the point where aircraft bottomed out at minimums to the tacan approach. When he called in a complaint, we listened. He not only identified the aircraft as to type, but model and sometimes tail number.

The visual approach had a turning point short of the junior college in Merced to preclude flying over it on the base leg. This was known to all instructors who in turn informed the students. I had bought a house about a mile from the college, and well out of the visual pattern. The instrument pattern was well to the north and east.

Occasionally, when I was home, I would hear a BUF over my house. After I became the bomb squadron commander, when one flew over, I would call the command post for the tail number and IP's name. I wanted to get a head start and be able to have talked to the pilot about it before anyone like the wing commander brought it to my attention from a civilian complaint. It helped.

I had also learned in the 4017th that the instructors would be more open with me when I was on their turf than when I asked someone to come to my office. It was even more evident in the bomb squadron. I spent a lot of time with the flight commanders. They were really the group that ran the training program in the squadron. I also recognized that my job was a lot easier than that of commanders in the field. My squadron members were, for the most part, older and more experienced. I had very few of the problems that plagued my contemporaries.

I also had another advantage. I had an executive officer. When I first arrived we had two, both female lieutenants. When it became evident we would lose one, we worked it so the one who had a weakness for SSGTs left. The other one was very efficient. She was married to an F-106 pilot assigned to the squadron on base.

Her desk was in an outer office adjacent to mine, but placed so we could see each other when the door was open. I had recommended a pilot to replace a departing flight commander. A major who thought he should have been selected came to speak to me about it. We talked about it. I gave the reasons we had selected whom we had. One of the reasons was that the major had a pending assignment. I had left the door open and Sue could not keep her facial expressions blank as she overheard the conversation which lasted about 20 minutes. Sue then came in and asked why I had put up with it. I explained that since he was not selected, he deserved to know the reason. I told her I wished I had been given the same consideration in the past when I was not chosen for something. He worked for me and was welcome to the time if he wished.

I received notice that an old friend from Clinton-Sherman was coming to the squadron from an ROTC assignment at Grambling. The last time I had seen Bill was at Minot AFB and he was preparing to leave for Grambling. He said he was going to drive onto the campus in his Buick

Riviera towing his Corvette and see what happened. It must have worked, for he now had a beautiful young lady as his wife.

I was walking down the hallway when he came in. We spoke and I welcomed him to the squadron. After a few minutes, he asked what I did around the squadron and I said I was the commander. His comment: "Oh shit! What have I gotten myself into now?"

I was in the DO's office shortly after that and Bill's name came up. The commander of the 4017th when I had left was now the DO. His assistant was an Air Force Academy graduate from the first class and went on to be the commander of MAC and Transportation Command, replacing a flying school classmate of mine. I mentioned that Bill was an academy graduate, and before I could identify West Point, H.T., the assistant, had a book out and informed us it was not the AF academy.

Bill did well at Castle. Several years later, he held the same job I had held at 15th AF. He also held the DCO job at Fairchild a few years after me. Unfortunately, he did not survive a BUF accident on a low-level route.

We had our annual ORI. The crews did the things they did best and we passed the inspection. However, not without some controversy. This was 1977 and the subject of haircuts was always a hot one. We had a young enlisted lady in the administration office, and she was always neat and kept her hair rolled in braids. On the first day of the squadron inspection she arrived with an Afro. This was not missed by the inspectors who spread the word that she was out of limits on hair length. By the time the word got to me, it was everywhere, but Sue had gotten a ruler and found it was three-eighths of an inch within the limits. I passed the word, but the damage had been done. It did not appear on the write-ups, but was always questioned.

The squadron did well otherwise, maybe because the flight commanders showed the inspectors around. The fact that most of them had flown with the flight commanders as crew members at one time might have been of help as well.

Bret was coming of age when the lure of driving a car became a goal he had to achieve. This was scary, for the TR-3 had reached an age when it began to appreciate in value. I did not drive it in bad weather any longer. I usually drove the 240Z, and Wendy drove the Toyota or the VW bus when Jami had the Toyota. One of the gunners in the squadron had a 1959 Bugeye Sprite which he wanted to sell. I made a deal with Bret. I would buy the car and he would be responsible for getting it running and cleaned up, while he paid me back. He could not drive it until he had received his license. He eagerly agreed and spent his spare time working on a car he could not drive. He did a good job. I often went into the garage and found him sitting in it with a girlfriend beside him.

He got his license. It took him years to finally figure out how I could tell him where he had been the afternoon or evening before. Like most young men, he went to where the young ladies were. Many of their fathers worked for me and would report his trolling their neighborhood. With their help he stayed out of trouble and never knew it.

I did have some unpleasant duties. I had to take action on several of the squadron members for DWI. I made a point of informing only the operations officer in the squadron, but the word was always out quickly, especially if it was a pilot. I would have to remove his name from Supervisor of Flying duty when he lost his driving privileges.

The last one I did was the easiest and the hardest. I got a call at 0400 one morning that a captain from the squadron was in the county jail for driving while intoxicated. I got up and went down to the jail to confirm it. Once that was established, I told them someone would meet him when he was released the next morning. The disturbing thing was that he was scheduled for a 1000 takeoff that morning. Of course, that same information was available for the wing commander when he came in the next morning.

We had received a new wing commander shortly before this. His policy was that anyone who was picked up DWI would appear at his office with his squadron commander as soon as possible. The first thing I did when I got to the squadron was to dispatch the IP's flight commander to escort the IP from the jail, home to change, and then to my office. The commander's exec called to inform me they had the word. I advised him I would be there as soon as the IP appeared.

I was on my way to the legal office when I met the flight commander and the IP passing wing HQ. I waved them down and we went by the DCO's office first. He had a few things to say, and then we went to the commander's office.

I reported to the commander with the other two officers. He then told the instructor he had let down his crew, flight commander, me, the squadron, wing, and Air Force. He promised him that he would never fly another aircraft at Castle. He emphasized the potential for disaster he faced if he had not been arrested. He then dismissed the two officers. He then asked what I intended to do.

I told him I was on my way to the legal office for advice as to whether an Article 15 was appropriate. He agreed and dismissed me.

The lawyer I talked to agreed that an Article 15 was indeed an appropriate action for the circumstances. It was easy to work with him for he had been a BUF IP at Castle, got out, completed law school and came back in the Air Force. I did not have to try to explain the complications and seriousness of the problem. The only kicker was that a general officer would have to administer the Article 15 since the recipient was an officer. He said he would work out the details.

I called the wing commander and informed him of my actions and he agreed. I then called in the IP and read him the required warnings. I informed him of the action I was taking and that he had three days to accept the punishment or take the option of a court martial. He immediately told me he would not accept it. I stopped him and informed him he must first confer with the area defense counsel, and after that discussion, make up his mind. I dismissed him. He came back the next day and accepted the punishment. The division commander came to Castle a week later and administered the Article 15. The instructor never flew a BUF again and elected to leave the Air Force.

The year had gone very quickly. I knew I was going to leave, but had no idea where I would be assigned. The DO assured me it would be a promotable job. I was assigned to 15th AF in the DOT shop. I had a group of super people to work with.

The big shock came in housing. I thought I was doing well to sell my house in Merced for twice what I had paid for it. Then I went to Riverside, California. The prices were double what I had just received when I sold mine.

Approach and Landing

The weather had changed and it was clear-severe when we returnedtothe Spokane area. I requested and received an enroute descent to the final approach at Fairchild. I lowered the nose as I reduced the power and milked the airbrakes up to position four, maintaining my penetration airspeed as the gear was lowered. We ran the checklists and followed directions from approach control to our final approach heading and altitude. We spent an hour doing pilot things; instrument approaches and touch and go landings. The time passed all too quickly. As we passed the Spokane International Airport on our final approach, I requested a touch and go followed by entry into the visual pattern for a full stop landing. It was approved.

I passed over the runway threshold on airspeed and slowly raised the nose as I decreased power and trimmed the stabilizer. The old lady settled into the proper attitude and gradually descended to touch so gently it was hardly noticeable. I raised the airbrakes to six and reset the stab trim. I lowered the airbrakes to zero and advanced the throttles to the vertical position and checked the instruments. They looked good. I pushed the throttles forward. We lifted off smoothly and climbed straight ahead to 500 feet and started a turn to the right. "Maggie 11 on the go, request full stop."

"Maggie 11 cleared, call turning final."

I continued my climb and turn to downwind and leveled off. We ran the checklist and I started my turn to final. "Maggie 11 turning final, full stop."

"Maggie 11 cleared to land."

I rolled out on final slightly above 500 feet and set up my airspeed and rate of descent. It looked good and I crossed the threshold as before and set up my flare, expecting the smooth, professional touchdown as on the previous landing. However, the nosegear touched down first and the aircraft went back into the air. I thrashed around on the controls, we touched down again solidly, and I called for the brake chute to make sure we stayed down. Oh well, I have never flown with anyone who could grease it in continually. It was a typical BUF landing we walked away from.

15TH AIR FORCE

The DOT at 15th AF had been the Combat Support Group Commander at Castle during part of my stay there. He was a super person to work with. He called me in one day and told me of a conference at SAC HQ which he wanted me to attend. The LG was also sending a representative. The purpose was to prepare the groundwork for a new training program for the BUF crew force. Representatives from throughout the command were attending.

We were briefed by the SAC Vice Commander who was rumored to be the author of the new program. Instead of flying the long missions, which had been the hallmark of the bomber force, we were directed to build a program to reduce the length of the missions, increase the number of missions, and the activity completed on each mission. This would also include dropping more ordinance versus using tones and electronic scoring. His comment was to the effect that pilots like to see things falling off of the aircraft.

It is not possible for a pilot to see something fall off of a BUF unless it is from a pylon, or he stands by the bomb bay. No one told him this and we had our marching orders.

I returned to March AFB and presented my report to the DOT and DO. They accepted the new course and directed us to get to work. I was in my office the next day when the LG came down and began to give me a hard time about caving in on a proven training program. Since he was a bird colonel, I tried to diplomatically tell him he had a representative at the meeting and he had not presented an argument either. I was told the long missions had been proven to be the best when maintenance was figured into the equation. I did not disagree with him but informed him we had been given no option. He insisted we should have stood up and disagreed. I gave up trying to reason and just listened.

Two weeks later another meeting was held at SAC. This time the DOT and LG went along. Several units which had been chosen to test the program were present. Their wing commanders had come along. This was serious. The vice commander came into the whole group and briefed us on how the program was to be planned. If anyone did not agree with it, they would be replaced with someone who could do the job. I waited for the LG to speak up. He did not. No one disagreed with the three star and we proceeded to lay out the program.

I was selected for promotion to colonel. I knew I would be moving to another job but had no idea what it would be. The deputy DOT, a full colonel, was reassigned to the 22nd Bomb Wing. His slot was open. I was moved into it before my selection, but could not actually have the position on my record because I was still an L/C. It was a full colonel position. Shortly after I was selected for promotion, the position was changed to an L/C position. This meant although I now held it, I would be moving, for I would be a rank higher than the manning required.

I shared an office with the DOT, and we spent a lot of time discussing things we thought would help the training program as well as the command. I expressed the desire to stay in the operation field. I had spent my whole career there and felt I could be more effective than in a field where I would have to learn everything from scratch. He agreed. As time passed we brought the Director of Personnel into our conversations, just in case he could help.

It was not unusual for some of the staff in the headquarters to take a half day off and play golf. The DOT was not a golfer, so he made it possible for anyone in his group, who wished, to go fishing once a month. I was not a fisherman and proved it when we went on a deep sea fishing trip out of the San Diego Naval Base. The golfing did slow down when a new commander, who was not a golfer, arrived and said something to the effect that he thought it was a waste of time. The fishing continued.

Since I was the assistant, I got to answer the telephone. The secretary would patch it to me rather than the DOT, unless it was specifically for him. I then got to argue or discuss the subject with the DOT listening. It was good experience. He let me work the problems, and only stepped in if he disagreed with my solution or had something additional to say. He spent a lot of time laughing at my end of the conversations.

He did teach me a lot of things. We had a staff meeting once a week with the commander and the rest of the senior staff. Each group would present information on slides and had people available to answer any questions which arose. They invariably did. The general would ask the colonels who would turn to the L/Cs and majors, who were expected to have the answers. We even sat or stood in tiers.

Prior to the first such meeting, the DOT went through our massive slide collection and reduced it by at least two-thirds. He explained that the slides he removed were required by the previous commander. We would start out with the required briefing items and only add as requested. It sure did cut down on the work load. We watched as the LG presented a slide on engine repair, which the commander did not like. At each meeting for several months a new slide would be presented to provide the information and each was turned down. They finally went back to the original. It was accepted.

I had been getting antsy, for I knew the date to pin on my rank was rapidly approaching. I would be leaving. I could not get any information except my name had come up for a maintenance slot. I doubled my efforts to stay in operations.

We were invited to a reception at the club to welcome the ADO from the 92nd Bomb Wing at Fairchild AFB, reassigned to the 22nd BW as the DCO. I was ordering a drink when the Director of Personnel asked me to step aside with him. I did. He asked me how the job of ADO at Fairchild sounded. I said it sounded pretty good to me. He told me it would be coming soon but not to tell anyone until I was notified. I assured him I would keep the confidence. He then said I could tell Wendy. I told him I did not think I should. He left and I next saw him in conversation with her.

I walked up to a group containing the 22nd BW/CC (H.T. from Castle), the new 22nd BW/DO, the 15th AF/DOT and their wives. The new 22nd BW/DO looked over and said he understood I was going to Fairchild as the ADO. I had just heard it five minutes earlier and had to keep my word, so I just indicated that it sounded pretty good if it were true. By the look on H.T.'s face I was sure he knew as well. Wendy came up. I knew that the DP had told her also.

There was not much time for planning. I had to sell a house. I would be on base at Fairchild. I did not want to be making house payments with two kids in college. We put it on the market and it was sold in six days. In fact, we had a final bidding in my living room as to which of three buyers would get it. We left within two weeks for Fairchild.

FAIRCHILD

I had been out of active flying for about two years and was anxious to get back to it, even in a new capacity. As the family settled in, I tried to catch up on all the things which I would need to know yesterday. One of the first things I had to do was to finish my office. The previous ADO had not completed a self-help project he had inherited for the short time he was in it before moving into the DCO position. I had to finish the paneling, if only to be able to move around in the office. Wendy and I did that in the evenings.

The eagles had their advantages. I did not have to run all over the base to process in. Everyone came to me. I had to get back into the books. I would have to requalify in the aircraft. This was in addition to my primary duties. I met some old friends from previous assignments and from Castle.

I had been on the base about three weeks when the wing commander called me in and gave me the hardest job I ever had to do in the Air Force. The government had decided to declare most of the Missing in Action in SEA as Killed in Action. I was to travel to Yakima, WA, to inform the parents of a pilot, shot down in 1967 and carried as MIA, that he had been declared dead. The notification had to be coordinated with one in Utah that was to notify his wife and children.

I left with a driver, a chaplain and a nurse. We arrived in Yakima and found the address. When we arrived at the house, the parents immediately recognized the nature of our visit. They welcomed us into their home and remained stoic while I presented them with the information and letters. It was difficult to do. They were so gracious and kind to us. We offered any assistance and stayed for a short while. They told us they did not believe what we had to say, not because of who we were, but that through other agencies they had information their son had survived, at least initially. This gave them hope that he might still be alive. I have seen nothing since to indicate their hopes have come true.

I had my first flight. It was a pilot proficiency with a stan-eval IP and an instructor receiving an instrument check. We had three pilots and an RN on board. At mission planning, the stan-eval pilot and I talked about the flight. I mentioned I had always felt more comfortable in the left seat; most of my flying had been with the throttles on the right and the control column flown with the left hand. I also mentioned that I had last flown the G and H, and during my simulator ride the previous week, I had automatically reached for the position of items as if I were in a D.

We had a late afternoon takeoff and returned to the traffic pattern at night. The weather was at minimums and the instructor was flying his checkride. I was to get into the seat after he completed. The weather did not improve. We found ourselves on an ILS approach. Our fuel had reached the point where we would have to land or go to our alternate if we did not break out of the weather soon enough to land. If the weather had been better we could have stayed in the pattern and continued to fly. It looked as if I would not get any activity since the IP's check was more important.

The first approach was well off the centerline and I saw the runway lights from the IP seat. The pilots in the seats did not. The wing commander and the DCO were at the end of the runway when we made our second approach. We did not break out and our fuel had reached the divert point. I told the pilot to get a clearance to our alternate, Mather AFB, California, and I would notify the command post. The commander came on the radio and said they had a visual on us during the missed approach. I explained we had not seen the runway lights and that we had reached divert fuel and were proceeding to Mather. After my go around at Kadena in '69, I was not ready to take a chance.

We returned the next day and completed the checkride. The weather was still marginal. As the IP made his last missed approach, the evaluator said he would get an extended pattern and make a three-way seat change. I told him if he had no problem with it, I would just as soon fly in the right seat. We could skip the massive seat change and maybe get more approaches. He agreed. I surprised him and myself with the ease with which I was able to adjust to flying the BUF after a two-year layoff. I found the seat made no difference. My confidence level went up proportionately. I knew the word would be around the wing quickly if I could not do it well. By the same token, the fact I could fly reasonably well would spread just as quickly.

My second flight was with the chief of stan-eval who had been at Castle when I first arrived there. The RN was experienced and had been on the Linebacker II bombing of Hanoi. He also had an all-expense-paid vacation at the Hanoi Hilton for several months.

We flew the typical profile with A/R and low-level. The A/R started a little rough but I was able to settle into a reasonable receiver and not fall off of the boom. Since the tanker was ours and the crews part of Operations, the word would be out as to whether I could do this as well.

Gene got out of the seat after A/R; it was just like it used to be. I felt pretty good when he let me fly the mountainous low-level terrain avoidance route with no coaching. It was as if I had only been on leave. Everything came back quickly.

One of the best compliments I have ever had was from the RN after our pattern work. He said he had not felt so comfortable in an aircraft in years. I asked why. He said that Gene and I had worked together well and the way we advised each other of airspeed, altitude and attitude when transferring control meant a lot to the crew. It was something we had learned early and always done, as well as taught.

In the spring of 1980 I got a call from the SAC DP. He asked how I felt about going to Guam as the DCO. I said I liked it and would like to talk to Wendy. He asked me to call back the next day. He had told me our present DCO would be replaced by someone who outranked me and I would be staying as the ADO. Guam sounded better for once.

I talked to the wing commander and acknowledged that my reaction was to take it. He agreed. I called back the next day with my answer and then sat back and waited. That evening, the wing commander called me at home and said to forget it. I would be staying in the 92nd and moving into the DCO position in June or July. I was ready to move, but this sounded better.

May 18, 1980, was a bright and sunny day, which showed off the Pacific Northwest at its best. Spokane was having its annual Lilac Festival. The annual base open house was in conjunction with it. Wendy had gone to Fresno, California, to pick up Jami who was attending Fresno State University. Bret was on a trip to Central Washington University. Jill and I were at home.

I was up and heard a noise which I thought was either someone breaking the sound barrier or someone had slammed the garage door shut. I thought nothing more of it until I turned on the TV and learned that the event that had been forecast for months had finally occurred.

Mount St. Helens had erupted. It is on the west side of Washington state and several hundred miles away. I did not expect it to affect anything I was doing. I was wrong.

I attended the Air Force Association brunch at the O Club. The hot topic was that the mountain had finally blown. At about 1100 the DCO and I went to the command post to check on the air show. They had been receiving reports from stations between us and the mountain. They were in the dark, literally. In the meantime, people were pouring onto the base for the open house and air show.

We had 45 visiting aircraft and eventually the crowd reached 60,000. The ominous reports kept coming. Communities to the southwest were reporting a heavy cloud overhead. We also began to receive reports of ash fallout. The division and wing commander called a battle staff meeting. It was decided to terminate the open house and move the people off of the base.

As the afternoon progressed, the people left with no accidents or incidents. Additionally, some of the aircraft began to leave. We had the alert crews button up the alert aircraft, sealing all of the sensitive points such as the pitot static system. We asked for and got a delay for alert response from SAC. We began to put aircraft under cover. We were able to get all except the bomber and tanker alert force, a WC-130, and an RB-57 under cover. Of course, they were packed in pretty close. Sixteen of the transients had been able to depart prior to the arrival of the ash cloud.

The cloud of ash was spreading across the sky from the southwest. The sun was blocked out. Visibility and light began to slowly disappear. We had been in contact with SAC and Boeing as to how to take care of equipment and what effect the ash might have on it. Initially it had a high sulphur content. The possibility of the ash getting wet caused some concern.

I called Jill and told her to stay in the house and make sure the windows and doors were kept closed. She had received a call from Bret, who was at Ellensburg. He told her the sky was black and things were falling out of it. I had not heard from Wendy who was supposed to return that afternoon. By 1600, it was pitch black outside and the ash began to fall like a quiet winter snowfall. It looked like an evening in January with the light gray ash covering everything.

The battle staff stayed in constant session with hourly updates throughout the evening. We had little response from SAC as to recommendations. Throughout the entire episode they were always 24 hours late on advice and it was usually the same as the action we had taken. I had called the bases to the east of us and informed them what we had and what to expect, as well as the actions we had taken.

I got home late that evening. Wendy had checked in from Dayton, Washington. She and Jami had gotten the last motel room in town. They were lucky. I think there was only one motel. I told her to stay until things settled down and we had more information as to what steps to take.

The next morning we had our battle staff meeting. I was given the duty of coordinating the departure of the visiting aircraft. I established the guidelines and a priority listing of the aircraft. The pilots were instructed to get directions from their units and then coordinate maintenance requests with their proposed departure times and dates with me. We established weather criteria of three miles visibility and a maximum of seven knots of wind for takeoff. I had launch approval.

Cleaning the runway had number one priority and the civil engineer worked the problem night and day. He finally found a solution which, when dispersed, would wash the ash away. The ash was very heavy and had a high silicon content. The established procedure was for the aircraft to be towed to a taxiway that would provide at least 10,000 feet of runway; then they were allowed to start engines. The runway had been cleaned three times but the departing aircraft still sent up large clouds of ash.

The morning of the 22nd, I had left the battle staff meeting and was proceeding to my vehicle to check the aircraft scheduled for departure. I heard the sound of a turboprop engine and hurried to the flightline. I found the WC-130 with two engines running and the crew chief moving to position for starting the third. The ash cloud behind the aircraft was tremendous. I motioned him over and told him to tell the pilot to shut down the engines. He told me they were leaving. I repeated my request and told him they would be towed to the runway. He answered that he had a full colonel in the pilot seat who said: "No Way." I reminded him that he had a full colonel in the car who was in charge of departures who said: "Shut it down." He immediately stood up and snapped a salute. I thought this odd until I looked over my shoulder and saw the division and wing commander in the general's car behind me. The pilot shut down and was towed. He was the only one who gave me any argument about our procedures. I decided it was because he was from a reserve unit and was not active Air Force.

A Navy F-14 was one of the first to leave and gave the best show. His takeoff was short and he built up his speed after he cleaned up the gear and flaps. He then did a double victory roll and rapidly disappeared into the blue (gray).

The next day was a no movement on the ramp day until the SR-71 had been fueled and departed. Since the Blackbird was a national resource, it had a high priority for departure, not only from its home station but from the Pentagon as well. A support KC135Q had arrived to prepare it for departure. The exterior had been vacuumed twice. The bird was finally towed to the intersection and started its engines. As it departed in a steep climb, we all gave a sigh of relief.

Bret came home in the middle of the night. As soon as it was possible, they had been loaded into a bus and left Ellensburg. They went north across the Canadian border and then down to Spokane. He said it was scary in Ellensburg. Later in the week it began to rain. Wendy drove up through Idaho and into Spokane. She said it was difficult to leave the high living and terrific night life in Dayton, but thought they should come home!

As the civil engineer continued to clean the base, we had to determine what we could do for continued training of the crew force. It was decided, with a great amount of coordination, that we would send the crews and aircraft to bases in California with a supplement of maintenance and operations support for the time it required to return the base to fully operational status. The alert force would remain and continue to have a delay built into their timing until such time that the ash presented no further danger to operations.

The first BUF departed the cleaned runway and was a thing to behold. The runway and taxiways looked clean, but when those eight engines went to takeoff power, the cloud behind the aircraft was so immense it looked as if the runway had never been cleaned.

The base continued to clean. The ash had to be picked up. It could not be diluted and washed into the ground. It had an estimated weight of 8,000 tons per acre. Fairchild is a big base with a large amount of ramp and other paved surfaces. Each LC was given command of a group of people and an area to clean with fire hoses, brooms and shovels.

The ramp was literally swept clean from one end to the other. Everyone on the base was involved—military, civilian, and dependents. It was normal to see everyone wearing surgical masks to keep from breathing the ash. Two months after the eruption, the wing was back to a semblance of normalcy.

We continued to get reports of small eruptions and had prepared local plans to immediately put into force if one of the eruptions approached the magnitude of the one of 18 May.

The wing changes had been made in the senior staff and it was August. I had not been assigned an assistant, so I moved the DOT into that position as temporary fill-in. Sid had been at Castle when I was there. He was the operations officer I replaced in the 328th Bomb Squadron. He was recognized as one of the best BUF pilots around and very knowledgeable in all aspects of operations. He had also been the squadron commander of the 325th BS at Fairchild. He came across as a good old boy with a country air. Those who took that to mean he was not too sharp always had a big surprise.

My brother was visiting and I had taken a few days of leave. We were in Coeur d'Alene, Idaho, when we heard the on the car radio that Mount St. Helens had erupted again. The ash cloud was estimated at 20,000 to 30,000 feet.

I drove home and called the command post for the latest. The battle staff had just been formed. I changed into a flying suit and went to the meeting.

Permission had been asked of SAC to evacuate the aircraft, except for the alert force, and the battle staff was awaiting the answer. In the interim, operations and maintenance were preparing to fly out everything which was flyable. It was an excellent example of cooperation between the two. I relieved Sid, although he was doing exactly what I would have done under the circumstances. We received permission to deploy; in record time we had the force in the air. The ash cloud turned out to be a light dusting but we knew our plans were viable. It could have only been done as it was—a commitment by the ops and maintenance units to do what was required and get on with it.

The wing had an ACE program for the copilots. The idea was to build flying time and confidence. This in turn would help those who took the program seriously to upgrade quicker. They flew T-37s. The ACE commander was a captain from ATC which owned the airplanes. He was continually asking the senior staff to fly with the copilots to generate interest. It was not always easy to schedule a flight with all of the other commitments we had. When we did it was worth it.

I flew with the ACE commander on my first flight and then with one of the wing copilots on the rest of the flights. One thing I never got down was the wheel steering on the T-37. I did not taxi it enough to get the hang of it. My takeoffs tended to wander all over the runway until we were airborne.

I had one flight with one of the copilots, which was a formation flight with another T-37 for about half of the flight. He was an up-and-coming young lieutenant and he asked if I wanted the takeoff. Naturally, I said yes . . . before I remembered the nose wheel steering. I was on the wing of the other aircraft, and the way I steered during the takeoff probably made the other pilot wish he had not asked. Once airborne I tucked it in and flew a reasonable formation. We were in and out of the clouds and it was a little bumpy, but with great perseverance, and a lot of luck, I stayed in position. It was then I remembered that this was the first formation I had flown in a light aircraft since flying school 21 years before. I mentioned it to the other pilot and I am sure he watched me even closer, for, in reality, he was an instructor and in command. We finally broke off and went to Lewiston, Idaho, for some touch and go landings before heading back to Fairchild. I enjoyed it and I think the copilot did as well.

One of the duties of the CC, VC, and DCO was to take EWO briefings from the crew force and certify they could complete the mission. This was done on an annual basis or anytime the EWO mission changed significantly. I had done it from the other side of the table many times. I tried to put the crews at ease in the sense that I wanted them to tell me what they knew and not be afraid I was going to play a game of *gotcha* with them. It seemed I took my share of certifications as well as many of the commander's. He had to take a minimum and always seemed to meet the quota. After so many, they tended to drag on. The certification always took at least an hour and one half with a tanker crew and two to three hours with a bomber crew.

The crew would have the briefing room all set up with maps, EWO bags, data, and manuals spread out. Their squadron commander or operations officer and other staff members were present. The drill was that the crew would brief the mission, and upon completion, the staff would ask questions. The briefing itself gave a good indication whether they knew what they were doing, and most questions were reasonable. If the crew appeared to be weak, there were ways to handle additional training other than embarrassing them.

I always tried to ask a question which the crew member should know, or be able to find the answer to, but which came under the area briefed by another crew member. It was not to catch them but to see if they had really comprehended the whole mission rather than just their own area of responsibility. It was also a hangover from the B-47.

One day I had a certification of a tanker crew with a brand new copilot. Each crew member gave the part of the briefing they were responsible for, and then the AC turned it over to the staff for questions. Each staff member had a question and the crew fielded them expertly. The senior staff member was always the last—in this case, me.

The boomer always covered the survival aspects of the mission, but everyone was responsible for the information. It could become very personal if required to be put to use. The copilot had not been asked many questions, and I posed one to him which everyone who had been through survival school and studied the survival information in the EWO package should know. I asked if he had to bail out and landed in the Arctic, and by chance killed a seal or even a polar bear, what parts would he be sure not to eat. The answer I was looking for was the internal organs, the liver in particular.

He thought and thought and then came out with: "Claws!"

The room erupted. Everyone knew what I expected him to answer. When the laughter had ended, I continued to query him until he had the right answer and had the boomer explain why. The tension ended; as we broke up, the squadron commander mentioned the copilot's nickname would thereafter be "Claws."

As a member of the senior staff, I had to carry a "brick"—a hand-held radio about the size of a brick. It has been known to be thrown like a brick when the holder's temper exceeded the boiling point. I never threw one although I was often tempted. At that time, only the senior staff carried them. We had a spare used by the Supervisor of Flying. It was also used in place of one that was down for maintenance.

When the new Deputy Commander for Resources came in he insisted on having the spare, which was a newer model rather than the older one his predecessor had used; the older one became the spare. The only problem was he seldom was called. When he was, he never answered, leaving the operator to keep calling him over the radio to everyone else's amusement.

Every news agency in Spokane had a receiver tuned to brick frequency. Any important conversation had to be done on a hard phone, which they could not monitor.

When I got home at the end of the day, although some days never seemed to end, I was to report: "In quarters." Any calls I received would be put through to the special phone, the same system, in my quarters especially for that purpose. My family called it the "funny phone" for it did not have a dial. We had to brief visitors which one to use as it was next to the regular one. Don't misunderstand; I loved it.

I had one in the kitchen and had another installed by my bedside. Wendy had always had the real phone on her side of the bed. The first time I got a call in the middle of the night, I answered and was in the middle of solving a problem. She was talking to the other phone, trying to get a response from someone who was not there.

I quickly learned that if I did not report: "Mobile" and take the brick with me into the bathroom in the morning, I would get a call on the funny phone when I got into the shower.

The most embarrassing event with the brick was the time I was at a party at the division commander's house and did not discover until I got home that I had set it down with the others and forgotten it when I left. It was embarrassing to return and ask for it.

The brick had its good point as well. A call in the middle of an especially dull meeting gave me the chance to wake up or step out for a hard phone. Sometimes it was a good excuse to just leave. I always arranged with the command post to give me a call during any dining in or out just to get a break and so I did not have to stand in line in the restroom.

It seems as if everyone carries one now.

The brick could make one's day miserable. The call always found the carrier. When a problem arose, it invariably was first known with a transmission on the radio. It always happened in a crowd. The transmissions could be monitored by anyone who had a brick or FM radio tuned to the right frequency. The recipient would try to go to a hard phone to continue the conversation and pass on directions or answers. The other brick carriers seldom monitored transmissions other than their own as a matter of courtesy, unless they were involved. However, anyone within hearing distance usually listened in.

Daily standup was a meeting involving the senior staff, squadron commanders, and other key members of the staff to review the activity of the previous day and cover what was scheduled for the following day. Any deviations from the flying schedule had to be answered by the responsible party. This was the DCO and the DCM in most cases. It was not always a pleasant experience. The two colonels developed a thick skin quickly, for the activity in their areas of responsibility were laid out for the whole staff to see. One became a better dancer in order to survive. Honesty was also an asset, although it could sometimes be detrimental. The other agencies were seldom questioned on their activities unless it involved the whole group or someone had screwed up something which would affect us all.

One day in standup the DCM and I had gone through our usual routine when the DCR's brick went off. This in itself was an event. The room became quiet as a matter of courtesy—as well as not to transmit anything over the radio which did not need to be told to the world.

The caller was the dispatcher from the transportation squadron. He immediately told the RM that they had a problem. The RM frantically tried to interrupt and go to a hard phone but the dispatcher would not be denied. He went on to say that one of the buses transporting survival students from the field had rear-ended a pickup truck in downtown Spokane. He went on to say that a second bus had rear-ended the first bus. The RM was somewhat crestfallen; he finally had one of his problems broadcast for the whole staff and anyone tuned in to hear. It was a good day for the DCM and DCO and we could be seen smiling as the meeting ended.

The Dining Out is a formal military dinner which the wives may attend. Their presence usually keep it from becoming too raucous. The Dining In is only for the military members. I have never been to one which got out of hand . . . loud and rowdy, yes. The event was run by the president of the Mess, who most of the time is the commander. The newest second lieutenant is selected to run the timing of the Mess and give punishment to those whose behavior is less than acceptable throughout the dinner. Punishment is in the form of visits to the grog bowl where the offender must address the mess through the grog bowl. Reciting a set litany, he must partake of the contents of the grog bowl. If he makes an error, the sequence must be repeated.

The Dining Out which stands out to me was at Fairchild. The room was full of officers in their Mess dress uniforms displaying their medals and rank in great splendor. The number and rank of the medals were not always in direct proportion to the wearer's rank. The ladies were dressed in their finest and presented a fine complement to their escorts. The guest of honor was the local representative to the U.S. House of Representatives and the majority whip of the Democratic Party.

The commander stood and began introducing those at the head table. Finally, he came to our guest of honor and introduced him as the Honorable Thomas Foley, the majority *lip* of the Democratic Party. It became deadly quiet until Mr. Foley began to laugh; then the place exploded with laughter. The commander, realizing his mistake, then made the correction, too late to save the moment.

POSTFLIGHT

The flight had been a good one. Now the mundane items had to be completed. Turn in the personal equipment, the water jugs, the classified, and go to maintenance debriefing. There is something to be said for the camaraderie of aviators, whether crewed together for a long time or just one flight.

The flight was one I would never forget because it was the last time that I strapped a BUF to my butt and slipped the surly bonds of earth as one of the BUF fellows. At the time I did not realize how much I would miss it.

ADDITIONAL THOUGHTS

The following thoughts are those of the author alone and did not fit into any particular area of the above narrative.

GUNNERS

Gunners are a breed unto themselves. They are independent souls who rely on an organization to keep track of each other. Anyone who can fly for up to twenty-four hours in a small compartment, facing backwards with barely enough room to move about, has to have true grit. Imagine flying low-level and feeling as if you are the last man on a game of crack- the- whip. They certainly have earned my respect and admiration. Of course, in the later models, G and H, they rode up front with the rest of the crew and consequently lost some of their independence. As the only enlisted man on a BUF crew, the gunners often ended up doing some less than desirable details. Some crews overdo it and others try to keep it to a minimum, recognizing they were a crew in the real sense. As a copilot in the B-47, I did a lot of the same things and therefore I fit into the latter group. A BUF crew operates together and often do things together even though the crew is made up of five officers and one enlisted man. We were no different.

The gunner's primary duty was aircraft defense. I always liked the gunner in the rear, simply because he provided an extra set of eyes to the outside of the aircraft. I flew with one gunner who was extremely good at identifying traffic out in front of the aircraft before the pilots could see it. There are some advantages to having him up front as well. The gunner operates a set of guns in the tail of the aircraft. He works in close coordination with the EW in aircraft defense. He contributes in many ways to the crew's ability to complete the mission.

I attended gunnery school at Schilling AFB, Kansas, after academics at McConnell, since one of the duties of the copilot in a B-47 was to operate the remotely controlled 20MM guns in the tail. This school consisted of some academic training with the bulk of the time spent on the gunnery range.

The range was set up with a series of B-47 tail turrets set at an angle toward the sky. Each had an operational system, including radar, just like the aircraft. We learned to operate the systems, fire the guns, and of course, complete the postflight, which consisted of de-arming and safing the system. This was referred to as a strange field postflight. The idea being, after using the guns, if the aircraft landed at an airfield without the proper maintenance capability, the copilot could complete the procedure.

The highlight of the school was the actual operation of the systems. The targets were small radio controlled drones. They would launch, fly out several miles and make passes at the turrets as if they were enemy aircraft attacking. The students each got a turn; each turret was used in order. The objective was to track the drone, and following the procedures, attempt to shoot it down when it came within the range of the guns and lockon was attained with the radar. If the copilot-gunner was accurate (lucky), he got a hit. We swore that some of the guns were set in such a way to guarantee a miss. A hit on a drone set off a loud siren and everyone was required to evacuate the systems shacks until the drone hit the ground. When a drone was hit, it deployed a parachute, the engine usually quit, and it fell gently to the earth. The siren and evacuation was for those times this did not work and the drone went where it wanted. I was one of the lucky ones; I got a hit and a probable in my three chances with the system.

Each copilot who completed the course received a Certificate of Training which stated he had successfully completed an Air Force Gunnery School. Gunners in the BUF did not attend a school such as this, nor get an opportunity to actually shoot at something until it happened for real. I always reminded my gunners that I was more qualified than they were as a gunner and could prove it. I had actually graduated from a real gunnery school. You can imagine how this was received.

Gunners have a somewhat closed community. The Gunner's Association can be found around any base which had BUFs. The group is made up of past and present gunners, active and retired, and can pretty much locate any gunner.

The gunners have adopted the bulldog as their mascot. I have never been told why but surmise it is because of the toughness and tenacity of the animal. Regardless, it is appropriate. I was made an honorary member of the Ancient and Honorable Society of Bulldogs in 1977 when I was the commander of the 328th BS at Castle. Two years later at March AFB, my old gunner and the 15th AF gunner, who worked for me, declared it was not done properly, and reinitiated me into the Society. The two certificates have a special place on my "love me" wall.

I was fortunate as an aircraft commander. I did not have the numerous crew changes that seemed to occur just to make the ops officer or scheduler's jobs easier. Unlike most, I can count the number of gunners I have had without taking off my shoes. I was also lucky to have run a crew before the practice of taking new airmen into the career field. I have nothing against the new guys, and they have performed admirably, but in the "old days" the gunners offered some advantages that the new ones do not. The requirements to be a gunner were such that they were more mature, having several years of service, and in most cases a maintenance background in aircraft systems. This experience paid off, not only in the operation of the gunnery system but in the ability to provide immediate assistance to the RN when he had difficulty with the bomb-nav system. It was like having an armament and electronics specialist on the bird. The problem often occurred out of radio range of ground assistance and the gunner's assistance was doubly helpful. Many missions were completed as directed because of it.

I had two gunners who stood out, not only in their field as gunners, but even today when their names are mentioned among gunners, they are not unknown.

I think everyone in the SAC during my career has known Louis. If they did not know him personally, they knew someone who did, or at least had heard of him. Louis was my gunner for about two years including two ARC LIGHT tours. Louis arrived at Clinton-Sherman shortly before we were to deploy to SEA. He was initially assigned to another crew. My gunner had decided to get out of the Air Force and was due to redeploy about two months into the first ARC LIGHT tour. The crew Louis was on broke up about the same time and he was assigned to the infamous E-13.

We were lucky. We returned to Andersen, Joe left for the States, and Louis was on the next mission. We did not have to go through a period of substitutions. There were rumors as to why his crew had broken up, and I am sure he knew we had heard them, for he appeared somewhat cautious in his approach to the crew, especially me. In addition, it was obvious he was going to try his best to get off on the right foot. The first thing he did was get his ass chewed.

We first met as a crew at the pre-takeoff briefing where he introduced himself to me as my new gunner. I had been advised beforehand and welcomed him as I would any new member. We proceeded to the bus and on to the aircraft. The other crew was dropped off first, and when we arrived at our bird, I went over the forms with the crew and briefed the crew chief. The crew began to unload the bus while I reviewed the 781 in depth, not paying too much attention to what was going on around me. I heard the RN roar out: "Goddamnit, Gunner! What the hell do you think you are doing?" My first reaction was that Louis had performed something really gross, for the RN was pretty easy going. I looked up and Louis was holding the chapkit box. This box contained chapkits which supplemented our survival kit in case we had to bail out in hostile territory. They were not light. The box held six of them and was locked until we were ready to board the aircraft at which time the gunner took his and went back to the tail.

"Put that damn thing down!" The RN said. The gunner complied immediately, unsure of what he had done to incur the captain's wrath.

The lecture began, with Louis standing somewhere near attention; he was not sure of himself, what to do, or anything else at that point. "Gunner, on this crew you do not carry that damn thing by yourself. You wait for someone to help you or you ask, even if you have to ask the pilot." The RN then turned to me and asked: "Right, pilot?" I nodded, and the RN turned back to the gunner. "Come on. I'll help you." Whereupon, he grabbed one end and they took the box off. From that point on, he was ours. I had to be very careful about what I said I would like or desired if it was within his hearing. When I did not, I would either get it or an apology from Louis as to why he could not come through.

For example, we were not authorized the canvas sided combat boot everyone else in SEA was wearing. We had quick-don all-weather boot or the normal leather combat boot. The canvas boot was much more practical in SEA.

The crew had seen them and we all expressed a desire for them, but no one had an old pair to turn in to supply in order to get a new pair. The subject came up on the bus one morning after a night flight out of UT. Of course, Louis heard us. We went back to the trailers and to bed about 0600. At about 0830, I heard the door to the trailer open and several thumps hitting the floor. The door closed and I got up to see what the noise had been. I found five pairs of very used canvas combat boots. Louis came back about noon, got everyone's size, picked up the used boots and disappeared. He reappeared an hour later with a new set of boots for everyone on the crew. I am not sure how he arranged it, but gift horses and all that. I decided not to ask.

They were pretty good boots. That was 1968. After three tours in SEA, and many stateside flights, they are still in good shape. I keep them in the trunk of my car in the summer time.

Louis had a slight speech impediment, noticeable as a slight stutter in normal conversation. In his environment in the air, whether calling out traffic, making a station check, or directing a trailing aircraft into position for a bomb drop, it was not apparent at all.

Gunners were known to maintain a large library of what could be described as borderline pornographic. We were in Kadena; Wiles was flying with us as ABC. He was an L/C and had run a crew the year before with us. He was presently serving as a Charlie. He was welcome. I knew I would have no interference and only assistance with him on board. We had a few minutes before the briefing when he came in and sat down. He took one look at me and said if he had known he was flying with us he would have brought a sex book to read. Louis disappeared and got back just as the briefing started. The ABC was seated in the row in front of us. I noticed Louis lean forward, slide a pocket book over the ABC's shoulder and heard him say: "Here you are, sir. Enjoy the flight." He did.

Clinton-Sherman closed when we returned in 1969. I went to Hooterville and Louis went to March and continued to rotate to SEA. I met him again in 1971 at UT and then did not see him again until after the war. His aircraft had been shot down in December 1972 and he was taken prisoner. He was repatriated several months later.

I first met John when I got to Blytheville. He was in stan-eval and when I went there several months later he was the gunner on the crew I took. We had G models and he flew up front. He sat facing backward next to the electronic welfare officer. He was a complete professional and an integral part of one of the best crews I was ever on or commanded.

We went to ARC LIGHT in 1971. John came to me one day and asked if I would mind if one of the staff gunners at UT flew in his place. Like all staff personnel they picked an experienced crew to fly with. I said I would prefer to have him in the tail, because of the confidence the crew had in him, but they were welcome to fly up front. He then told me that was what he had told them and just wanted to confirm his own feelings. He added that when his crew flew he wanted to fly with them. Talk about making you feel like you are doing the job right.

John eventually went to Fairchild and I went to Castle. He then moved to the Air Force Personnel Center working in gunner's assignments and was a Chief Master Sergeant as well. Therefore, every gunner in SAC knew his name.

I saw a picture of Louis in a national magazine in late December 1972. He was a POW and being marched through a village with a bayonet at the back of his head. He later said his captors wanted his head down, but he kept it up as much as he could, for he knew his picture was being taken and he did not want to appear defeated. We had a long visit at Castle when he returned.

The last time I saw Louis was at March. I had just been promoted to O-6 and was to be reassigned to Fairchild. Louis, along with the 15th AF gunner, decided to reinitiate me into the Society of Bulldogs along with the wing commander. HT had impressed the gunners by flying a full mission in the tail of a D model.

Unbeknownst to me at the time, Clean Gene, the 15AF gunner, had called ahead to Fairchild and told the wing gunner to take care of me when I arrived.

Shortly after signing in at Fairchild, an invitation appeared on my desk inviting me to attend a dining out to be held by the base NCOS. I replied that I would attend with Wendy and was contacted several days later by a Senior Master Sergeant from the Security Police Squadron. He identified himself and informed me that he would be my escort for the event and would meet me at the door of the NCO club.

Wendy and I arrived at the NCO Club on the night of the event and were met by the wing gunner, a C/MSGT. He informed us he and his wife were our escorts and welcomed us to the base and evening event. When I explained I had been notified of another escort, I was told that he had orders from the 15thAF gunner to personally take care of me and he had made the change. He said gunners took care of each other even when some were only honorary gunners. The evening was a very pleasant one and started a strong working relationship and friendship.

Several months later the gunner's annual Christmas party was held. I received an invitation as well as the DCO and the bomb squadron commander. The active duty gunners as well as retired gunners in the area attended. After the meal, the squadron commander and the DCO were inducted into the Society of Bulldogs as honorary members and each spoke to the group when introduced. The DCO went on and on about the great honor it was to be included in such a group. An undertone could be heard from adjacent tables. Recognizing that I would be introduced next, and the group was restless, I quickly prepared my remarks.

"As an honorary bulldog, thank you for including Wendy and me. We have enjoyed it. I am proud to be included in an organization which includes two of my previous gunners, Louis and John." The place exploded with comments, and for the rest of the evening we swapped stories about the two until it was time to go.

Since I started this, the gunners have been dropped from crew duty. It is a shame, for there have been no prouder, and rightfully so, group of professionals. I am honored to be a gunner, real in the B-47 and honorary in the BUF.

MUSIC

The music was everywhere. Some good, most bad. It was always loud. Most of it was some form of rock-and-roll. In the room we had contemporary music from the local FM stations. It was on from the time we moved into the room until we left for the next base.

Each of the bases had some sort of music in the clubs. The bars had juke boxes. I recall hearing Johnny Cash more than anyone else. The dining room at Andersen had a large band from the Philippines which featured a very good vocalist. She sang everything, but was especially good with show tunes. The background provided a good break from the reasons we were there.

The O Club at UT in 1968 was not air-conditioned. It had a patio that served as a dining area, bar and entertainment theater. Most of us ate outside, weather permitting. At one corner of the patio there was a stage. The entertainment was mostly small bands which performed the current music just like it was recorded by the original artists. Most of the performers could not speak English, but had the lyrics down cold. Some were good and some were not. The favorite songs were *Jello Liver* (*Yellow River*), *Jello Bird* (*Yellow Bird*), and *Sixty-nine is all right on a Monday night*. The night in the song changed according to the night they were singing it. They were not as good as the Andersen group, but they were all we had.

The longest and most tiring part of the flights were the returns to Andersen, especially at night. The EW was the keeper of the tapes. When the recorder was not in use, he would put a tape of music on. It could be heard by selecting private interphone. It did not interfere with normal activities.

The copilot and EW had selected some music and had it recorded on five-inch tapes while at Kadena. We carried them on the long flights. Once level on the way home, lunches would go into the oven and everyone got comfortable.

There was little radio traffic. The only noise was the drone of the engines interrupted occasionally by the interphone oxygen checks or the radio. Those nights the music helped the most. A clear sky full of stars and the dulcet tones of Nancy Wilson were an incomparable combination. I never hear her without recalling those flights. I became a fan overnight, so to speak.

The first year our wing staff and maintenance unit was at Kadena. We had a representative at Andersen. The second year, our wing commander spent most of the time at Andersen. He had taken the wing between ARC LIGHT tours. The advance word was that he was a hard taskmaster. He demanded his staff work and work hard. I saw no problem with that. I had been a B-47 crewmember at Pease when he was the DCO and recalled that he wanted the truth and honest work. I never had a problem with him at Clinton-Sherman, nor did most of the crews. He did something no other commander I know of did. He held a Friday meeting at the club at Andersen for those available. It was a combination happy hour and staff meeting. He used it to keep us up-to-date on things, especially from home. I guess the best thing was that he showed an interest and did not isolate himself from the crews. He put together a beach party just before we returned and helped get as many crew as possible off duty so they could attend.

I do not know if he was the one responsible for the following, but always felt he was. The last few weeks, as the wing was rotating back through

Andersen and then deploying home, the band/orchestra at the O Club did something special for us. Each evening the music was dedicated to the crews from Clinton-Sherman. It was the complete score from *Oklahoma*. I have never heard it performed better, nor appreciated it more.

The most hilarious incident I can recall about music occurred at Minot AFB, North Dakota, much later than the general time frame of this narrative. The event was a special dinner at the O Club for the Commander in Chief, Strategic Air Command (CINCSAC). It was "By Invitation Only" and each colonel received an invitation. The dinner went well and the company was excellent. The entertainment for the evening was also very good. The Officers' Wives Chorus sang. The first song set me giggling until my shins were sore from the kicks from Wendy. It was *Send in the Clowns*. The line: "Don't bother, they're here," really did it.

SUPERSTITIONS AND HABITS

We all have them. Pilots are as bad or worse. If some action is taken and everything turns out right, especially if one's rear end was on the line or in jeopardy, there is a tendency to repeat everything that can be recalled that was done prior to the event—just in case. For example, we were told early in pilot training that it would be a good idea to carry a small survival kit which would fit into a flight suit pocket. A good strong knife was also recommended. We were issued a survival knife which we carried in a special pocket on the left leg of the flying suit. The knife was secured with a cord attached to it and a small grommet hole in the pocket flap. The knife's primary purpose was to cut parachute cord in case of a bailout. It had a curved blade just for that. The additional blade did not hold an edge too well, but was good for bruising butter. I purchased a very good two-bladed knife and put a small survival kit together. They both served me well for the rest of my flying career and I never flew without them. Other than replacing or adding to the kit, I never had the occasion to use either. I always thought it was because I had them. The fact that I always put them in the same pocket had nothing to do with it either.

As a SAC crew member, I flew at all times of the day, although it seemed as if it was mostly at night or a flight which required rising in the middle of the night. In order to get a little more sleep and not to disturb the family, I always put my flight suit with all of the items I carried in it together before I went to bed. Once I had my shower, I could put it on and leave. The fact that I spent a lot of time waiting for other members of the crew while they gathered their items also played a part. Once I began to pull alert duty, this was a habit.

I had one friend who always went to the rear truck of the B-47 and urinated on the tire prior to each flight.

I smoked a cigar during mission study prior to my first ARC LIGHT mission. The flight went well. Therefore, the cigar had to have been a good omen. It became an action to repeat so as not to disturb the gods of war and flight.

I had a very smooth refueling one night and had just happened to have put an orange in the window to keep it cold so I could enjoy it after A/R. The A/R was a snap. I have never tasted a better orange . . . other than those I carried from then on. I was not sure it was the presence of the orange or the anticipation of enjoying it which was important. I was not about to stop and find out.

Refueling can be frustrating, sometimes easy, sometimes difficult, but always requiring concentration. The secret is to relax and do as little as possible to screw it up. Easily said, not so easily done, when the weather was not cooperating, the sky was dark, and an engine was shut down. The first time this happened to me for some reason the song *The Girl from Ipenema* kept running through my mind. I got the off-load with no disconnects and we pressed on. Guess what I sang in my mind (and some-times out loud if the situation demanded) on every refueling from then on?

THE BACKBONE

It has always been said and probably always will be, that the air crews (some argue pilots), get all of the glory while the maintenance crews get all of the work. This is true to a great extent, depending upon who's talking. It is easier to picture the crew defying the laws of gravity and challenging the wild blue yonder than it is the technician challeng-ing the idiosyncrasies of a jet engine or radar system under the pressure of weather, crew impatience, senior NCOs, scheduled takeoff times, and the mission itself. If he is successful in repairing the problem, he gets little credit. If not, he gets a lot of blame.

The crew expects to get a perfect aircraft. They seldom do, but not because the crew chief or line chief or MA desires it that way. If the aircraft is in good shape, the crew chief has less to do and he is like the crews in that he appreciates it. He is not lazy, but practical, for he knows it will not last. The next time he may spend the night before nursing his charge back to health.

The crews get to know the crew chiefs as well as the crew chiefs get to know the crews. Some receive more respect for some than others. There are a few of each who make it hard for the rest.

There are some pilots who will take the aircraft if the engines start and others who will not take it if the ashtrays are full. There are crew chiefs who pride themselves on presenting a clean and flyable bird while a few seem to be affronted if anything is questioned. Fortunately, there are only a few of the latter.

The crew arrives at the aircraft, preflights, flies the mission, lands and walks away. The maintenance crew shows up several hours prior to prepare the bird, sweat out the preflight and takeoff, and then wait until it returns to do the postflight maintenance, which could literally take all night. I have often wondered what the incentive was; they worked for little pay, less rec-ognition, and a ration of crap from everyone. Occasionally, if the problem warranted it, the technician would be allowed to go with the crew for the flight. I think they enjoyed it. They usually had little to do except hand out a cup of coffee and observe the equipment they had worked on to see if it was repaired or restored to its previous condition.

It is a very simple formula. If the birds are kept up, the crews fly and are happy, and maintenance has an easier workload. If they are not kept up, everyone works harder, especially the ground troops, who will lose a lot of sleep. The aircrews on the other hand have a lot more at risk.

Here's a belated thanks to a lot of guys who helped keep me alive.

MISCELLANEOUS

I remember WWII. I was almost six years old when someone burst into church on December 7, 1941, telling us the Japanese had bombed Pearl Harbor. I did not really know what that meant except it was not good. The years that followed brought the war to us and I began to understand to a greater degree. It was more personal. At one time I had nine uncles in the military. I do not know what the particular influence was, but flying always appealed to me. Maybe it was the way aviators were portrayed. Maybe it was Doolittle's raid on Tokyo. Or it might have been something more mundane such as *Terry and the Pirates* and *The Air Adventures of Jimmy Allen* on the radio and in the comics. Regardless of the reasons, I eventually was able to fulfill at least part of the dreams of childhood.

Like most kids of that time, one of my heroes was Jimmy Doolittle. His raid on Tokyo made him even more of a hero. I was at 15th AF when a message came across my desk to the effect that the Air Force Association's annual conference was to be held in Los Angeles. The attendance of as many local Air Force personnel as possible was requested. Anyone interested could sign up and would be excused from duty to attend. The invitation included a $35.00 a person buffet, with no cost to the attendee. The only catch was that transportation had to be arranged by the attendee. It was a 60-mile trip. I asked my boss if I could attend and he approved.

The day was filled with briefings from the CINCs of the major commands, Defense Department officials, and other interested aviation parties. I met old friends and generally had a good time. I waited and attended the buffet in the evening and it was worth the wait. The food was good and the company excellent. My evening was made when a short, bald gentleman stepped into the line beside me and began a conversation. Here I was, someone who had achieved nothing of any great importance, talking to one of my childhood heroes, and one of aviation's greatest: General Jimmy Doolittle. I could not have asked for a better evening. I hope I sounded halfway intelligent to him.

Air Force headgear has always been questionable. Everyone longed to wear something like a 50 mission crush, but the rules had changed.

While some commands allowed no hats on the flightline, SAC insisted one be worn. In most B-47 units, the overseas cap (military types have a more descriptive name for it) was the hat of choice. This was the most practical; it could be folded and put in a flight suit pocket. The BUF units wore a simulated leather ball cap, in the primary squadron color. Even among crew members there was an ongoing disagreement as to which should be worn. It was not until the SAC units began to go to SEA that the normal baseball cap was worn.

The baseball cap gave identity to individuals as well as units. It had to be in the unit color. We were given some do's and don'ts. One of the do's was to remove all patches and means of identification from our flying suits except for name, rank and wings. This made it more difficult to identify the unit to which we were assigned. While the original intent was to deny any potential enemy the information, it also made it difficult for those of us involved. Thus, the baseball caps were in squadron colors and sometimes identified the unit. They would not be with us if we had to bail out.

Those who chose to wear the baseball cap usually bought them in Okinawa. The local embroidery shops were kept busy making patches, words and other displays on them. The only rule was that it must be the squadron color with rank displayed, and not have obscene displays. There was the average run-of-the-mill cap and then there were those which showed some ingenuity and a sense of humor.

For example, a gunner had one with the words 'no step' on the crown. "No step" being a common phrase found all over the aircraft to designate areas where one was not supposed to step.

One whole crew had their rank on the front and the name "Yossarian" on the back after the main character in the book *Catch 22*. Most of the hats had innovative ideas and some were downright funny. Some bordered on the obscene and some were just raunchy. All in all, they provided an insight into the individual, and the crew in many cases.

My first one was dark blue with captain bars in the front and three feathers on the back to support the idea everyone had that I was of American Indian extraction. BUF DRIVER was written under the feathers. Without my asking, the rest of the crew had the feathers added to theirs as well.

I had another made the second tour and I still have it. It is also dark blue with a major's leaf on the front. On one side is a patch with the cartoon character Major Hoople from *Our Boarding House*. I had a lot of the patches made since I had picked up the nickname Major Hoople. On the left is a diving bird of prey with a bomb in its talons. It is from the patch of the 6th BS. The words Flying Dutchman are on the back. It has had two tours and still looks good.

My flying helmet, on the other hand, has always been decorated. The helmet itself had to remain solid white. The visor cover could have some decoration. I have always been taken for an Indian, because my name sounds like something they think is Indian. There may be some Indian blood somewhere. If so, fine. I consider myself an American with no hyphen. Anyway, I have always played the game and had my visor cover painted like a war bonnet. I have had a few disagreements with over-zealous personal equipment people until they realized I would always repaint it when they cleaned it off.

THOUGHTS ON THINGS

There are many things in the Air Force and military life which irritate the members. Some of them have been present for as long as there has been a military. Others are personal . . . and some are personnel. The Air Force has some which are inherent in the mission. Additionally, as one rises in position and rank, he may become the irritant to others. Sometimes this is necessary and sometimes it is not. The following things have at times irritated me, and I am sure others have had similar experiences.

The portrayal of the military. Why is it in the movies and TV the actors always wear their hats indoors and seldom outside? It is not done that way in the real world. Also, they always have someone saying: "That is an order!" In twenty-eight years I never used it or heard anyone express it that way. Military people are not stupid. If the ranking man directs some action, *it is an order.* Only idiots have to tell the recipients.

MAINTENANCE

I may have given the impression that I do not like or respect the maintenance side of the house. That is absolutely not true. It is true that I have had occasional disagreements with them. One must remember that these revelations are not the norm. Most of the flights have no difficulty, but who wants to hear about them? These are just the daily incidents of give-and-take between ops and maintenance, both intent on completing the mission.

I never thought they intentionally tried to give me an aircraft that was not safe. Sometimes the aircraft had problems that I was not willing to deal with or had questions about. Since I was the one who was flying it, I insisted upon the best I could get. Any honest pilot will tell you there are some days he would take anything with wings and the right number of engines. There are other days when he would not.

All one has to do is watch the activity of the maintenance people, from the 0-6 to the newest airman when an exercise or the real thing is occurring. Every one of them knows the mission is to get the birds in shape and eventually in the air. They do it and they do it well. We could not ever have done our job without them. They get little glory and a lot of grief, but they make it happen. If you want to see dedication, go to the flightline at Minot in the middle of the night in January when an aircraft has to be ready to fly in a short time. Very seldom is a launch not met, and the maintenance crew quietly go on to the next one.

FOOD

The military has a word for food service. Whether chow hall or O Club, it is referred to as a *mess*. Sometimes, it is an accurate description. The troops must be fed. The general rule is that a good officer ensures that his men are fed before himself. Some of the mess halls and O Clubs I have eaten in make this a good rule of thumb for anyone intent upon survival. The food is prepared to the average of many different palates, influenced by the chef. The food in the mess hall is wholesome, but like any food it can become tiresome, especially when the same menu is served on the same day of each week, week after week. This is not to say the food service people are not trying. The situation, the food available, the training and supervision all make a big difference. Also, what the NCOIC and OIC are willing to accept are what they will receive.

The mess at Webb AFB, Texas, during my ROTC summer camp was my first chance to try military food service. The activities which we engaged in required a high daily caloric intake. The food was good, wholesome and plentiful. Not fancy, good. I often sat at a table with a gentleman from the northeast who continually berated the quality and selection as nowhere near what he was accustomed to in his civilian job. He expounded on this three times a day, seven days a week, while shoveling in quantities that surpassed what the rest of us could eat.

Flying at high altitudes creates many problems in a physical sense. Obviously, above 12,000 feet one needs to have oxygen supplied to prevent the loss of consciousness. At the time I started flying, pressurization was available and made the atmosphere in the cockpit much more livable. It also reduced the altitude of the cockpit to much less than that of the actual aircraft altitude. This enabled the crew to perform without being on oxygen at all times. Just to have it available within reach was enough. This depended to some extent upon the aircraft. For example, the B-47 crew had to wear helmets at all times, and be on oxygen unless cleared off by the pilot, even though the bird was pressurized. Naturally, we all adhered to that rule, at all times, especially during check rides.

The ingestion of certain food could also create difficulties. At preflight training at Lackland in 1958, and through flight training, we were taught what to eat to preclude excessive gas buildup in our systems at high altitude. The wives were also indoctrinated into the preparation of foods which did not produce gas. Anyone who has ever been at altitude with little or no pressurization can vouch for the expansion of even small amounts of gas. It gets uncomfortable real quick. However, the mess halls, and the alert shack in particular, either did not have the same training, or could not comply; the food often produced gas in prodigious amounts at sea level. Of course, they operated on the assumption that we would not be flying, and thank heavens we never had to. Flight lunches sometimes provided enough gaseous foods that the requirement of a tanker was often questioned!

Survival rations which were in our survival kits in the aircraft were good under some conditions—survival conditions. They were high in calories and vitamins and designed for use in conditions requiring quick energy to sustain strength. I would not recommend them as a constant diet. Improvements have been made since I ate them in survival school, but there is still room for improvement.

One of the best meals the mess halls serve is the holiday dinner. Christmas and Thanksgiving they go all out. They serve everything, literally from soup to nuts. They never seem to get the recognition they deserve for the magnificent effort they make. Families are welcome and the sponsor pays the normal cost and a surcharge for himself and each family member. It was always well worth the minimal cost. It was impossible to serve the same at home for the cost. The alert facilities would open the alert shack for the families on those days as well. The crewmember only had to give the names and escort them as long as they were present. The normal alert routine would be broken with the shouts of children and the movement of women through the halls. It must be remembered, there were no women flight crew members in my crew days. Usually, about the time the football games were ready to start, the hints would begin to the families that they should think about leaving.

The best alert food I ever had consistently was at Clinton-Sherman. The whole wing staff seemed to come out, and the line was always long on the day they served Mexican food. My EW went to Houston about every six weeks and would take orders for seafood from anyone who wanted it. The only seafood in the Burns Flat area was prairie oysters. He made a deal with the alert shack chef and would bring him oysters, which the chef would turn into oyster stew, a very rare item in mess halls. I spent two years at Pease and I never saw it served. He would ration it so that it lasted for a changeover and most of the crews could enjoy it.

Greenham Common in the UK was also good. We only had two meals, late breakfast and early dinner. This was brought about due to the reduction in per diem by Secretary of Defense McNamara. The new per diem did not cover the cost of three meals. It almost covered the two. Nothing being too good for the troops, that was usually what they got. The mess hall supervisor was an Irishman and he could not bear to see someone not eat what he thought was enough. He always insisted that my AC take more than he could eat. No amount of arguing by Mac could change his mind. Mac was about five foot five and weighed about 130. He never had a big appetite.

The worst alert food was at Columbus AFB. Air Training Command owned the base, and we were on satellite alert from Blytheville. The mess hall did not have too many customers, for there were not too many available. The staple served at every meal but breakfast was black-eyed peas. The staff did not seem too enthusiastic. No amount of complaints to the staff made any difference, maybe because they did not have to eat there.

In the old days, the mess halls in the alert facilities were left open and the crews would sit at the tables and discuss everything while drinking untold amounts of coffee. A lot was learned at those tables, for the subject always turned to flying. We still had some people who had flown in WWII and Korea. That changed about the time I left the crew force. I have always felt that hangar flying done at those times in the mess halls was some of the best. The atmosphere was different from the classroom or the instructor-student relationship.

One Saturday morning at Little Rock, we were sitting around drinking coffee, waiting to go to the morning briefing. There had been no paper napkins for the past two days. We had been on alert two days and no amount of requests had helped. Unannounced, the division commander happened to come in and sit down with us. As he set his coffee cup down, he spilled some on the table. Someone said: "Have a napkin, General." When he did not see any, he asked why and was told the problem. We had to go to the briefing, but when we came out fifteen minutes later, he was standing in the hallway with a big grin. He told us we now had napkins and the base commander had not liked being wakened on Saturday morning to deliver them. He was one of the good guys in many ways.

At Neuasseur the Reflex crews ate most of their meals in the O Club. It was so-so. The best meals were those you could wash down with iced tea or the local wine. Of course, drinking while on alert duty was forbidden. The best part of the meal was the bread. It was always fresh, crusty, and delicious.

One evening we arrived for dinner. The special was spaghetti. We all ordered it; it went well with the bread. The waiter asked us if we were sure and we asked why. He told us the chef's recipe called for a slight amount of cinnamon, and he might have overdone it a little bit. We had never heard of cinnamon in spaghetti, but were assured it was a normal ingredient. While we awaited our meal, we watched the stray cats walk the ledge around the ceiling of the dining room looking for rats. Real atmosphere. The spaghetti arrived and sure enough the chef had overdone the cinnamon. It tasted a lot like pumpkin pie. At least the bread was fresh and good.

In SEA, all beef was sold as Kobi beef . . . at least that was what it was called. I have a strange feeling that much of it in Thailand was water buffalo someone named Kobi before it met the butcher.

The O Club at UT used local girls as waitresses. It was not at all uncommon for the language difference to get in the way. There is a famous story about blueberry pie. That is all I will say about it. Those who have been to SEA know it.

We stopped for lunch one day shortly after arriving on our first trip. One of the group ordered a hamburger and was told: "No hab hamburger!" He pointed to a nearby diner who had a cheeseburger and again asked for a hamburger. He was emphatically told: "No hab hamburger, hab cheese-burger!" He did not press the issue, and you can guess what he ordered.

INFLIGHT FOOD

Flight lunches all depend upon the ability, desire and pride of the inflight kitchen. Some are good; some are not so good. All lunches are pre-pared, and the time by which it should be consumed was noted on the box. This is not always consistent with mission requirements. For example, the expiration time is usually about two hours after pickup. The aircraft which I flew had not even gotten off of the ground in most instances. I always thought it was an out for food service if someone got sick.

The lunches were varied and all cost the same amount. Things have changed since I pulled crew duty. The best box lunch was made at Little Rock. It contained about eight ounces of bite size pieces of steak. It also included a can of fruit juice, two half pints of milk, an apple, sometimes some carrot and celery sticks, and some kind of dessert or candy bar. In the early days it also included a pack of four cigarettes.

The kitchen had menus which included sandwiches of all kinds, fried chicken, and cans of soup which could be heated. Additionally, there were frozen dinners that were much better than the commercial ones. These were available only on aircraft such as the BUF, which had an oven avail-able for heating. A six-ounce steak with mashed potatoes, corn, and a des-sert always provided a lift, which a cold box lunch could not.

Twenty-four-hour Chrome Dome airborne alert sorties always provided an interesting meal selection. The crew would meet at the alert shack for a steak and eggs meal, or whatever else we wanted. The day before, each crewmember had ordered what he wanted for food on the flight. I usually had a box lunch and a frozen dinner to enjoy in the middle of the night somewhere over the frozen north. Some crews took the makings for bacon, ham, and eggs for breakfast. I always thought this was too messy for the in-side of the aircraft.

The inflight kitchen at Blytheville was not too good. The crews would complain but little was ever done. The senior staff said they always had good meals. I always thought this was because the kitchen would get a flight schedule, and in most cases see that the colonels and commanders were flying, and provide food accordingly.

Additionally, most gunners told the kitchen the commanders were flying when they called in the lunch orders. I told my gunner not to let them know. I felt if they got what we ate on a normal basis some changes might be made. I never could tell the difference, however.

The flight lunches were so bad out of Andersen most of the crews went to the commissary and bought TV dinners to eat on the missions. Fruit was also in big demand.

COFFEE

Air Force coffee is probably like all military coffee . . . strong enough to stand on its own, do an about face, and march away. I know. I have drunk my share. The crews in my day would get a jug of coffee and a jug of water from the inflight kitchen when they picked up the lunches. It was a big surprise when I flew with a crew years later; they carried Koolaid. No coffee. I always thought coffee was a mandatory item.

There was no way of knowing when the coffee had been brewed. The first cup was usually drunk several hours after pickup. The jugs in the B-47 were very good, and the coffee would stay hot for hours, sometimes for the whole flight. The jugs in the BUF were not as good, and the coffee would have to be reheated in the hot cup. It was always strong and bitter. It did do the job; it woke one up.

While on ARC LIGHT, my RN modified an electrical cord and we could use the hot cup to heat things in the room. I took this even further. I modified the cord to an electric coffeepot. I bought coffee in cans which had premeasured packages. At 12,000 feet, I would clear the gunner forward (G model), he would plug in the coffee pot, and by level off we had fresh hot coffee. The smell alone was enough to lift the spirits. He would brew a fresh pot after low-level. The crew morale seemed to improve after we began brewing our own.

CHAPLAINS

I found the chaplains were pretty good guys, for the most part. Regardless of denomination, they were interested in the welfare of troops. The good ones were seen and heard but not obtrusive. Their duties involved getting out with the troops in the work areas no matter where. Some even flew with us. A few were never seen.

The chaplain visits to the work areas were required to be noted. The signoff of this seemed to be the only reason some came around. They always made sure it was noted and spent minimum time. The good guys were there often enough not to worry if they were filling all the squares.

The biggest surprise I ever had with a chaplain was at Andersen. The crews would receive the mission briefing and the chaplain was required to be present for any needs of the crews prior to going off to war. He also offered a prayer at the end of the briefing. One stood out among the rest. He always prefaced the prayer with a joke . . . a dirty joke. I mean dirty. The first time I heard him I could not believe it. It became like everything else, something to be endured.

The most impressive chaplain I have met was the 15th AF chaplain. He was a Roman Catholic. He was a pleasure to be around and to listen to; he was intelligent and witty. He knew where he fit in the organization and he fit very well. His blessings over meals and benedictions were works of art. While asking blessing on the food and people, he would weave in other items which were amusing but appropriate, but not expected in the prayer. He was respected more than any other chaplain I ever met.

Supply

The supply system often was less than desired, but only in items which were required as soon as possible. It was not always responsive in the manner we wished. With the advent of computers the system changed, not always for the better. At preflight in 1958 we were issued a whole complement of flying equipment. When we broke something or wore it out, we could take it to the Individual Equipment, the flyer's supply store, and trade it for a new one. It worked most of the time and served the troops well. However, sometimes the supply people acted as if the equipment belonged to them and were reluctant to part with it. This was usually taken care of by asking to see the supervisor or asking the individual to call the squadron commander and explain why the item was denied.

The one item which seemed the most difficult to keep in stock was the watch issued to flying personnel. Generally, they were very good wrist watches and envied by others not authorized the equipment. They always seemed to be on back order. I went into supply one day and asked for a replacement watch. The person behind the counter finally admitted he had one left. He traded it to me for my broken one. The AC asked to have his replaced and was told there were no others in stock and no date when there would be any available. Dain pointed to the watch the airman was wearing (Air Force issue for flying personnel) and told him it would be satisfactory. Without any comment the airman removed it and made the trade.

Several months prior to leaving Pease, I had finally gotten a helmet which fit perfectly. It was comfortable and had replaced a large one with a lot of padding. I turned it in at Clinton-Sherman and never saw it again. When I went to get it to take to Castle, I was told I had not turned one in. I had used it several times at Clinton-Sherman. I found my card in the file and then, while the supply man complained, went through his cabinets. I did not find my helmet but found the bag with my name on it. Service improved quickly.

Since I had not been to Castle and was not on a crew, I had not been issued any cold weather gear. When I returned from Castle, I did not get it all. Most of the items were on back order, or so I was told.

Once a year, each crew member is required to certify on his personal equipment form that he has the listed items. When my turn came, I went down and was given the form for my signature. I mentioned that I did not have certain items and had never been issued them. I was told they had been issued. I repeated they had not. The sergeant then pointed to the form and told me I had initialed for them.

I asked if he wanted to get the OIC or if he wanted me to. When he asked why, I explained that I had not initialed the forms, and that if I had, I would have used my initials, not the ones on the form. Without another word, I was issued the items and the forms were corrected. I can only guess someone decided to make up a shortfall, or prepare for an inspection and was not too careful or smart.

PROMOTIONS

Promotions are necessary. They bring higher pay. If you are not promoted, you do not stay in the Air Force. Generally, if you could make the rank of major and did not screw up too badly, you would be able to stay for 20 years and retire. Naturally, everyone wanted to advance as high and as quickly as possible. Promotions are never a sure thing. Some people you expect to be promoted are not and some who you think would never be, are. In a way, it is a crapshoot. However, there is something to the advice to do the job you have as well as you can and things will work out.

Promotion to 1st lieutenant is automatic unless one really steps on it. Mine came at the 18 month active duty point. At the time, those silver bars looked so much better than the gold. It was possible to rub the gold bars until they looked silver and many of us did. I signed into Little Rock the first day of my 19th month of active duty. I did not have any orders to indicate it and had to wait until they were cut to change the insignia.

The next step is to captain. Until 1962, a board was held and the promotion point was anywhere from six to eight years. My nav at the time was promoted this way at almost the nine- year mark in 1961. The next year the rules were changed and it became automatic at four and one half years unless one had really screwed up. I was on alert at Zaragoza, Spain, during the Cuban Crisis when I pinned on the railroad tracks. They sure looked better than the single silver bar.

Promotion to major was next. I was in the air over SEA when the list was released. I had not expected to make it, for I had been a copilot forever. I did not turn it down either. Those gold leaves looked so good against the blue uniform. I might even make it to 20 years and be able to retire, at least as a major. This time Wendy knew it before I did. I was not at home for the second time.

In 1974, I was at Castle and again did not expect to be promoted. At every gathering of those of us who were eligible, I heard stories of OERs at the highest rating for the last x number of years. I knew mine were not in that category. The more I listened to others, the more I resigned myself to a passover.

The day the list came out I was on TDY at Carswell AFB, working on a television tape for the new system to be installed in the G and H BUFs. The individual who told those of us interested, said it would be released the next day, but if we knew the wing commander, he might tell us that night. I knew him, but did not feel confident enough to pursue the matter. I went back to my motel room at the end of the day and kept putting off calling home to tell Wendy where I was staying. I finally called about 2200 and we talked for a few minutes until she asked if I had heard anything. I said no and she told me I had made the cut. Apparently, my squadron commander had called Carswell billeting and asked for me and was told I had checked out. They did not tell him I had been moved downtown, so he assumed I was on the way home. This was the second time Wendy knew before I did.

The chance for promotion to colonel was about 50% of those eligible. Since I had held several positions which were generally acknowledged to be promotable positions, I thought I had a little better chance. The board met and the list was to be released momentarily. I was at the BX at March when my boss, the DOT, came up to me and held out his hand. I put mine out and then looked at what he had put in it. It was a set of eagles. I asked if he was telling me something. He said he was, and that he had to twist the arm of the DP to get him to tell him. He said that one of the pilots who worked for us had learned from a friend at the Pentagon and he wanted to tell me before the pilot had a chance.

That evening, when I walked into the house, I intentionally had my hands full and asked Wendy to get something out of my jacket pocket. She removed the eagles; it took a minute or two for the significance to dawn on her. At least I knew before she did this time. I got a call later that evening to report to the 15th AF Commander the next morning at 0730. It turned out to be a very rainy morning. He gave us the real word and congratulated us.

I went into my office and met the gang I worked with. I was told they figured out that the list had been released and that I was on it, or we had gone to war. When I asked how they arrived at that, I was told they had seen the TR-3 in the parking lot and they knew I did not drive it in rain unless something important had happened.

PAY

There is a belief among many civilians that the military member does not pay taxes. I don't know where this idea originated, but I can assure you it is false—or the government took a large amount out of my paychecks for something of the same name.

One of the continual gripes we flyers heard from groundpounders was on the subject of flight pay. They never seemed to realize that was for flying. Flying is recognized as a somewhat dangerous activity, especially when combat is added. Just ask any life insurance agent. In SEA we flying officers received combat pay ($55 a month) and a tax break ($500 a month), as I recall. The enlisted men got the combat pay and paid no tax on their base pay. Everyone in the theater of operations received these breaks, not just the flyers. The combat pay was earned by some more than others.

I overheard a conversation between a flyer and a missile type about the pay and the missile man was griping about the fact that flyers were paid these in addition to base pay, housing allowance and subsistence, and the missile combat crews were not. The flyer replied that he did not recall seeing any Minuteman Missiles while he was in SEA, or the crews in the air in the states. There was no reply.

HEADQUARTERS

There will always be differences between those in the field and those in headquarters. Most pilots do not like to fly desks. All want the opportunity to change things they feel need changed. Few get the chance; fewer get it right. Directions from above are seldom given with reasons or background that would make them easier to accept and which the field would accomplish with less frustration.

Nothing is ever done with a long suspense. It must be done immediately. The results are often reflective of this. In 1979 the retention rate of pilots was poor, especially among tanker pilots. Many were joining the National Guard and the airlines—in many cases both. I was at 15th AF at the time and the word came from SAC HQ to query the units and find what the crews thought about everything and what changes they would recommend. The suspense date was 0800 Monday morning Omaha time. The message hit us on Friday.

The units responded well on such a short suspense. The number one item was the request for information which required the units to work over the weekend. They did not have the time to obtain information and scrub it before submitting it to us where it would have to be compiled and then sent forward. To my knowledge, this has not changed, at least not before I retired.

The irritants were not new and had been brought up many times before. Fewer additional duties was number two. It seems each time some one up the line has a new idea or passes a law it requires data to be gathered and records kept. This takes time and a new duty is created, without an increase in manning. Most of these had little to do with the primary or secondary duties of crew members.

I often wondered if anyone ever read the final reports. Things never changed on the items from the crews and most of them required little or no cost. Instead, ideas such as a snappy new uniform to wear while on alert were suggested from HQ. Either the HQ people had never been on alert or had forgotten.

WAR STORIES

A group of fliers together can be considered a critical mass. A string of war stories you wouldn't believe begin to emerge. Sometimes one is not expected to believe them, at least in their entirety. This is not to indicate they are lies, but like fish stories, they tend to grow. It seems as the passage of time increases, the ratio of fact to fiction decreases. Do not misunderstand, it is not intentional lying, but one must retain the interest of the listener and we have all heard the old adage that flying is hours and hours of boredom, interrupted occasionally with moments of sheer terror. The interesting thing is that most have little direct reference to the execution of the war but are more pleasant memories of the periphery of the war that time has not erased. The stories get embellished with each telling and sometimes have little resemblance to what had actually happened. It is always interesting to hear a story in which you were a participant, told by someone else. You get another viewpoint, sometimes from someone who was not even present. The following are a short collection of some of those I have heard and cannot substantiate through personal observance, but are worth repeating.

My first flight instructor, Glenn Sheets, attempted to teach me to fly in 1957. He talked little about his background and we asked even less. He was much older, wiser, and definitely more experienced. He told us of his younger days when he was flying Condors in South America. He worked for a company which flew gold from the mines to the cities. His praise for the Condor was high, until it lost an engine. If a full load was carried, it could not maintain altitude, much less stable flight. Naturally, on one trip, as they were returning with a full load of bullion, an engine failed. The jungle lay below and was not hospitable to emergency landings. The decision was made to jettison the cargo in order to save themselves and the aircraft. With much reluctance, they began to toss the cargo overboard. This action did indeed save the crew and the aircraft. They reported their actions and the general location where they had unloaded the gold. The company sent a search party, which included Indians of the region. They returned with the complete cargo. Think about it, and the precision navigation of the time.

An experienced crew run by an AC, for want of a better name, Gross Grogan, went on a shopping spree in Thailand. You could buy just about everything there, some legal, some not. However, most goods purchased were gems, clothes, brassware, carvings, temple rubbings, etc. What inspired this crew is difficult to discern, a liquid one is possible. It could have been close association with the Clinton-Sherman snake crew, or just a wild hair in a body orifice. Who knows? Who cares?

Whatever the motivation, the end result was the purchase of a real live monkey. He became a member of the crew. It was rumored he could pass for and complete the duties of some of the members as well or better than they could, especially peeling bananas. Crew members other than pilots appreciate that. Supposedly, the plan was to eventually have a flying suit made to fit, log enough flights, and enter him for an air medal. I might say, for those who doubt, with little to do but fly, the mind creates distractions which are often put into words and then into action. It is for the moment. This appears to be such a case.

The crew, so the story goes, prepared their new member for his first flight, which was to be about three and one half hours long. This proved to be about three and one half hours too long. The crew chief was no longer their friend when the flight ended. It seems from the time the engines were started, until they were shutdown, the noise, vibration and everything else was in opposition to the monkey's digestive tract which went into action, and he lost control of his anal sphincter. This obviously was too sensitive an issue to try to explain as a reason for abort, so the crew persevered and the monkey shit . . . for three and one half hours. Upon landing the crew initiated a grounding ceremony for the monkey.

Many stories have evolved concerning extra people on board the aircraft. Notice, I do not refer to passengers. The BUF does not carry passengers as a rule, although there are provisions to do so if absolutely necessary. Anyone flying on a normal mission, training or combat, must be qualified to do so. This consists of training in the altitude chamber, emergency procedures, and general operation of the position requirements for that which they will be flying.

The story, as it was related, involved a crew that took off out of Andersen on a bright and sunny day. Their departure was normal. At level off, the crew went about their station checks. The copilot was taking a fuel reading and comparing it to his programmed fuel curve. He completed the check, advised the pilot of the fuel status and accepted control of the aircraft, while the pilot completed his station check. The copilot gazed about the sky and saw a slight movement around the windscreen. Further investigation revealed two bright, beady eyes, and what appeared to be a grin on the face of a large rat between the instrument panel and windscreen. The sudden face-to-face confrontation left him in a mild state of shock, nearly requiring an airstart to get his heart pumping normally. When he had recovered sufficiently to speak, he advised the pilot that there was a stowaway on board and pointed to the rat. The rat immediately reacted by disappearing behind the instrument cowl, but not before the pilot got a glimpse of it.

The pilot, being a resourceful and intelligent fellow with lightning reflexes, punched the interphone and advised the crew, except the gunner who was sealed into his own compartment in the tail, of the situation and ordered them to go to 100% oxygen and check in. The crew complied; the copilot depressurized the aircraft, the idea being that lack of oxygen would eventually cause the rat's demise. The cabin pressure changed from about 7,000 feet to 30,000 feet above sea level. It also began to cool off in the cabin. In theory, there is not enough oxygen to sustain life at this altitude. So the crew thought. After a reasonable period of time (until the EW started to complain) they repressurized and went about their business, convinced they had caused a combat casualty.

Shortly thereafter, the rat returned to its perch. The grin was not evident. The pilot ordered the crew back on oxygen and the aircraft was depressurized again for a longer time. The rat returned. The aircraft was depressurized. The rat returned. The aircraft was depressurized. The rat returned. This continued the whole flight except during refueling and the bomb run, but not without some trepidation. Just imagine refueling with the thought of a rat climbing into your lap. The mind can do wonderful things. The last sighting indicated no harm done to the rat, and although he was written up in the forms, he was never found nor sighted again.

The aircraft Form 781 is a notebook about nine by twelve inches and contains loose-leaf pages, some of which are permanent and others for entering problems encountered in flight with the aircraft and/or its systems. When these are cleared, they are removed and stored. It is usually the pilot who makes the entries and signs the write-ups, but anyone discovering a problem can do it. The maintenance people would then send the appropriately qualified person to correct the problem. When this is done, the write-up is cleared by the authorized individual.

Those making write-ups are encouraged to enter as much information as possible as to the time in the flight the malfunction occurred, and flight conditions, if applicable.

The story is told of a B-47 pilot who was known for his ability to write up any and everything he noticed, but not necessarily write it up too well. He entered the following write-up after a flight.

"Lost number one engine."

The corrective action read. "Found number one engine in number one nacelle" and was signed off.

The last flight back to Bartow from Drane field after a thunderstorm could be interesting indeed. Sometimes it would still be raining when the pilots climbed into the aircraft for the return trip. It was always late in the afternoon as well. The engines would come to life with the pilots who were to ride back in the bus, standing fireguard. The birds would start to taxi as soon as they could. One day the rush was on, the pilots strapped in, the engines started, and the firebottles put away. The aircraft were launching into a constant stream of T-34s which had just enough spacing to allow a safe landing and clearing the runway when the next one was landing.

Things were often overlooked or left behind. Such was the case of one solo pilot who got halfway down the runway and realized he did not have much airspeed. He noticed a long red streamer flapping in the breeze. It was his pitot tube cover. Not wanting to abort and suffer the derision of his instructor, he pressed on, reasoning he would fly by the seat of his pants and just keep the proper distance from the bird in front of him. The pitot cover's purpose is to keep the pitot head clear on the ground. It must be removed prior to flight in order to receive proper airspeed indications. He recognized he had a problem. This can be serious with an experienced pilot, let alone a newly soloed one.

Once stable, he evaluated the situation and followed the aircraft in front of him, maintaining a constant distance and being careful not to overrun it or stall his own. Anyway, it sure beat returning to Drane and trying to land with no reliable airspeed reference except his eyeballs, lack of experience, and the seat of his pants. Of course, by now the seat of his pants had become very puckered and was of little value. Mainly, he did not want to try to explain it.

His idea worked quite well, and if he was lucky, he might be able to get on the ground and parked before anyone noticed. He flew what has been his most concentrated approach, maintained his distance, kept from being sent around and landed the airplane with a great deal of relief, pulling up beside the aircraft he had followed to complete his after-landing checklist. Feeling quite proud of his quick thinking and still hoping to get away scot-free, he glanced over at the airplane he had been following for the last 20 minutes. There, attached to the pitot tube, and flapping gaily in the breeze, was the other bird's pitot cover and streamer.

Primary flight training in 1958 was run by the Air Force, but employed civilian flight instructors. These instructors, for the most part, had spent time in the military as pilots during WWII and/or Korea. They were all men. Women filled positions around the base, such as Link Trainer instructors, but none as fliers. One of these ladies worked in the tower at Bartow Air Base. I personally never saw the lady to recognize, but spoke to her through the radio many times. I was fortunate never to be the object of one of her responses, which could be somewhat acerbic.

The bolder aviators-to-be would phrase their request for altimeter and time in a poetic fashion. These stories are in this section because I cannot personally vouch for their accuracy. However, I have heard the call which never identified the aircraft. The request would be: "Little flower in the tower, please give altimeter and hour." After a long pause, the reply would come, and in a manner that left no doubt of her opinion of the tormentor's heritage.

The story has the lady in question arriving at Bartow with experience as a pilot and instructor. She applied for a job as a civilian flight instructor. Unable to fulfill the physical requirement of the time for bilateral testicles, she was denied the position. She was hired to work in the tower. It was noted at times she, like all male instructors, showed little patience with the efforts of the fledgling pilots as they went about their daily activities, trying to prove to the world they were the next Chuck Yeager. Her patience was tried to the extreme one day when a student called in with an emergency.

The pilot was not coherent in his description of the problem, not too cool in the execution of the corrective action. In short, the kid was scared. This is not uncommon when a pilot encounters his first emergency situation and is solo. He entered the pattern; with the help of cooler heads, he prepared for his approach and landing.

The Flower was working the tower that day.

In his anxiety to put the aircraft on the ground, he convinced himself the approach was not proper and went around. One of the first things we learn as pilots, if it does not look right, take it around and do it again correctly. Recognizing the potential for disaster with the mounting tension in the cockpit, the IPs continued to work with him trying to build his eroding confidence. He continued to break off his approaches and go around.

After several of the aborted attempts, the pilot was asked the status of his emergency. His voice rising higher with each transmission, he replied: "I smell something! I smell something!"

There was a slight pause, and then a feminine voice came over the tower frequency. "That's shit! Now land the airplane!"

He did.

We went through the whole six month period of Primary with no accidents in our class. In fact, there was only one accident while we were at Bartow. It involved a Korean student. We were in T-28s at the time, and the word quickly spread that a T-34 had gone down. Eventually the report was that no one was injured. That in itself created an indefinable feeling of relief. Of course, rumors were rampant for several days until the real story came out.

It seems, according to the final word, a Korean student was flying solo out of Drane Field. He had flown before in Korea, P-51s. Not the comedown you might think. They were here to upgrade to jets by going through our flight program. The word had it that in the P-51 when the fuel system was set up, it fed automatically. If this is in error, this is the way I heard it. Regardless, the T-34 fuel system required a change. The fuel selector valve handle had to physically be moved from one tank to another. Otherwise, the engine would not continue to operate. It seems the student had failed to make the change. He was on a touch and go landing. The engine quit at about 300 feet above the ground. He landed straight ahead in the swamp. The crash tore off both wings and knocked some holes in the canopy. The bird was recovered, jacked up, fuel put in the empty tank, and the engine started and ran as advertised.

It was an accident. Some were to be expected when the number of flights made each day and the experience level of the pilots was considered. Only one accident in that time period was unusual for those days. The pilot was slapped on the back and congratulated for having had no injuries . . . by the Americans. He was ostracized by his fellow Koreans. He had bent an airplane and they were not about to forgive him.

Most of us ate lunch in the mess hall. When his class came in, he was not allowed by his fellow countrymen to sit at the same table with them. I have heard of the practice of shunning by some religions. We saw it in action. The system finally reacted and washed him back to the next class and, as far as I know, he completed the course. We took it for granted that his survival was important and rejoiced with him. Obviously, his fellow Koreans saw it differently.

A similar story surfaced at Greenville. In December 1958 we had just begun our training in basic when we broke for Christmas. The students went in all directions. The most memorable were the students from Cuba, who did not return immediately after the first of the year. According to the third stool on the right, the Cuban pilots had returned home for the break and flew combat missions for Castro during the Cuban revolution. Whether it is true or not, they did not return until well into January 1959.

We had an AC at Clinton-Sherman named Terry. It is easy to guess that he and his crew were referred to as Terry and the Pirates. They played the game. Although I never personally observed it, I have no reason to doubt that when they landed, the EW raised a skull and crossbones flag through the sextant port . . . at least until they were told to cease and desist.

The air traffic control system had not come into its present state in the late '50s and early '60s. There were more traffic centers at that time and they did not have positive control airspace except in a few crowded areas. We flew in an environment of IFR (instrument flight rules) hard altitudes and VFR on top, a condition in which the flight was made in visual flight conditions at altitudes which were normally reserved for instrument flight rules. Theoretically, the flight was always VFR, although sometimes to complete the mission, this was stretched a bit. The altitude was always 500 feet above the normal IFR altitude depending upon direction of flight. It simplified the mission of the SAC bomber force immensely.

The system for practice bombing was also different. This was before most of the RBS sites were for low-level activity. The wing scheduling would schedule each aircraft for a specific time for a bomb run. It was then up to the crew to contact the site in flight, confirm that time, and complete the bomb run. It was not unusual to plan a mission and hope to get a bootleg run (one that had not been scheduled or someone else cancelled for some reason). The aircraft would hold in a nearby orbit until time to make the run. If the scheduled aircraft showed up, it would complete its bomb run and the others would continue to orbit and reschedule a bootleg run.

The bomb plot would track the aircraft by radar, using information the crew gave them, such as the specific target, the altitude, the initial point, and airspeed. The crew also passed the call sign, crew number and names of the bombardier and copilot or ECM operator. The aircraft would call leaving the IP, and at once become a target for the defensive radar, which the copilot would attempt to counter with his electronic jamming gear within given time constraints. The bomb plot tracked the aircraft. A stylus on a map would provide a line of the aircraft route and position. The aircraft bombing system would direct the aircraft. Twenty seconds prior to bomb release, the radar/nav would turn on a tone which was projected over the UHF radio. At the point which the bomb would have been released, the tone would stop and the stylus at the bomb plot would raise off of the map. The bomb plot would use the information of wind, airspeed, altitude and heading provided by the aircrew and plot the point at which the bomb would have landed. They would then pass a score back in terms of azimuth and distance from the target. It was always encoded. The termination of a tone was extremely important for a score within the circle of reliability. Without it the stylus would continue to lay out a line until the tone broke.

My radar nav at the time told a story about a night on which several aircraft were orbiting in the area of St. Louis bomb plot awaiting their turns for a bomb run on the Gateway to the West. This particular night (it seemed SAC never flew in the daytime) the scheduled aircraft called leaving the initial point and was immediately followed by a transmission by another aircraft. The new transmission informed the bomb plot that they were also leaving an initial point for a bomb run. The crew information was given and the radar nav's rank was given as colonel. The first aircraft tried repeatedly to inform the second aircraft that the release time was theirs and they were already on the bomb run. The second aircraft refused to acknowledge, even to bomb plot when they got into the act. The first aircraft eventually aborted the run and let the second continue with the plot tracking it. The tone come on at 20 seconds to go. At least one other tone came on and stayed on. A voice came over the radio several minutes later when the tone broke. "Eat that one, Colonel!" it said. The release was scored somewhere near Kansas City. Crew dogs are resourceful.

The electronic tone was the safe way to score a bomb run and gave the crew experience in all of the procedures they would use if they were required to do it for real. There was a mission the crew flew at least once a year that actually involved the release of a live bomb. It was an MB-4 and carried a ten pound charge. Most of these missions were flown against Matagorda RBS at Matagorda Island, Texas. The plot would score the hit by sight using triangulation on the smoke from the charge. The charge was not always visible. Regardless, the crew was required to visually inspect the bomb bay to ensure the bomb had been dropped. This was especially important if activity at another bomb site was scheduled.

The procedure to inspect the bomb bay was to descend to an altitude where oxygen was not required and depressurize the aircraft. A crew member then would inspect the bomb bay. In the B-47 this was normally accomplished by the copilot or the fourth man, if one was on board and was willing. The inner pressure door was opened, the crew member would descend the entrance ladder and proceed to crawl through the crawlway to the bomb bay and inspect it. If the bomb had not been released, then subsequent activity could not be accomplished.

A B-47 out of base X had flown a mission and dropped an MB-4. The bomb bay check was made and they continued to Atlanta bomb plot for a scheduled run. The target was, as I recall, the northeast corner of a building at the Atlanta Prison. We never dropped on big targets, just coordinates. The crew made the bomb run, passed the information and waited for their score. It came back. It was outside the reliability circle. However, when they landed, they learned while they had a bad bomb score that they had actually released an MB-4 and it hit the northeast corner of the building. No damage or injuries. The crew never recovered, especially the copilot who had made the bomb bay check. Forgiveness was not known to be widespread in SAC in those days.

The academic portion of survival school was very instructional. Many of the instructors had real experience from previous wars and conflicts. They covered subjects from Arctic survival to POW camps. The object of the course was to prepare the crew member for the possibility of bailout and survival in any situation or conditions during peacetime and conflicts up to and including nuclear war. I think everyone paid attention.

I cannot vouch for the accuracy of the story we were told when we first arrived, but we all were briefed on it the first day. It seems one of the officer instructors had been sent on leave when our class signed in. The reason given was that he had been a POW in Korea, hanging by his thumbs during an interrogation, when a member of our survival class was brought into the room, also a POW. The new arrival at the interrogation was given a cigarette and treated with kindness, which he accepted. The officer hanging by his thumbs was interrogated. The school felt it best that the instructor not be present for obvious reasons. Whether or not the story is true, it did bring one of the lessons of the school home to us.

Emergency procedures are practiced as often as possible when learning to fly. One of the favorite tricks of the instructor is to put the student in a situation and pull the throttle back to idle and announce a forced landing. The student then simulates the actions of cutting the throttle, fuel, ignition, and battery switches, while setting up an approach to an area he has selected to set the aircraft down. The items are called out over interphone to the instructor to indicate the student knows the procedures.

There is the story of a student at a training base in Texas. He was flying the T-28. The student had difficulty getting the items in the correct order, especially for the forced landing. Warned of the seriousness of his shortcomings, he had hit the books with great fervor. Then he went to fly. Shortly after takeoff, the instructor pulled the throttle to idle and announced a forced landing. The student immediately cut the throttle, mixture, and prop controls, and went on to do the same to the battery, ignition, generator, and fuel switches. For real. They landed in a plowed field straight ahead before the instructor could intervene.

A friend of mine deployed to Zaragoza, Spain, on Reflex and was not scheduled to assume alert until the day after arrival. The crew decided to spend the evening in downtown Zaragoza. He returned early and was in bed when the AC came in three sheets to the wind and went to bed. Shortly thereafter, he awakened to the sound of the AC selling Buicks (puking). He then heard him roll over and go back to sleep. He spent the night wondering how bad the room would be when he got up. In the morning, he got up and gingerly went to the bathroom. He saw no evidence of the previous night's problems and thought the AC had gotten up and cleaned up after himself. He then heard the pilot exclaim from the other room: "Oh shit!"

He stepped into the room and observed the pilot with his foot in his flying boot with vomit oozing out of it around his ankles.

MISSION COMPLETE

The assignment at Fairchild terminated my direct association with flying. A few things of note regarding BUF days did occur.

I was in the 42nd Air Division at Blytheville. It was no better than the first time, but the rank difference did help. As we went to different bases in our division, I constantly met people who knew me. One of my assistants asked me how everyone seemed to know me. I explained that some I had served with in B-47 units, others I has served with in BUFs or met during ARC LIGHT tours. The rest had gone through Castle when I was there and while in the 4017th. I gave each class the introduction briefing for two to three years. Many had gone through the bomb squadron while I was the operations officer and commander. There were even a few who referred to me as the AC of the snake crew.

I was on an exercise in Germany. One of the people in my group came back from a meeting with representatives from other nations and he was shaking his head. He said that a British Wing Commander had discussed the capabilities and use of the BUFs as if he had flown them. He admitted the Brit knew some things he didn't.

I asked what his name was and he told me Ward. I asked if he had large bushy eyebrows. He said he did. I then explained to him that Wing Commander Ward probably did know a great deal about the BUF. He had spent three years at Castle as an academic and flight line instructor during the period I was there. I then looked up Derek and had a good long visit with him.

I spent twenty-eight years in the Air Force and in all that time never got any real say in what I would be doing and where I would go to do it. I could have easily turned down some assignments and gotten out, but that was not my desire. I never got an assignment that I had on my wish sheet. I did serve in some positions I desired and that was worth it all.

In retrospect, it all worked out for the best and there is little I would change if given the opportunity to do it all again. However, I still would like to have been turning the double play at Busch Stadium.

The Air Force is unusual. The word is that when you retire, you are finally shown the big picture, get to meet the regular crew chief, and unlike other organizations, if you are a pilot, you turn in your watch.

Descriptions

T-34A-Beech Mentor
Length - 25 feet, 10 inches   Wingspan - 32 feet 10 inches
225 HP Continental piston engine. Cruise 160 MPH 140 K
Tandem seating

T-28-North American Trojan
Length - 32 feet   Wingspan - 40, feet 1 inch
Wright R-1300-1A radial engine, 800 HP
Cruise 190 MPH 160K   Tandem seating

T-33A-Lockheed T-Bird
Training version of the F-80 Shooting Star
Length - 37 feet, 8 inches   Wingspan - 38 feet, 9 inches
J33-A-35 centrifugal compressor turbojet engine
4600 lbs of thrust. Cruise 580 MPH 505 K
Tandem seating

T-37-Cessna Tweet
Length - 29 feet, 8 inches   Wingspan - 33 feet, 7 inches
Two Continental J69-T-25 engines   1025 lbs of thrust
Cruise 507 MPH   438 K. Side by side seating

T-38-Northrop Talon
Length - 46 feet   Wingspan - 25 feet
Two J85-6E-5 engines   3850 lbs of thrust with afterburners
Maximum speed Mach 1.6   Tandem seating

C-45-Beech 18 Expeditor, Bugsmasher
Length - 35 feet, 2 inches   Wingspan - 49, feet 8 inches
Twin engine, low wing, twin tail monoplane
Two Pratt and Whitney R-985-AN-3 radial engines
Cruise 185 MPH 160K. Side by side seating

C-47-Douglas DC-3 Skytrain, C-47 Dakota, Gooney Bird
Length - 64 feet, 5 inches   Wingspan - 95 feet
Two Pratt and Whitney R-1830-92 radial engines
Cruise 194 MPH 152 K. Side by side seating

B-47E-Boeing Stratojet
Primary mission - nuclear bomber
Length - 107 feet, 1.5 inches   Wingspan - 116 feet, 4 inches
Height (to top of tailfin) - 28 feet
Design gross weight - 125,000 lbs
Maximum takeoff weight (with external tanks) - 221,000 lbs
Six J47-25 axial flow turbojet engines with 5970 lbs of thrust;
with water augmentation thrust increased approximately 23%.
Capable of carrying 33 ATO bottles for additional thrust for takeoff.
Equipped with two 20mm cannons in tail.
Three man crew: pilot, copilot and navigator/bombardier with
tandem seating. Pilot and copilot are seated under a
jettisonable bubble canopy and the navigator in a
compartment in the nose. Additional seating for one or two in the aisle.
P, CP, and Nav have ejection seats.
Copilot duties included ECM, navigation assistance, gunner,
engineer, radio operator and finally, pilot.
Maximum speed 425 KIAS without drop tanks or Mach .86
G limit - 3 positive at design gross weight
1359 B-47E models built. 2012 of all models built.

B-52-Boeing Stratofortress, BUF
Mission - nuclear bomber. D models, modified for use in
Southeast Asia as conventional bomber in addition to nuclear
role.
All models listed were equipped to carry two AGM-28 Hounddog
missiles. The Hounddogs have since been retired.

D Model

Crew of six with positions for four additional personnel.
Crew consists of pilot, copilot, radar-navigator, navigator,
electronic warfare officer and gunner. Everyone but the
gunner is situated in the forward compartment. The gunner's
compartment is in the tail section.
Length - 156 feet, 6 inches   Wingspan - 185 feet   Height to top
of tailfin - 48 feet, 3 inches.
Maximum takeoff gross weight - 450,000 lbs
Eight Pratt and Whitney J57-P-19W turbojet engines. Water augmented.
Two 3000 gallon underwing drop tanks.
Maximum airspeed 390 KIAS 595 MPH Limiting Mach .90
Maximum G limit 2 positive   .67 negative
Big Belly modification allowed aircraft to carry eighty-four
500 lb bombs in bomb bay. An additional twenty-four 750 lb bombs
could be carried on wing pylons. There were many
combinations of 500 and 750 lb bombs.
Armament - four fifty caliber machine guns mounted in tail.

G and H Models

Crew of six all in forward compartment. Four additional
positions available. Gunner and EWO sit side by side facing
aft. Gunners have since been deleted from the B-52.
Length - 160 feet, 10 inches. Wingspan - 185 feet   Height to
top of tailfin - 40 feet 8 inches.
Maximum takeoff gross weight - 488,000 lbs
Two 700 gallon wing tanks
Equipped with Electro Optical Viewing System
Equipped to carry AGM-69 SRAM short range attack missiles
Armament: G - four fifty caliber machine guns mounted in tail
               H - 20 mm multi-barrel Vulcan cannon mounted in tail
Engines: G - Eight Pratt and Whitney J57-P-43WB turbojets.
               Water augmented.
               H - Eight Pratt and Whitney TF33-P-3 turbofans
Many modifications have been made to the G and H since I had my
last flight. The D models have all been retired.